Digital Image Processing

A Systems Approach

Digital Image Processing

A Systems Approach

Second Edition

William B. Green
TDC
Moorpark, California

VNR VAN NOSTRAND REINHOLD
———————————— New York

Copyright © 1989 by Van Nostrand Reinhold

Library of Congress Catalog Card Number: 88-5630
ISBN 0-442-23052-4

Printed in the United States of America

Published by Van Nostrand Reinhold
115 Fifth Avenue
New York, New York 10003

Van Nostrand Reinhold International Company Limited
11 New Fetter Lane
London EC4P 4EE, England

Van Nostrand Reinhold
480 La Trobe Street
Melbourne, Victoria 3000, Australia

Macmillan of Canada
Division of Gage Publishing Limited
164 Commander Boulevard
Agincourt, Ontario M1S 3C7, Canada

15 14 13 12 11 10 9 8 7 6 5 4 3 2 1

Library of Congress Cataloging-in-Publication Data

Green, William B.
  Digital image processing.

  Bibliography: p.
  Includes index.
  1. Image processing—Digital techniques.   I. Title.
TA1632.G727   1988   621.36′7   88-5630
ISBN 0-442-23052-4

With affection and appreciation,
this book is dedicated to
my family
Barbara
Robert Cheryl Richard Jennifer Kimberly
Max Dorothy Yetta Nathan
and the memory of
Albert Zimmerman

Preface to Second Edition

It is now about a quarter century since computers were first used to process images. When I arrived at JPL almost twenty years ago, Robert Nathan, Fred Billingsley, and other pioneers of this technology had just completed an "interactive display." That display was designed to use the core memory of a mainframe computer as the refresh buffer for a gray scale raster display. The result of applying an algorithm could be viewed when the computer had completed the specified series of operations on the image; because of the processor hardware and software limitations, no other work could be performed on the processor while it was busy continually refreshing the display screen. In those days, "interactive" meant that the processed image could be viewed as soon as the processing had been completed, and the user did not have to wait to view the results of the computer processing until the processed image was written to tape, recorded onto film with a separate device, and then processed by the photo lab.

Today image processing technology is widespread. Commercial vendors provide high-resolution image processing and display equipment that can operate peripheral to a host processor or as highly capable self-contained stand-alone systems. Image processing peripheral boards provide personal computer users with image processing and display capability superior to the mainframe-based systems of twenty years ago, at a cost comparable to or less than the cost of a new automobile.

In the five years since the first edition of this text, technical evolution in this field has proceeded at an accelerating rate. The evolution of hardware specially designed to incorporate the most common computationally intensive image processing operations continues to make possible the economical application of this technology to an increasing number of applications areas, and the cost of equipment required to support the use of imaging technology continues to drop rapidly. The personal computer revolution and related development of PC-compatible hardware designed for efficient image processing has made the technology accessible to a broad base of users. The evolution of reliable optical disk storage media and rapid image scanning equipment has begun an evolution of document storage systems from a historic reliance on micrographics technology to emerging systems incorporating digital image technology.

In developing this second edition, material from the first edition has been updated to reflect the current state of the art in several areas. Chapters 1 and 2 have been extensively revised to include descriptions of the new earth resources satellites and sensors placed into operation since publication of the first edition, and the commercialization of the United States earth resources program. An introduction to convolutional filtering has been added to Chapter 4. Chapter 5 has been extensively revised to reflect advances in display technology, and a new section describing the various formats of optical storage media has been added. The appendices have been completely updated to provide the latest available information regarding sources of imaging data from various spacecraft. Two completely new chapters describing image processing with personal computers and computer processing of digitized document imagery have been added.

I wish to thank Don Bane of the Public Information Office at the Jet Propulsion Laboratory for again assisting in providing recent examples from that outstanding institution for use in this revised edition. The Public Affairs offices of both EOSAT and SPOT Image Corporation were extremely helpful in providing dramatic illustrations for use in this new edition. I wish to thank the many sources of illustrations at various equipment manufacturers, each of whom has been recognized appropriately in the figure captions. At Unisys Defense Systems, I appreciate the support of Will Sardelli, President of the System Development Group and John Potate, Vice President and General Manager of the Logistics Systems Division during the development of this revision. John Addington, Ken Kiss, Jim Young, and Eric Wels of Unisys provided new material for this edition, using the image processing facilities at the Camarillo, California location. Mike Rothbart, David Krar Hutton, Jim Schwartz, and Herman Pass at Terminal Data Corporation have encouraged this effort, and I am grateful to them for their support.

Finally, again, I thank my family for supporting this revision. The dedication page of this text has changed from the first edition, to accommodate other new developments during the past five years, and its a pleasure to thank all of them for their encouragement and continuing support.

William B. Green
Granada Hills, California

Preface to First Edition

Computers have been used to process pictures for approximately twenty years, and the technology of digital image processing is continuing to expand rapidly. The increasing number of digital image sources includes remote sensing satellites and systems, film scanners, video digitizers, digital sensors, biomedical systems, and military systems. A variety of data types can be compactly stored, processed, and displayed in digital image format. Applications in diverse fields, including geology, astronomy, planetary science, meteorology, land use studies, forestry, cartography, agriculture, medicine, and military applications, effectively utilize digital image processing technology.

Several recent texts have been published dealing with the basic techniques of digital image processing. The majority of the material published to date is mathematical or theoretical, and deals almost exclusively with the algorithms associated with computer processing of images. The main emphasis in this text is the reduction of theory to practice. Two chapters outline the mathematics of the most basic generally applicable image processing techniques. The algorithms described in this text can provide a foundation on which image processing systems can be built. Most of the material in the book deals with issues related to implementing image processing systems, including design concepts for computer software used for image processing, description of the various systems that acquire digital imagery, and descriptions of the specialized computer peripherals that are employed in the field.

The format, structure, and content of this text have evolved during the past several years. They reflect the author's experience gained by working in the field as well as experience in structuring and teaching this material from a systems perspective. Teaching experience gained in the Physics and Astronomy Department at California State University Northridge and at the Harvard University Graduate School of Design Laboratory for Computer Graphics and Spatial Analysis seminar series have been invaluable in developing the approach and content of this textbook.

This book can be used as a basic text for a one semester upper division or graduate level course in image processing system design, within computer science, engineering, physical science, or life science curricula. It can also be used as a supplemental text for courses in which the major emphasis is on the mathematical foundation of digital image processing. It is intended to be especially useful for the working engineer or scientist who has decided that image processing technology can be of benefit to a particular problem or application, and is suddenly faced with the need to design and implement a computer-based system.

It would not have been possible to produce this textbook without the assistance and guidance of several individuals. Dr. Paul Richter and Dr. John Lawrence of the California State University Northridge helped formulate this approach to the subject, and Dr. Richter was especially helpful in structuring the content of the one semester course taught in the Physics and Astronomy Department. Alan Schmidt, Director of the Laboratory for Computer Graphics and Spatial Analysis, supported the incorporation of an information management seminar taught from a systems perspective, and Marjorie Maws and Barbara Tarlin of the Center for Management Research were especially helpful in structuring the course content at Harvard.

Don Bane of the Public Information Office at the Jet Propulsion Laboratory was patient and helpful in providing many of the illustrations used in this text. The System Development Corporation provided encouragement and cooperation during the preparation of the text, and the SDC people in the Systems Division involved in SDC's image processing activities were helpful and cooperative. The staff at EROS Data Center provided assistance and detailed information in several key areas. John Addington provided the analytical structure for the color coordinate systems described in Chapter 4, and also shared many of the trials and tribulations of manuscript preparation during some long carpool rides to the office.

The majority of the examples used in this text to illustrate processing techniques have been provided by Cal Tech's Jet Propulsion Laboratory. I was fortunate to spend ten years at JPL working in the finest image processing facility in the world; much of the material presented in this text represents the distillation of a philosophy developed during an exciting period that was rich in experience, friendships, and the high adventure of planetary exploration in the 1970s. The large number of JPL examples used in this text is a testimony to the outstanding group of individuals with whom I was privileged to work, and to the cooperation and assistance I have received since leaving JPL.

This text has been prepared during evenings and weekends over an extended period of time, and I need to especially thank my family, to whom I have dedicated this book, for their patience, support, and understanding.

Granada Hills, California   William B. Green

LIST OF COLOR PLATES

Plate I

Figure 1-12. Geometrically projected view of the Los Angeles basin.
Figure 1-15. Two different LANDSAT Thematic Mapper images of the Hubbard glacier area in Alaska.

Plate II

Figure 1-14. Color ratio enhancement of a LANDSAT.

Plate III

Figure 1-18. GOES satellite image with wind bars.

Plate IV

Figure 1-23. False color rendition of digitized image of comet Kohoutek.

Plate V

Figure 2-16. LANDSAT 4 Thematic Mapper image of the Washington, D.C. metropolitan area.
Figure 2-19. SPOT color image of the New Orleans metropolitan area.

Plate VI

Figure 3-20. Color composite rendition of LANDSAT scene of East Pilbara region of Australia.

Plate VII

Figure 3-22. Color composite enhanced image of the limb of Io, one of the satellites of Jupiter.

Plate VIII

Figure 3-24. Color ratio composite rendition of the LANDSAT Australia scene.

Plate IX

Figure 4-19. GOES satellite image with geographical boundary overlay.

Plate X

Figure 4-28. Thematic map depicting results of supervised classification of agricultural test flight path.

Plate XI

Figure 4-29. Classification of degrees of Wisconsin lake eutrophication based on multispectral classification of LANDSAT imagery.

Plate XII

Figure 4-32. Color composite image of Mars constructed from a series of Viking orbiter images.

Plate XIII

Figure 4-33. Hue/saturation enhancement of the color composite Mars image.

Plate XIV

Figure 5-12. Example of use of region-of-interest.
Figure 9-12. Four screens driven by commercially available PC-based image processing software.

Plate XV

Figure 7-1. Color composite processed astronomical image.

Plate XVI

Figure 7-2. Color composite LANDSAT-1 image of Iceland.

Contents

Digital Image Processing

A Systems Approach

1
Introduction to Digital
Image Processing

The concept of using digital computers to process pictures is over 25 years old, and digital image processing has now emerged as a technology in its own right. A complete mathematical formulation for the discipline of image processing has been established. In addition, a wide variety of specially configured equipment, including special-purpose digital processors and specialized computer peripherals, is now available. A new industry has emerged that involves the development and sales of computer-based systems, peripherals, and software, all specially designed to access, process, and display image data.

Digital image processing technology has evolved rapidly because of several factors:

Digital imaging systems are capable of acquiring imagery that has a wider dynamic range than the human eye or photographic film. The eye can discern fewer than 100 discrete shades of gray, and black and white film can typically reproduce on the order of 50 to over 100 shades of gray, depending on the film contrast. Digital imagery can be used to represent several hundred, and even several thousand, shades of gray. Color digital imagery can also represent a wider tonal range than the eye can resolve or than can be reproduced on film.

A single digital image can present a very large amount of information in a compact and easily interpreted form. A digital image containing several million bits of information can be displayed on a single photographic print or display monitor. Image format is a natural format for compact display of large amounts of data that cannot be readily viewed in any other manner; the use of the image format provides the advantages inherent in the human visual process, including the mental processes inherent in human perception. The image format provides an effective display mode that can be interpreted by a wide range of observers with disparate background and training.

Digital computers can process and manipulate imagery using methods that cannot be duplicated with nondigital technology. Computers can be used to apply a variety of transformations (including nonlinear transformations) to imagery that cannot be performed optically. Digital information extraction techniques can fully exploit the statistical nature of digital imagery, in terms of both the two-dimensional statistics inherent in a single image and the mathematical relationships that exist between multiple images acquired of the same scene. Digital techniques can also be used for analysis based on correlation of image data with nonimaging data, including correlation of remotely sensed imagery with nonimaging georeferenced data bases.

1

The growth of all phases of digital computing technology has enabled the development of digital image processing technology. The trend toward faster and cheaper computational elements, large-capacity high-density digital data storage devices, and improved display technology have made possible the processing, manipulation, and display of large volumes of digital imagery.

This chapter begins with a summary of the historical development of digital image processing technology. An overview of the various applications areas in which digital image processing is making a significant contribution to progress is presented after a definition of the basic terms used throughout the text. The chapter concludes with an overview of image processing systems. The three basic capabilities found in all image processing systems (image acquisition, image processing, and image display) are described, along with their relationship to the structure of this text.

HISTORICAL BACKGROUND

The use of computers for processing image data had its most visible origins in the NASA unmanned planetary science program. Digital computers have been used to process images returned from space for over 25 years. The use of digital techniques for processing imagery has been a contributing factor to our successful exploration of the solar system, and these techniques have more recently been applied to a variety of earth-based applications, ranging from monitoring of the earth's natural and agricultural resources to biomedical applications. Image processing technology has proceeded along with parallel developments in digital computing technology, information display, and communications. This section presents a brief historical overview of the major events leading to the development and application of digital image processing technology. Figure 1-1 contains a summary overview of the evolution of this technology.

The use of computers for image processing first became generally visible to a broad community during the early unmanned lunar and planetary exploration missions conducted by the National Aeronautics and Space Administration (NASA) in the mid-1960s. The Ranger spacecraft[1] returned hundreds of images of the lunar surface from a series of missions. Many of these images were converted from analog television format to digital format and then computer-processed. The Surveyor series of unmanned lunar exploratory missions was designed to evaluate landing sites for later manned missions.[2] The Surveyor 7 spacecraft shown in Figure 1-2 returned 21,038 television images from its landing site on the lunar surface. Many of these images were computer-processed in an attempt to improve knowledge of the composition and structure of the lunar surface. The processing included digital filtering performed to improve the resolution of the video imagery as an aid in determining surface characteristics.

The Mariner 4 spacecraft shown in Figure 1-3 was launched in 1964 and returned 22 digital images of Mars as it flew past the planet. This was the first space mission to utilize an all-digital imaging system. The spacecraft returned imagery at a data rate of approximately 8 bits per second and provided low-resolution imagery of a small portion of the planet's surface.

The Mariner 6 and 7 spacecraft also incorporated digital imaging systems, and they provided several hundred images of Mars during flights past the planet in the

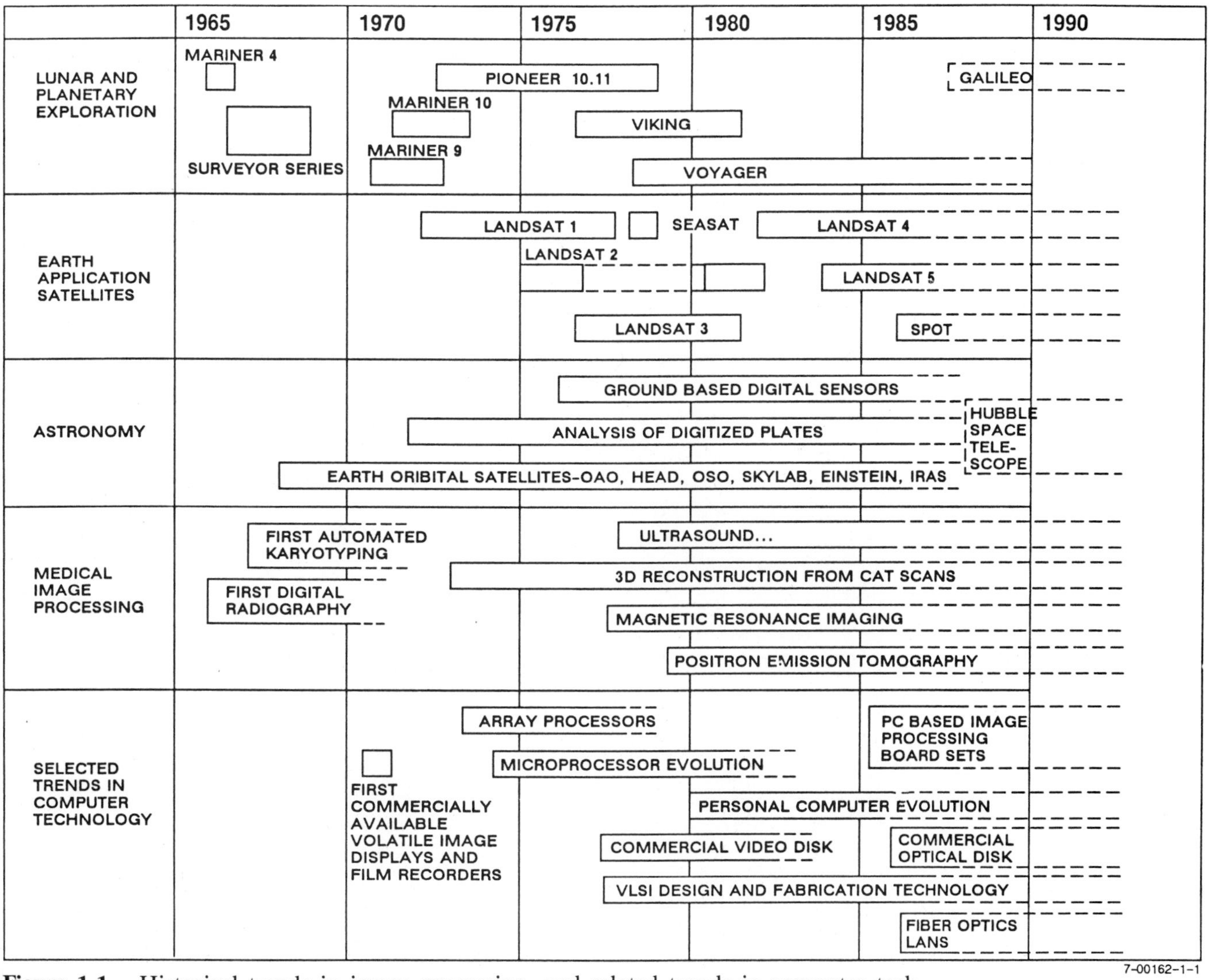

	1965	1970	1975	1980	1985	1990
LUNAR AND PLANETARY EXPLORATION	MARINER 4 ☐ ☐ SURVEYOR SERIES	MARINER 10 MARINER 9 ☐	PIONEER 10.11 VIKING	VOYAGER	GALILEO	
EARTH APPLICATION SATELLITES			LANDSAT 1 ☐ SEASAT LANDSAT 2 LANDSAT 3		LANDSAT 4 LANDSAT 5 SPOT	
ASTRONOMY			GROUND BASED DIGITAL SENSORS ANALYSIS OF DIGITIZED PLATES EARTH ORIBITAL SATELLITES-OAO, HEAD, OSO, SKYLAB, EINSTEIN, IRAS		HUBBLE SPACE TELE-SCOPE	
MEDICAL IMAGE PROCESSING	FIRST AUTOMATED KARYOTYPING FIRST DIGITAL RADIOGRAPHY		ULTRASOUND... 3D RECONSTRUCTION FROM CAT SCANS MAGNETIC RESONANCE IMAGING POSITRON EMISSION TOMOGRAPHY			
SELECTED TRENDS IN COMPUTER TECHNOLOGY	FIRST COMMERCIALLY AVAILABLE VOLATILE IMAGE DISPLAYS AND FILM RECORDERS ☐	ARRAY PROCESSORS MICROPROCESSOR EVOLUTION COMMERCIAL VIDEO DISK VLSI DESIGN AND FABRICATION TECHNOLOGY		PERSONAL COMPUTER EVOLUTION	PC BASED IMAGE PROCESSING BOARD SETS COMMERCIAL OPTICAL DISK FIBER OPTICS LANS	

Figure 1-1.   Historical trends in image processing, and related trends in computer technology.

7-00162-1-1

late 1960s.[3,4] In 1971, the Mariner 9 spacecraft became the first spacecraft placed into orbit around another planet, and it returned over 7,000 images of Mars during an extended orbital operational period. Mars became the first planet to be mapped entirely from digital remotely sensed imagery based on the Mariner 9 image data.[5-7]

Mariner 10 was equipped with digital camera systems similar to those employed on the Mariner 9 spacecraft; it was launched on a trajectory designed to carry the spacecraft past Venus and Mercury and into orbit around the sun. The spacecraft encountered Mercury twice again during its solar orbit while the data and telemetry systems remained operational, and thousands of digital images of the two planets were acquired.[8-10]

NASA digital image processing activities continued with the Viking missions to

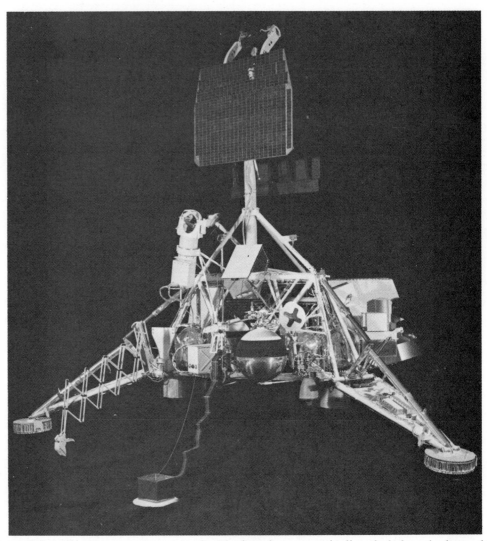

Figure 1-2. The Surveyor 7 spacecraft. The imaging sensor is directly below the lower left corner of the solar panels (Jet Propulsion Laboratory).

Mars, beginning in 1975. Two orbiting spacecraft and two lander spacecraft utilized digital imaging systems to return thousands of images of Mars to earth during an operational lifetime of several years. The Orbiter systems alone returned over 100,000 images; it is interesting to note that a single image from one of the Viking Orbiter cameras contained as many bits of data as the total image data volume returned by the Mariner 4 spacecraft a decade earlier. A major ground processing facility was required to extract the image data from the telemetry returned from the mission, process the image data in a variety of ways, display the processed imagery, record the images on film, and produce the required photographic products for the Viking mission.[11-17]

Two Voyager spacecraft were launched in 1977 on trajectories designed to take the spacecraft past Jupiter and Saturn and their associated satellites starting in 1979 (see Figure 1-4.[18,19] Following successful encounters with Jupiter and Saturn, Voy-

Figure 1-3.   The Mariner 4 spacecraft. (Jet Propulsion Laboratory).

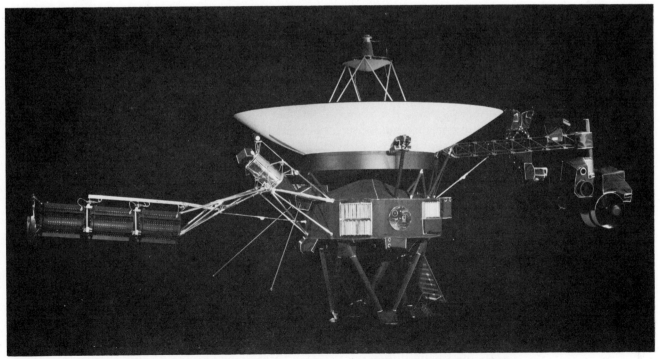

Figure 1-4.   The Voyager Spacecraft. The imaging system is located at the far right of the
spacecraft (Jet Propulsion Laboratory).

ager 2 flew past Uranus in January 1986, passing within 50,600 miles of the planet. The Voyager 2 spacecraft is now traveling on a trajectory that will provide an encounter with Neptune in August 1989. Computer image processing was used to provide the first color close-up views of these planets, and played a key role in the scientific discoveries of this mission.[20] These discoveries include discovery of a new Jovian satellite, discovery of a ring around Jupiter, analysis of the complex ring structure of Saturn, and discovery of ten new moons around Uranus.

Earth-Orbiting Systems

NASA began sponsoring a series of earth-orbiting spacecraft equipped with digital multispectral imaging systems with the launch of LANDSAT 1 on July 23, 1972.[21] The imaging data acquired by the LANDSAT spacecraft series have been made available to the public for many years, and a diverse user community now utilizes the LANDSAT imaging data.

Five LANDSAT spacecraft have orbited the earth and returned multispectral imagery to date. The spacecraft provide data to ground stations located around the world. LANDSAT 1 operated from 1972 until January 1978. LANDSAT 2 operated from January 1975 through November 1975, and was then reactivated for service from June 1980 until July 1983. LANDSAT 3 operated from 1978 through September 1983. LANDSAT 4 and LANDSAT 5 incorporated a new multispectral imaging system, providing improved spectral coverage and spatial resolution. LANDSAT 4 was launched on July 16, 1982 and LANDSAT 5 was launched March 1, 1984.

Operation of the LANDSAT systems was initiated by NASA in 1972. During the 1980s, Congress determined that the earth resources program should transition into the private sector, and the Earth Observation Satellite Company (EOSAT) now operates the systems and provides data products as a commercial venture.

The Satellite Pour l'Observation de la Terre (SPOT) was launched in February 1986 by the Centre National d'Etudes Spatiales of France. Image data is available commercially from this system. In the United States, the SPOT Image Corporation provides access to these data products. Both the LANDSAT and SPOT systems are described in Chapter 2.

NASA operated the SEASAT satellite in the late 1970s, acquiring high-resolution synthetic-aperture radar imagery during a 90-day operational period. Other remote sensing systems incorporating digital imaging systems have also been used in a variety of applications areas. The Heat Capacity Mapping Mission returned data designed to map the earth's heat capacity in imaging format in the late 1970s.

A series of spacecraft designed to aid in analysis of weather and climate have been operational since the mid-1970s. The TIROS and NIMBUS spacecraft have carried a variety of sensors, including imaging systems and spectral instruments that return data in image format. A series of synchronous satellites, the GOES series, provides frequent imaging that is routinely used for weather forecasting, analysis of weather patterns, and measurement of cloud motion.

The trend toward digital imaging systems for remote sensing applications has also been followed by the military. Military satellites now return imagery that is processed digitally for military applications.

The increasing utilization of earth-orbiting satellites for remote sensing applications has led to the development of a full technology, incorporating specialized processing techniques useful in a wide range of applications areas.[22-24]

Biomedical Applications

The success achieved in using digital image processing techniques in planetary and earth remote-sensing applications has led to the use of this technology in an increasing number of other areas. One emerging applications area is medical image processing. Digital image processing techniques were applied to analysis of X-ray imagery as early as 1968.[25] Other early work included automatic classification of chromosomes.[26] Digital processing techniques have been applied to quantitative diagnosis of atherosclerosis, using arterial X-ray imagery.[27]

A wide range of medical applications currently utilize digital image processing technology.[28,29] Computerized tomography involves multiple X-ray views and three-dimensional reconstruction of imaged areas within the body from the multiple views. Magnetic resonance imaging involves application of a magnetic field to areas of interest. The magnetic field changes the alignment of hydrogen atoms, and the realignment of these atoms after the magnetic field is removed generates a detectable electric signal. Organs in the body in which water density is higher than other areas can be imaged using this technique. Other techniques utilizing digital imaging technology include ultrasound imaging (application of high-frequency sound waves and detection of their reflections), digital subtraction angiography, and positron emission tomography which involves multiple imaging after irradiation.

Astronomy

Digital image processing has been applied to images acquired through earth-based telescopes as well as those acquired by earth-orbiting outward-looking astronomy satellites.[30,31] Initially, digital techniques were applied to photographic images obtained with earth-based telescopes. More recently, digital imaging sensors have been used in conjunction with earth-based telescopes. Digital sensors can provide better radiometric resolution than film. Digital sensors are placed in the focal plane of earth-based telescope systems, and the image acquisition and processing are performed digitally.

Astronomy has also benefited from the ability to place satellites in earth orbit, outside the earth's atmosphere. Several spacecraft have been used to obtain celestial maps in a variety of spectral regions, including ultraviolet and X-ray regimes. In the early 1980s, the Infrared Astronomical Satellite (IRAS) obtained a high resolution infrared map of the celestial sphere.

The Hubble Space Telescope will be placed into earth orbit sometime in the near future using the Space Shuttle, and periodic refurbishment of the imaging systems is planned to extend the operational lifetime of the system.[32,33] After the system is placed into orbit, it will be operated in the same manner as an earth-based telescope system, with data available to the scientific community who will request observation time based on planned scientific investigations. The exact schedule for deploying this system is still not definite as of this writing, due to the rescheduling of Shuttle flights necessitated by the loss of the Challenger in January 1986.

Summary

The early space probes provided high public and scientific awareness of the capabilities provided by digital image processing technology. In recent years, computer processing of images has been accepted as a necessary component in many applications areas.

The development of computer technology has made possible the economic utilization of digital imaging techniques in operational systems. Several key computer-related developments are shown of the bottom of Figure 1-1. In the early 1970s, the first commercially available volatile image displays and film recorders appeared on the market. The volatile displays were the forerunner of today's proliferation of raster-based computer terminals and workstations. Array processors made it possible to improve the computation time for the more complex image processing algorithms by orders of magnitude. The evolution of microprocessors, and the integration of electronic circuitry achieved through the development of design and fabrication tools for very large scale integrated circuits made it possible to develop the economically viable components required for digital image processing systems. The evolution of personal computers, and the associated commercial products that now support image processing on personal computers, are broadening the penetration of digital image processing technology into new applications areas.

Compact storage requirements for digital imagery are being met through development of optical disk-based storage systems. These systems provide for economic storage of large archives of digital image data. The use of commercial video disks for the storage and display of low-resolution imagery provides a compact and inexpensive storage mechanism for imagery. The development of fiber optics local area networks should provide the high bandwidth required for the development of large distributed image processing and archival storage systems that will support many users simultaneously.

The evolution of the technology enabled by the new developments in computer technology has been rapid, and the rate at which new commercial products are introduced into the market continues to increase. Compact, highly capable, and economical systems for computer processing of digital imagery will continue to evolve in the foreseeable future.

BASIC DEFINITIONS

A *digital image* can be thought of as a matrix of numbers. A simple example of a digital image is shown in Figure 1-5. The scene is a black square on a white background. One possible digital representation of that scene is shown on the right of Figure 1-5. The digital representation of the scene is a sampled version of the continuous scene that is present in object space. Each point within the digital representation corresponds to an area in object space, and a digital value is assigned at each point in the digital image that is related to the intensity of that area in object space.

Several decisions were involved in generating the particular digital representation of the scene shown in Figure 1-5. One decision involves the sampling frequency used to generate the discrete digital representation of the continuous real scene. In Figure 1-5, it can be observed that the sampling frequency was selected so that an object the size of the black square would appear in the digital image as a 2-element by 2-element object. A higher sampling frequency would produce more matrix elements to represent a square of the same size, and a lower sampling frequency might mean that an object the size of the black square could not be detected in the digitized representation of the same scene.

The second decision relates to the representation of intensity within the sampled

OBJECT   IMAGE

```
          1   1   1   1   1   1   1   1

          1   1   1   1   1   1   1   1

          1   1   1   0   0   1   1   1

          1   1   1   0   0   1   1   1

          1   1   1   1   1   1   1   1

          1   1   1   1   1   1   1   1
```

Figure 1-5.   Digital image example.

image. In Figure 1-5, a single bit is used to represent intensity at each sampled position. The black square has an intensity represented by a zero, and the white background intensity is represented by a 1 in the digital image.

Digital imagery in which only a single bit is used to represent intensity may at first glance appear relatively uninteresting. There is a wide range of applications for this type of imagery, however. Images of document material are often digitized, using a single bit for intensity so that characters appear at zero intensity and the background is digitized with an intensity of 1. Single-bit document imagery is now used in many areas, including facsimile transmission of text and document material, optical-character-recognition equipment, and digitized document storage and retrieval systems. Processing, manipulation, and display of digitized single-bit document material is addressed in this text as a specific subject in Chapter 8.

Figure 1-6 illustrates some basic terms used in this text to refer to the components of a digital image. The two-dimensional matrix of numbers is called a *digital image.* In order to establish the spatial orientation of sampled imagery, the rows of the matrix are called *lines,* and the columns are referred to as *samples.* Line numbers increase in the row direction, and sample numbers increase in the direction of increasing column number.

The individual component elements within the digital image are referred to as *picture elements.* Two common abbreviations for this term are *pixel* and *pel;* the

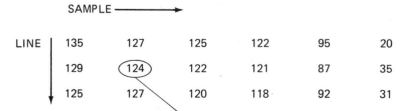

Figure 1-6.   Basic definitions.

term *pixel* is used in this text. The digital value of each pixel that represents intensity is referred to in this text as *digital intensity*. Using this notation, the digital intensity of the pixel at line 3, sample 4, in the digital image shown in Figure 1-5 is zero. As a convention in this text, low digital intensities represent low intensity in the actual scene. In a black and white image, a digital intensity of zero represents black.

Figure 1-7 contains a different digital representation of the same scene shown in Figure 1-5. The same spatial sampling frequency has been used to generate this digital version, but the number of bits used to represent digital intensity has been increased from 1 to 8. Digital intensity values can range from zero to 255, with zero representing black and 255 representing white. Several common effects that occur when a sampled digital representation of a continuous scene is created can be seen in Figure 1-7. First, note the digital intensity values representing the black square. The 4 pixels representing the uniformly black square have digital intensity values of 3, 2, 2, and 4. Most systems that provide sampled digital representations of a scene introduce a degree of random noise into the sampled image. If no noise was introduced during the sampling process, the digital intensity values of the 4 pixels would be the same. System-induced random noise has caused a random fluctuation about a mean digital intensity. This effect can be caused both by system electronics and by the analog-to-digital conversion process involved in converting input light intensity into a sampled digital pixel intensity value.

The second effect that can be observed is the lack of a sharp transition in the sampled digital image at the edges of the black square. In Figure 1-5 the square is sharply defined at the boundary, but Figure 1-7 more accurately represents what actually occurs when a sharp boundary is sampled to create a discrete digital representation of the scene. The spatial resolution within a sampled digital image will be less than the resolution of the actual continuous scene. The frequency degradation that occurs when a scene is sampled can be determined by imaging targets containing sharp high-contrast boundaries and measuring the frequency response across the boundary. The degradation is due to two causes. The first is the sampling process itself, which causes a degradation in resolution because of the attempt to represent

OBJECT   IMAGE

255	255	255	255	255	255	255	255
255	255	255	126	132	255	255	255
255	255	119	3	2	120	255	255
255	255	123	2	4	119	255	255
255	255	255	121	118	255	255	255
255	255	255	255	255	255	255	255

Figure 1-7. Digital representation of the same scene as Figure 1-5, with digital intensity represented as 8 bits per pixel.

a continuous signal with a set of discrete points. The second cause might be the optics used in the particular digital imaging device, which may contribute to the resolution loss. Most digital imaging systems are designed so that the sampling process rather than the system optics is the limiting factor in system resolution capability.

In Figure 1-7, the sharp black-to-white transition in the scene occurs in the digital image over a 3-pixel range (note the transition from 255 to 119 to 3 going from line 3, sample 2, to line 3, sample 4, as an example). A higher sampling frequency would provide sharper definition of the high-contrast boundary; the resolution degradation effect would still be present, but it would be less severe with a higher sampling frequency. A higher sampling frequency would also generate a larger digital representation of the same scene. The trade-offs involved in system design relative to choice of spatial sampling frequency and intensity resolution are described more fully in Chapter 2.

Figure 1-8 shows an enlarged region of a Voyager 1 image of Saturn's rings taken in November 1980. This image is approximately 150 lines by 200 samples in size. The digital intensity values are quantized to 8 bits. The individual pixels are clearly visible in this enlargement. Each spot, or dot, in this illustration represents 1 pixel in the sampled image. The digital intensities would be near zero for the near-black pixels in the image (e.g., the upper-left corner), near 128 for midgray (e.g., in the regions between the two broad bright elliptical rings), and near 255 for the pixels that are near white. The black spots in the image that appear in a regular pattern within the image are called *reseau marks* and are incorporated in the imaging device so that they appear in every image acquired by the Voyager 1 camera system. The location of these dots within the digital image indicates the degree of geometric distortion present in every region of every image. Subsequent computer processing can be used to remove this distortion on the basis of the location of the reseau marks and a knowledge of the original reseau geometry.

This small image segment illustrates the compact display capability inherent in digital image processing. This image contains a total of 240,000 bits of information (150 lines by 200 samples by 8 bits per pixel), and this volume of information can be displayed compactly in an image format that is amenable to analysis and interpretation.

Multispectral Imagery

The examples shown so far in this definition section all demonstrate imagery acquired in a single region of the electromagnetic spectrum. Digital image processing techniques are not inherently limited to "black and white" or "single-color" images. Figure 1-9 shows one concept of a sensor that acquires digital imagery of the same scene in different parts of the electromagnetic spectrum. The same input image is passed through three spectral filters, which separate the image into three separate spectral components. Each separate component is then digitized so that a three-component color digital image representation of the scene is produced. In this example, the three filters might correspond to the red, green, and blue response regions of conventional color film, and the three digital images would thus represent the red, green, and blue spectral components of the original scene.

A variety of techniques are used to process, manipulate, and display multispectral imagery, and several of the most commonly used techniques are described later in this text. It should be noted, however, that the concept of multispectral imagery is

Figure 1-8. Enlarged Voyager image of the Rings of Saturn. The individual picture elements can be seen in this enlarged version (Jet Propulsion Laboratory).

quite general; multispectral image processing techniques can involve manipulation of imagery containing more than three spectral components. Figure 1-10 illustrates the more general concept of a multispectral image, in which a large number of component images are present. On the left side of Figure 1-10, a multispectral image is shown containing 11 separate spectral component images. On the right side of the figure, still more generality has been introduced. Several components of the multispectral image are not originally derived from imaging sensors. The "multispectral image" on the right of Figure 1-10 includes three image components (red, green, and blue) plus other component images that represent values of population, elevation, and air quality. In this case, the digital image format has been used to represent data that are not originally acquired by an imaging sensor. Digital image processing

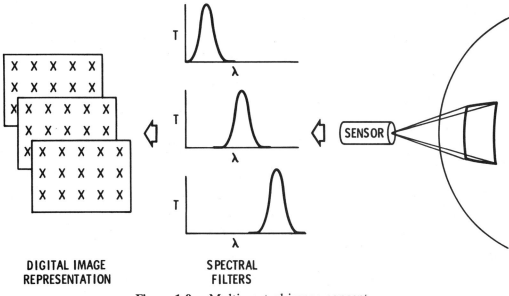

Figure 1-9.   Multispectral image concept.

provides a set of techniques for combining, merging, analyzing, and displaying multiple disparate data types.

APPLICATIONS OVERVIEW

This section contains a descriptive overview of a variety of applications of digital image processing techniques. The text describes various types of algorithms, hardware devices, and software design concepts. The overview is intended to illustrate the broad applicability of image processing technology and to demonstrate that a general set of image processing capabilities can support a broad range of applications.

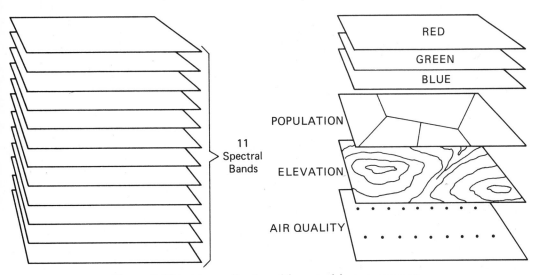

Figure 1-10.   Generalized multispectral image concept.

Planetary Exploration

Image processing techniques are used to support several scientific disciplines involved in planetary exploration, including the following:

Geology. Involves study of the structure of the planets and their satellites, including surface composition, surface dynamics, and surface structure. The image processing techniques include digital filtering, image enhancement, and multispectral analysis.

Cartography. Digital imaging techniques have been used as an aid in mapping the planets and their satellites. Techniques include geometric transformation (to project digital images into standard cartographic projections), digital filtering, digital image mosaicking, and determination of elevation from stereo imagery.

Figure 1-11 shows the first photomosaic globe of a planet constructed from remotely sensed imagery. Over 1,200 individual images from the Mariner 9 Mars orbital mission were processed to remove camera-system distortion; the images were then filtered and enhanced to emphasize structural detail and were cartographically projected to an orthographic projection for final assembly onto the globe, which was 3 feet in diameter.

Figure 1-12 illustrates the combination of elevation data with remotely sensed imagery. A LANDSAT multispectral image of the Los Angeles basin was combined with elevation data to produce a three-dimensional representation of the area. The LANDSAT image was projected to the same geometric reference as the elevation data, so that the image data and elevation data were spatially registered. Computer techniques were then used to manipulate and reproject the imagery to provide a three-dimensional representation. The vertical scale was exaggerated by a factor of two in order to emphasize elevation variations in the region. A series of 3,336 images was processed using this technique, with each image produced at a different viewing orientation, and the resulting images were used to produce "LA: The Movie." The movie is a two-minute film that provides the sensation of an aerial ride over a three-dimensional Southern California landscape.

Atmospheric Sciences. Image processing is one tool used to determine atmospheric composition and radiometric properties and to analyze the dynamics of atmospheric motion. Processing techniques include image enhancement, digital filtering, radiometric analysis (based on both monospectral and multispectral images), and generation of movie sequences, using time-sequential imagery.

Figure 1-13 is an illustration of the use of time-sequential imagery in analyzing the atmospheric dynamics of the planet Uranus. Four sequential images acquired through the orange filter of the Voyager 2 imaging system in January 1986 are shown. These images were acquired over a 4.6-hour period. The motion of a bright cloud in a counterclockwise direction during the observation period is visible in the four images. A smaller, fainter cloud is also visible closer to the planet limb in the last three images. From analysis of these images, the relative motion of the clouds at two different latitudes was determined; this information can be used to develop models of the atmospheric dynamics on this planet.

Figure 1-11. Three foot photomosaic globe of Mars, constructed from computer-processed Mariner 9 images (Jet Propulsion Laboratory).

Earth Applications Remote Sensing

Earth applications remote sensing involves the use of imaging sensors and other instruments mounted on aircraft, spacecraft, undersea vehicles and platforms, or other systems designed to measure or monitor the earth's characteristics. Many spectral instruments now return data that can be processed using image manipulation technology. The major subdivisions of remote sensing that involve the use of imaging sensors include the following:

Mineral Exploration. Normally involves the use of multispectral imagery for analysis of surface composition that may indicate mineral deposition and for analysis of

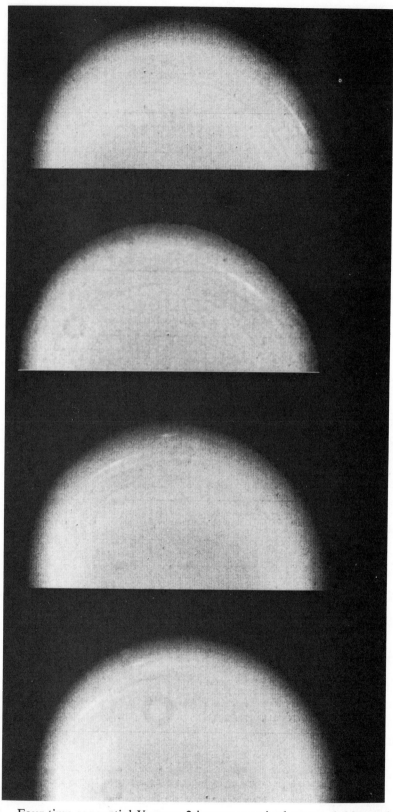

Figure 1-13. Four time-sequential Voyager 2 images acquired over a 4.6-hour time period in January 1986, used to analyze atmospheric dynamics (Jet Propulsion Laboratory).

surface structure. Image processing techniques include image enhancement, multispectral classification, image ratioing, and correlation of image data with other geographically referenced data bases.

Determination of Surface Composition. Surface composition can be estimated from a knowledge of the reflectance properties of various types of materials. Multispectral imaging provides one mechanism for determining surface composition. The most frequently utilized techniques include multispectral image enhancement and classification, and image ratioing. Figure 1-14 illustrates the use of LANDSAT multispectral imagery to attempt to identify areas of potential limestone structure in the Coconino plateau region below the Grand Canyon. The color imagery has been processed so that areas with a spectral reflectivity close to that of limestone will be displayed as a light orange color. This analysis was performed in order to identify porous limestone regions on the plateau that might serve as potential drilling sites for new water sources within the relatively arid region.

Change Detection. Multiple images acquired of the same area support analysis of changes occurring in the selected area. The images are generally geometrically projected to the same orientation, map projection, or viewing angle. Figure 1-15 shows the surge of the Hubbard Glacier in Alaska that sealed off the Russell Fiord in 1985–1986. The left image is a LANDSAT Thematic Mapper (TM) image acquired in August 1985 and the right image is a second LANDSAT TM image acquired in September 1986. Both images have been registered to the same viewing geometry and orientation. The two images illustrate the movement of the bluish-white glacier and the ice blockage that turned Russell Fiord into Russell Lake.

Land-Use Analysis. Remotely sensed imagery can be used to determine various categories of land utilization. The image processing techniques include cartographic projection, correlation of image data with nonimaging geographically referenced data bases, image differencing, and multispectral image classification and analysis. Figure 1-16 shows a land-use classification of Portland, Oregon, that is based on analysis of LANDSAT multispectral imagery. The various classes of land use are indicated by the shading of the image. The land-use map produced from LANDSAT data has been registered to the data base containing the United States Census tracts in Portland. This registration aided in later analysis, when land-use patterns were correlated with data contained in the Census Bureau statistical data base for this area.

Agricultural and Forestry Applications. The use of multispectral imagery and images acquired at different times of the year can provide an indication of crop types in agricultural areas and of forest cover types of forested regions. Remotely sensed imagery can provide a basis for monitoring and for detection of significant changes as well as for developing inventories of various crop types or forest cover.

Ocean Monitoring. Multispectral imagery can be used to monitor the quality of ocean water, especially near coastlines. High-resolution imaging devices can be used to determine wave patterns and ice pack structure. Synthetic-aperture radar systems are ideal for these applications, and the SEASAT satellite demonstrated the viability

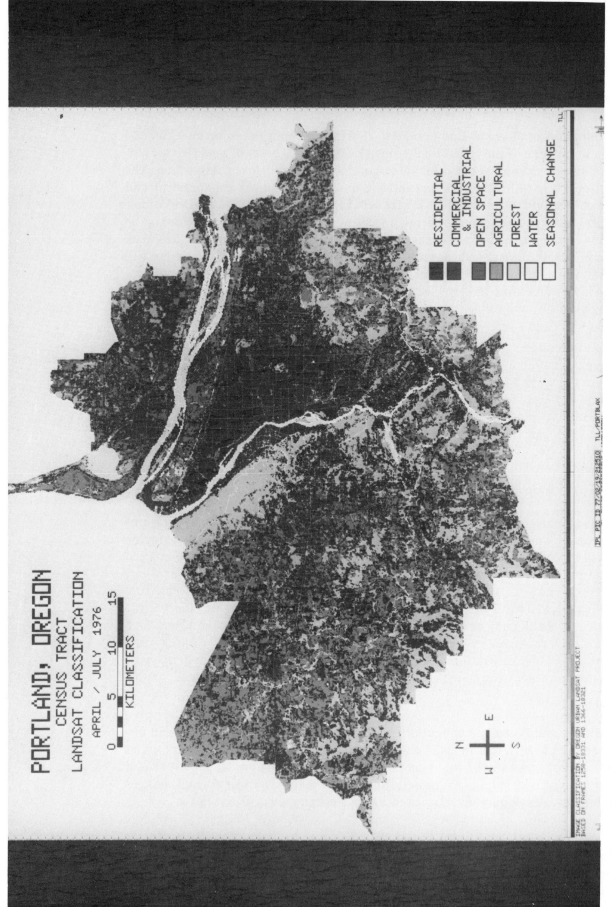

Figure 1-16. Land use classification of Portland, Oregon, with census tracts overlay (Jet Propulsion Laboratory).

18

of this technique for monitoring ocean dynamics. The major image processing techniques used in this type of application include image enhancement, multispectral image manipulation and classification, digital filtering, geometric projection and cartographic registration, and image differencing. Figure 1-17 shows the use of aircraft-mounted synthetic-aperture radar system to monitor a portion of the Arctic ice pack. Several strips of radar imagery acquired on several passes over the ice field were computer-processed to provide a consistent geographic reference scale and to remove a variety of radiometric distortion effects (including range-dependent shading). The multiple strips were processed and then displayed as a single registered digital image with the same radiometric properties throughout. The analysis was directed toward determining the relative orientation of the "leads," or cracks in the ice field, as a function of time. The imaging was repeated in the same region 2 weeks later, and the image data were compared quantitatively, using digital Fourier transform techniques to determine the change in orientation of the leads during the 2-week period.

Weather and Climate Analysis.   Weather patterns and atmospheric properties are continuously monitored from spacecraft-based systems. Synchronous satellites such as the GOES spacecraft monitor a particular area from a constant location above the area in earth orbit, providing periodic imagery and other sensor data that can be used for weather forecasting. Wind speed and cloud motion dynamics can be determined from time-sequential imagery of the same region. The image processing techniques most commonly used include image enhancement, image differencing, and multispectral analysis. Figure 1-18 shows the second of a pair of GOES satellite images used to determine wind speed and direction, using observed cloud motion in the image pair. The "wind bars" indicate wind speed and direction. The data determined at discrete locations in the image pair can be interpolated to provide a contoured pattern indicating wind speed and direction, as shown in Figure 1-19.

Undersea Exploration.   Imaging sonar systems and other sensors are increasingly being used to determine the structure and composition of the ocean floor. The image processing techniques include image enhancement, geometric correction, and digital filtering. Figure 1-20 shows a pair of images obtained from a digital side-looking sonar system. Both images have been computer-processed to correct for geometric distortion caused by the sonar sampling process and by the wandering of the ship about the central desired track (the black area in both images is caused by the fact that the side-looking system cannot look downward). The two images have received different types of enhancement. The version on the right has been processed with an enhancement filter designed to display maximum structural detail.

Medical Applications

Digital image processing is becoming an increasingly important tool in medical diagnosis. There are several broad areas in which the technology is playing an important role, including the following:

Chromosome Karyotyping.   Analysis of chromosome samples can provide important insight into disease and genetic defects. Computers have been used for over 10 years to perform chromosome classification under the guidance and control of hu-

Figure 1-17. Computer processed synthetic aperture radar image mosaic of Arctic ice field (Jet Propulsion Laboratory).

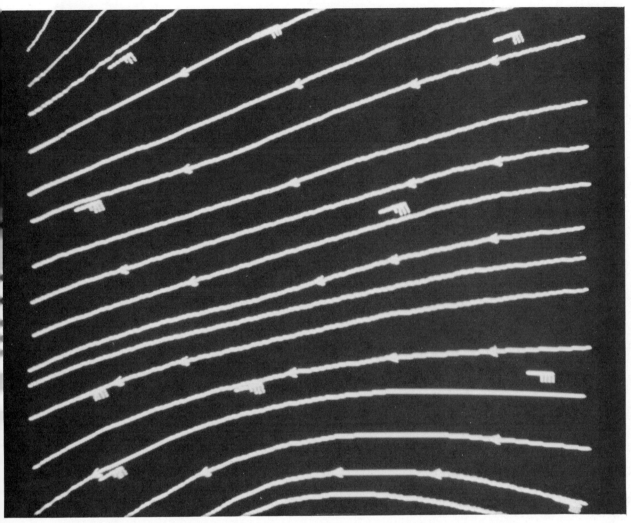

Figure 1-19.   Interpolated graphical display of wind velocity and direction derived from multiple weather satellite imagery (Unisys Defense Systems).

man operators. Chromosome classification is performed in several steps. A microscope slide containing a set of randomly oriented chromosomes is obtained and converted to digital format. Each of the chromosomes is isolated as a single object, and the object is then classified according to type, using a variety of pattern-recognition techniques. Figure 1-21 shows the process at the second step; at this point, all the chromosomes located within a sample have been extracted from the image and labeled with a numeric identifier. The next step involves classification of each object according to type.

Radiography.   Analysis of X-ray imagery was one of the earliest medical applications of digital processing. The basic techniques involved in radiography include image enhancement, image averaging and differencing, geometric transformation, edge detection, and digital filtering. Figure 1-22 shows one typical application. Time-sequential X-ray images are often averaged to improve the signal-to-noise ratio as an aid in image analysis. There are difficulties in achieving geometric registration of multiple images of coronary arteries since the blood vessels move as a result

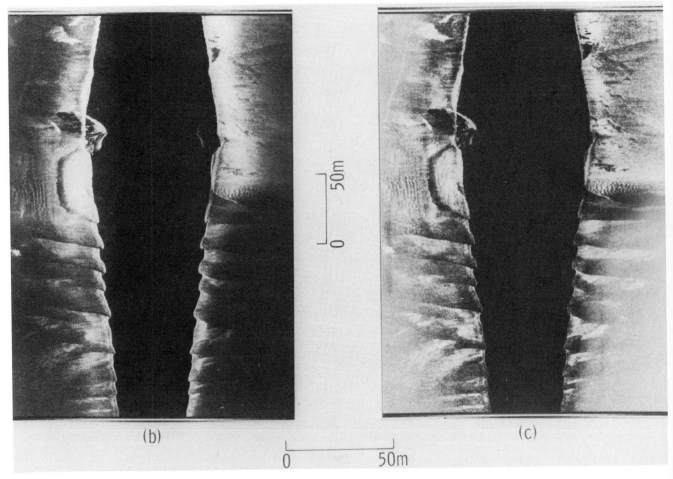

Figure 1-20.   Side-looking sonar images of the ocean floor. Two different computer enhancements have been applied to the same image (Jet Propulsion Laboratory).

of heart action between successive exposures. Figure 1-22*a* and *b* are a pair of time-sequential images. The original version of Figure 1-22*b* could not be directly aligned with Figure 1-22*a* because of varying degrees of blood vessel motion that had occurred relative to the geometric orientation of Figure 1-22*a*. Digital image processing techniques were used to correlate subregions of Figure 1-22*b* with corresponding subregions of Figure 1-22*a*, using fixed landmark reference points (e.g., a vessel branch or intersection).

Figure 1-22*b* is a geometrically corrected image that is precisely aligned with Figure 1-22*a*. The resulting average of the registered image pair is shown in Figure 1-22*c;* the averaged image has improved the overall signal-to-noise ratio, as originally desired. If the two images had not been geometrically aligned, the resulting average image would have been more blurred, and the signal-to-noise ratio might well have been degraded instead of improved.

Astronomy

Digital techniques are widely used in astronomical applications. Digital techniques are used to process imagery originally acquired on film and also in conjunction with digital sensors that are used with ground-based telescopes. Digital techniques and

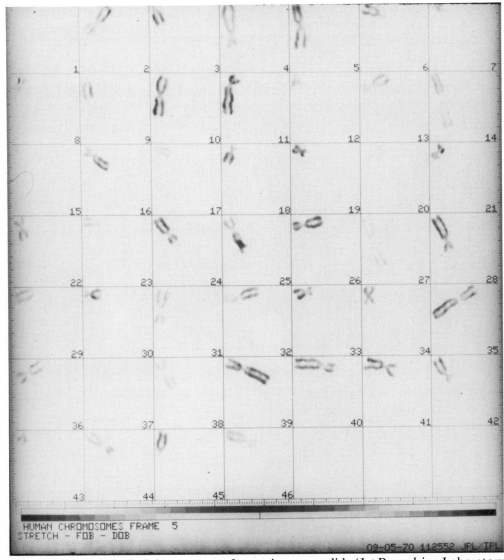

Figure 1-21.   Isolation of chromosomes from microscope slide (Jet Propulsion Laboratory).

digital images sensors provide improved resolution and dynamic range for astronomical applications. Typical image processing techniques used for astronomy applications include radiometric analysis, image enhancement, false-color display, digital filtering, image ratioing and differencing, multispectral classification, and feature extraction and classification. Figure 1-23 illustrates the use of "false color" for image enhancement in an astronomical application. An image of the comet Kohoutek originally acquired in black and white has been enhanced, using false-color techniques, in an attempt to analyze the radiometric properties of the head of the comet. The image intensity data have been contoured and produced in false-color rendition so that small changes in intensity appear as large color differences in the displayed image. The enhancement displays almost every intensity level in the head of the comet; the false coloring also enhances the system random noise in the background surrounding the comet and its tail.

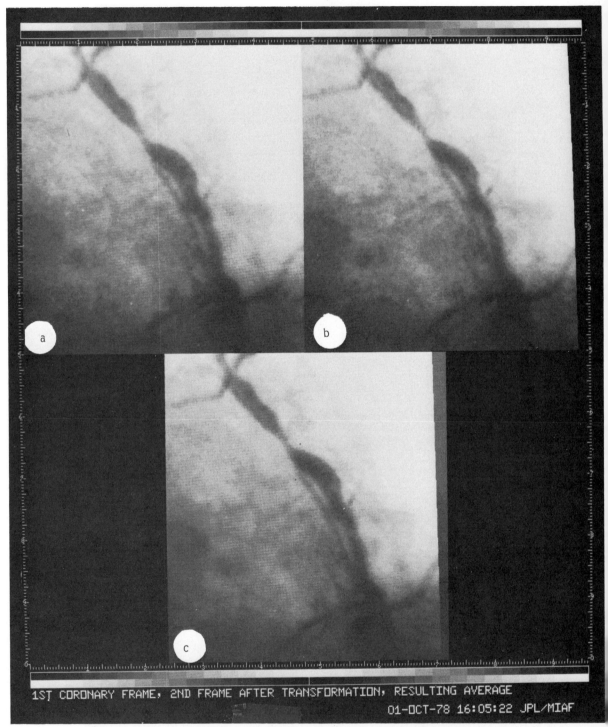

Figure 1-22. a and b) Pair of x-ray images that have been geometrically aligned. c) Average image produced by averaging images a and b (Jet Propulsion Laboratory).

DIGITAL IMAGE PROCESSING—A SYSTEMS APPROACH

The preceding introductory sections of this chapter have demonstrated the utility of digital image processing technology in a wide range of applications areas. The development of the technology has been characterized by the transfer of techniques and associated hardware from one applications area to another. Each applications area eventually develops specialized algorithms and equipment that enhance the utility of computer-based techniques for that particular application. There remains, however, a central set of image processing capabilities that is relevant to a wide range of applications. It is also true that much of the commercially available image processing hardware can be used in many applications areas and that many of the fundamental software system design concepts are relevant to all applications areas.

The remaining chapters of this book outline the basic technology foundation on which an image processing system can be developed. The intent has been to extract the techniques and concepts and to describe the hardware system components that can be broadly applied to a variety of different applications.

Every digital image processing system can be represented by a block diagram containing three main elements, as shown in Figure 1-24. The three major elements of every image processing system include the following:

Image Acquisition.   Involves the conversion of a scene into a digital representation that can be processed by a digital computer. Image acquisition can be performed by a sensor system specially designed to view a scene and provide a digital representation of that scene; image acquisition can also involve the conversion of image data from an existing medium (television, film, etc.) into a digital representation.

Image Processing.   Provides digital processing of one or more images to produce a desired result. The processing can range from simple enhancement of an individual image for improved display of scene detail to more complex processing involving several component images (e.g., multispectral classification) or several hundred component images (e.g., a photomosaic of a large region of a planet).

Image Display.   Provides for generation of an output product that can be seen by a human observer. The display can be achieved by using volatile display techniques on a video monitor or in hard-copy form (e.g., film). This element provides the required conversion of digital data into some analog form (e.g., video signals or film products) for viewing.

Specialized computer peripheral devices are now available that perform many of the functions contained within these elements. In addition to the specialized computer peripherals, general-purpose (or customized) digital computers are required for many of the functions. All three elements require computer software both for image processing and for control of the flow of data within the overall system. It

Figure 1-24.   The three basic components of an image processing system.

is often necessary to develop or adapt a data base management system just to keep track of input images, processed versions of input images, and output image products of a variety of formats.

The remainder of this book is organized on the basis of this systems view, as shown in Figure 1-25. Chapter 2 describes the various types of digital image acquisition systems. Several digital imaging systems used in remote sensing spacecraft are described, with special emphasis placed on the LANDSAT and SPOT multispectral scanning systems. The various devices used for converting image data from film and video format into digital format are also described, and a summary of the trade-offs involved in designing image acquisition systems is included.

Chapters 3 and 4 provide an introduction to the basic image processing algorithms that are generally useful in a broad range of applications. The intent in these chapters is to provide an introduction to the most commonly encountered algorithms, and so a basic set of general purpose algorithms is described in these two chapters. A series of "implementation notes" is also provided to aid those who wish to implement these algorithms. References are provided to other sources that present more detailed descriptions of the algorithms presented here as well as additional material not included in the text.

Chapter 5 describes the devices that are used to display image data, including volatile image display systems and film recorder systems. Chapter 5 also includes a review of techniques used for compact storage of image data bases, including microfilm, microfiche, and video disk systems. It also describes some considerations relative to the calibration of display devices to ensure consistency of image display.

Chapters 6 and 7 contain basic concepts for design and implementation of computer software that are relevant to all three system elements. Chapter 6 outlines the concepts of image processing software system design. It includes a discussion of the formats used to store digital image data, a description of the use of software modules and system-level subroutines as components of image processing software systems, and a section dealing with software design for interactive image processing. Chapter 6 concludes with an overview of a complete image processing software system, including top-level executive, data base management system, utility routines, and individual input, processing, and display modules.

Chapter 7 deals with concepts involved in image data base management. The

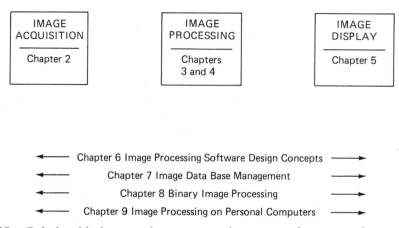

Figure 1-25. Relationship between image processing system elements and organization of the text.

chapter includes a description of methods used to identify and index individual images within a system so that user query and image retrieval operations can be accommodated efficiently. The use of image descriptors for data base query and image retrieval operations is discussed, and the topic of annotation of image data products is addressed extensively.

Chapter 8 treats the special topic of systems designed for the processing of binary imagery. These systems are most often used for processing digitized document material. The chapter includes an overview of the specialized systems used for digital document processing, a summary of the equipment used to scan and display digitized document imagery, a description of the data compression techniques used to reduce storage and communication time requirements within these systems, and a summary of halftoning techniques used to display gray-shaded imagery using binary representation.

Chapter 9 describes personal computer (PC) -based systems used for image processing. The limitations of image processing in a PC environment are outlined, and the general architecture of PC-based image processing systems is described. The application of special purpose boards used for image acquisition, processing, and display in a PC environment is described. The chapter also includes a discussion of software considerations for PC-based image processing systems.

The three appendixes contain (1) a description of the digital image data currently available from a variety of earth observations and planetary exploration spacecraft and a list of the agencies distributing that data within the United States; (2) a list of LANDSAT receiving stations and data sources around the world; and (3) a bibliography listing additional sources in several categories.

REFERENCES

1. Hall, R. Cargill, *Lunar Impact–A History of Project Ranger,* Washington, U.S. Government Printing Office, 1977.
2. *Surveyor Project Final Report, Part II–Science Results,* JPL Technical Report 32-1265, June 1968.
3. Collins, S. A., *The Mariner 6 and 7 Pictures of Mars,* NASA SP-263, Washington, U.S. Government Printing Office, 1971.
4. Rindfleisch, T. C., J. A. Dunne, H. J. Frieden, W. D. Stromberg, and R. M. Ruiz, "Digital Processing of the Mariner 6 and 7 Pictures," *J Geophys Res* 76 2, pp. 394-417 (1971).
5. Hartmann, W. K., and O. Raper, *The New Mars–The Discoveries of Mariner 9,* NASA SP-337, Washington, U.S. Government Printing Office, 1974.
6. Green, W. B., P. L. Jepsen, J. E. Kreznar, R. M. Ruiz, A. A. Schwartz, and J. B. Seidman, "Removal of Instrument Signature from Mariner 9 Television Images of Mars," *Appl Opt* 15, 105 (1975).
7. Levinthal, E., et al., "Mariner 9 Image Processing and Products," *Icarus* 18, 75 (1973).
8. Dunne, J. A., and E. Burgess, *The Voyage of Mariner 10,* NASA SP-424, Washington, U.S. Government Printing Office, 1978.
9. Davies, M., S. E. Dwornik, D. E. Gault, and R. G. Strom, *Atlas of Mercury,* NASA SP-423, Washington, U.S. Government Printing Office, 1978.
10. Soha, J. M., D. J. Lynn, J. J. Lorre, J. A. Mosher, N. N. Thayer, D. A. Elliott, W. D. Benton, and R. E. Dewar, "IPL Processing of the Mariner 10 Images of Mercury," *J Geophys Rev* 80, 12 (1975).
11. *The Martian Landscape,* NASA SP-425. Washington, U.S. Government Printing Office, 1978.
12. Spitzer, C. R. (ed), *Viking Orbiter Views of Mars,* NASA SP-441, Washington, U.S. Government Printing Office, 1980.
13. Green, W. B., "Computer Image Processing—The Viking Experience," *IEEE Trans on Consumer Electronics,* Vol. CE-23, 3 (1977).
14. Green, W. B., "Viking Image Processing," *Proc SPIE* 119, 209 (1977).

15. Levinthal, E. C., W. B. Green, K. L. Jones, and R. B. Tucker, "Processing the Viking Lander Camera Data," *J Geophys Rev* 82, 28, p. 4412 (1977).
16. Liebes, S., and A. A. Schwartz, "Viking 75 Mars Lander Interactive Video Computerized Stereophotogrammetry," *J Geophys Rev* 82, 28, p. 4421 (1977).
17. Ruiz, R. M., D. A. Elliott, G. M. Yagi, R. B. Pomphrey, M. A. Power, K. W. Farrell, J. J. Lorre, W. D. Benton, R. E. Dewar, and L. E. Cullen, "IPL Processing of the Viking Orbiter Images of Mars," *J Geophys Rev* 82, 28, p. 4189 (1977).
18. Morrison, D., and J. Samz, *Voyage to Jupiter,* NASA SP-439, Washington, U.S. Government Printing Office, 1980.
19. Morrison, D., *Voyages to Saturn,* NASA-SP-451, U.S. Government Printing Office, Washington, D. C., 1982.
20. Jepsen, P. L., J. A. Mosher, G. M. Yagi, C. C. Avis, G. W. Garneau, J. J. Lorre, E. P. Korsmo, and L. R. Doyle, "Application of Image Processing to Voyager Imagery," *Proc SPIE* 292 (1981).
21. Short, N. M., et al, *Mission to Earth–LANDSAT Views the World,* NASA SP-360, Washington, U.S. Government Printing Office, 1976.
22. Colwell, R. N. (ed.), *Manual of Remote Sensing,* American Society of Photogrammetry, Falls Church, VA., 1983.
23. Bernstein, R. (ed.), *Digital Image Processing for Remote Sensing,* New York, IEEE Press, 1978.
24. Sabins, F. F., Jr., *Remote Sensing–Principles and Interpretation,* San Francisco, Freeman, 1978.
25. Selzer, R. H., "The Use of Computers to Improve Biomedical Image Quality," *Proc Fall Joint Computer Conf* 33, 817 (1968).
26. Castleman, K. R., J. Melnyk, H. J. Frieden, G. W. Persinger, and R. J. Wall, "Computer Assisted Karyotyping," *J Reproductive Medicine 17* 1, p. 53 (1976).
27. Crawford, D. W., S. H. Brooks, R. H. Selzer, R. Barndt, E. S. Beckenbach, and D. H. Blankenhorn, "Computer Densitometry for Angiographic Assessment of Arterial Cholesterol Content and Gross Pathology in Human Atherosclerosis," *J Lab Clin Medicine* 89, 378 (1977).
28. *IEEE Trans. on Biomedical Engineering.* Special Issue on Computerized Medical Imaging, *BME-28* 2 (1981).
29. Sochurek, H., "Medicine's New Vision," *National Geographic* 171, 1 (1987).
30. Lorre, J. J., D. J. Lynn, and W. D. Benton, "Recent Developments at JPL in the Application of Digital Image Processing Techniques to Astronomical Imgages," *Proc SPIE* 74, 234 (1976).
31. Elliott, D. A. "Applications of Digital Image Processing to Astronomy," *SPIE* Vol. 264 (1980).
32. Janssen, K., "Grounded," *Air and Space* 2, 2 (1987).
33. Bahcall, J. N. and L. Spitzer, Jr., "The Space Telescope," *Scientific American* 247, 1 (1982).

2
Digital Image Acquisition Systems

INTRODUCTION

A digital image acquisition system is a device that generates a sampled digital representation of a scene. A scene can be many different things. A digital image acquisition system operated on a spacecraft can be used to acquire imagery of an area of a planet. A microscope slide can be viewed by a closed-circuit television camera system that feeds analog input to a digitizing module, generating a sampled digital version of the scene being viewed by the camera through the microscope. A CAT system can acquire a set of images that will be analyzed to determine the three-dimensional coordinates of the various organs within the human body. In each of these cases, the continuous scene being viewed by some type of sensor is converted into a discrete set of samples that can be processed by a digital computing system.

Imagery can be acquired in one single region of the electromagnetic spectrum or in more than one region. The term *multispectral image* refers to an image acquired by viewing the same area of scene in more than one spectral band. A color image that portrays the scene as it would be seen by a human observer can be acquired with an imaging system that views the scene through three spectral filters (red, green, and blue) sequentially. This system would in effect produce three separate digitally sampled images, and those images can be merged into a single color rendition, using techniques described later in this text.

Multispectral imaging systems can acquire image data in spectral regions for which the human eye is not sensitive. Digital imaging systems are often used to acquire imagery in the ultraviolet, infrared, microwave, and X-ray regimes. In all cases, however, the output is of the same general form. A scene viewed in a particular wave-length region will be represented digitally as a two-dimensional matrix of numbers, where the numerical value of each matrix element is related to the brightness of the scene at that point within that spectral region. A multispectral image will be represented as a set of individual matrixes, one for each spectral band sampled by the image acquisition system.

There are four broad categories of digital image acquisition systems:

1. *Digital Imaging Sensors.* These devices acquire digitized imagery of the scene viewed by the sensor. The output of these systems can be multispectral.
2. *Film Scanners.* These devices are used to convert film transparencies to digital representation for computer processing. A variety of mechanisms are used to scan the transparency point by point, producing a digital intensity for each point scanned. Film scanners can also scan multispectral imagery.
3. *Video Digitizers.* Conventional television systems provide analog imagery of a scene approximately every one-thirtieth of a second. Video digitizers either "freeze" a single analog video frame and digitize it point by point or scan the

camera field of view for a few seconds, digitizing point by point as sequential imagery is acquired.

4. *Paper Scanners.* These devices are used to scan document material. The most common paper scanners image individual pages and produce binary (one bit per pixel) images. The scanner acquires gray scale data, performs image enhancement processing, and converts the gray-shaded enhanced pixel into either black or white, based on a threshhold.

This chapter describes the first three categories of image acquisition systems. Paper scanners are described in Chapter 8, where document image processing systems are described. This chapter also includes a discussion of the design trade-offs performed in designing a digital image acquisition device, and the data communications and computer processing systems often associated with these devices.

DIGITAL CAMERA SYSTEMS FOR REMOTE SENSING

This section describes several types of camera systems used in remote sensing applications. The systems described here have been selected to provide a representative but not complete description of the remote sensing devices currently in use. The designer of an image processing system must develop a fundamental understanding of the sensors that acquire the data in order to develop or utilize the algorithms best suited to the individual applications analysis that will be supported by the image processing system.

Vidicon-Based Systems

Vidicon tubes are frequently utilized to acquire imagery in remote sensing applications ranging from planetary exploration to ground-based television image acquisition. The main component in a vidicon system is a glass tube containing a scanning electron beam mechanism with a photosensitive surface at the end opposite the electron beam source (see Figure 2-1). The photosensitive surface is designed to produce a buildup of electric charge on the back surface, proportional to the amount of light

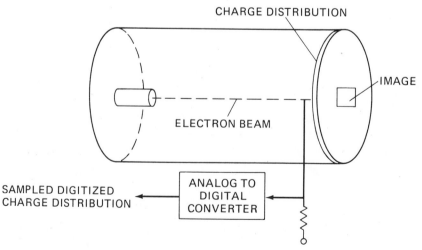

Figure 2-1. Vidicon tube schematic.

falling on the front (outer) surface of the photosensitive material. The back surface is flooded with electrons before image exposure, producing a uniform saturated charge distribution. When the image is focused on the front surface, the electron charge is depleted in proportion to the amount of light incident on the front surface of the material. The resultant charge distribution is characterized by a high number of electrons in the dark regions of the image and a low number of electrons in the lighter regions.

The scanning electron beam then scans the charge distribution line by line. The scanning beam replaces the electron charge in the regions where the charge was depleted by exposure to light. The fluctuations in the electron beam current caused by replacement of depleted charge are proportional to the light intensity, and the fluctuating beam current is read out through a load resistor. The sequential scanning produces a series of lines of analog data. The analog signal is sampled a fixed number of times for each scan line and then is digitized. This process produces a two-dimensional digital image that is then available for computer processing. Vidicon systems are available with a variety of spatial resolutions. Most vidicon systems provide at least 512 scan lines, with 512 points digitized per scan line.

A variety of scanning speeds are also available, and the choice of photosensitive material used in a vidicon system is often based on the desired scanning speed. A system in which the charge distribution is read out over a period of many seconds requires a photosensitive material that will retain the charge intensity and spatial location for that period of time. Faster scanning requires material that will not retain the charge distribution for long periods of time. Vidicon systems can be troubled by residual image problems because of the need to retain the charge distribution long enough for the image-scanning process to be performed. The retention capability may cause incomplete readout of the charge distribution, and a portion of the charge distribution may then be present in the next image that is scanned. Residual image problems are usually reduced significantly by saturating the surface with electrical charge between exposures. In this manner, any residual image will be spatially uniform and unstructured and thus less distracting in the next sequential image.

Vidicon systems often introduce a variety of artifacts into imagery. The scanning electron beam is not perfectly linear, and some geometric distortion is often introduced by vidicon systems as a result of nonlinear scanning of the charge distribution. The electron beam can also be deflected toward or away from high-contrast boundaries in the charge distribution during scanning (caused by high contrast detail in the scene). This effect can introduce local geometric distortion at locations within the scanned image. Vidicons may also introduce artifacts into scanned imagery because of defects, or blemishes, within the photosensitive material used to acquire the imagery. The degree of charge retention may also not be uniform within the photosensitive material, and additional charge depletion, or "leaking," can occur during the scanning process. If a few seconds is required to scan the charge distribution, the charge at the lower regions of the image may deteriorate somewhat before the electron beam arrives at that area to replace the depleted charge. It is possible to compensate for some of these distortions with computer processing; techniques for distortion removal are discussed in Chapter 4.

Figure 2-2 shows a schematic of the Viking Orbiter remote sensing system that employed a vidicon tube as the imaging sensor.[1] The two Viking spacecraft placed into orbit around Mars in 1976 each carried two vidicon-based imaging systems. These systems returned over 100,000 images during a 4-year operational period. The

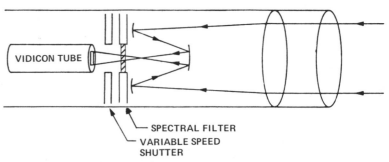

SPECTRAL FILTER
VARIABLE SPEED
SHUTTER

Figure 2-2. Viking Mars Orbiter Vidicon-based camera system.

optics system was designed to achieve a particular ground spatial resolution, and the image data were focused onto the front surface of a vidicon tube placed in the focal plane of the camera system. The system included a variable-speed shutter, which permitted control of exposure. A filter wheel was positioned in front of the shutter, and a variety of spectral filters could be placed in front of the shutter to select a spectral range for each image. An image was acquired by positioning the filter wheel and opening the shutter for a prescribed period of time. The charge distribution was read out and digitized in slightly over two seconds, and the tube was then conditioned to reduce residual image before the next exposure. Each image was approximately 1,000 pixels square. The two camera systems on each spacecraft were operated in an alternating manner; one image was acquired while the image from the other camera system was being read out and digitized.

Figure 2-3 shows the twin camera systems mounted next to the main radio antenna

Figure 2-3. The Viking Mars Orbiter Spacecraft. Note the twin camera optics visible on the silver coated science instrument scan platform located to the right of the high-gain antenna just above the solar panel (Jet Propulsion Laboratory).

adjacent to one of the Viking spacecraft's solar panels. The camera systems and other scientific instruments were mounted on a "scan platform." The cameras and other instruments were pointed at particular target areas on the planet's surface through a combination of scan platform orientation and modification of the full spacecraft orientation.

Facsimile Systems

Facsimile systems have been used on remote sensing lunar and planetary landing vehicles. They acquire imagery by performing sequential single-line vertical scans of scenes. The horizontal dimension is achieved by scanning multiple adjacent vertical lines.

The Viking Mars Lander camera system is one example of a facsimile system (Figure 2-4).[2] The imaging sensors consisted of 12 solid-state light-sensitive diodes located in the base of the camera system; each diode was equipped with a spectral filter. The vertical line scan was achieved through the use of scanning mirror. Light entered the narrow quartz window slit in the camera housing and struck the scanning mirror. The scanning mirror rotated upward, and a narrow slit of object space was swept across all 12 diodes as the mirror performed the scan. A command sent to the spacecraft would select the diode to be read out on each scan.

The 12 diodes provided a wide flexibility in imaging the area around each of the two Viking Lander spacecraft. Four of the diodes were equipped with wide-band spectral filters that passed light corresponding roughly to the spectral range of visible light. Each of these four diodes was placed at a different position along the camera optical axis; the position along the vertical optical axis determined the focus of each of these four diodes. The diodes were positioned to provide optimal focus range from areas located directly below the camera system on the surface to areas

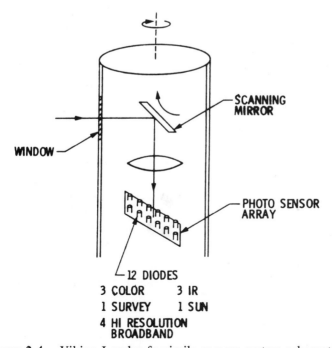

Figure 2-4. Viking Lander facsimile camera system schematic.

far out on the horizon (focus at infinity). Narrow-band spectral filters were placed on six other diodes, providing three-color bandwidths (red, green, and blue) in the visible region of the spectrum and three infrared bandwidths. One diode was equipped with a dense filter so that the sun could be imaged directly through the Martian atmosphere without damaging or saturating the photosensitive diode. The twelfth diode was used in "survey" mode, providing broad-band spectral coverage at lower spatial resolution than the other diodes.

Commands sent to the spacecraft would determine which of the signals acquired by the 12 diodes would be read out and digitized for each scan of the mirror. A full two-dimensional image was acquired by rotating the entire camera housing between line scans. For multispectral imaging, the camera housing was held stationary between line scans, and a series of different diodes would be read out sequentially before the housing was rotated. A three-color image would appear in the telemetry stream as a series of red pixels, followed by a series of green and then blue pixels; these three pixel streams would correspond to the same geometrical strip in object space. Figure 2-5 is a cutaway view of one of the camera systems, revealing the complex electromechanical nature of these imaging systems.

The analog signal derived from each diode during an individual mirror scan was sampled 512 times, providing 512 digital intensity values for each vertical line scan. The camera housing could be rotated almost a full 360°. The sample increment was 0.04° per scan line horizontally and vertically, except for the survey mode, in which the sampling increment was 0.12° per pixel. If high-resolution imagery at 0.04° spacing was desired over the full 360° range around the camera axis, approximately 9,000 vertical scan lines were required for that image in each spectral band. The image format acquired by the Viking Lander systems was thus a variable-size format; it is illustrated in Figure 2-6. The selection of spatial and spectral resolution for the camera system and the choice of a facsimile system were dictated by the stringent scientific objectives of the Viking science mission,[3] and the final choice of each parameter occurred only after extensive debate and trade-off studies.

Two cameras were mounted on each of the Lander spacecraft. A full-scale mock-up of the Lander spacecraft is shown in Figure 2-7. The two cameras were mounted on either side of the surface sampler arm. That arm could be rotated and extended to acquire samples of surface material that could be placed in the various biological analysis instruments located in back of the camera systems. The two cameras were positioned to provide stereoscopic coverage of the surface area directly in front of the Lander spacecraft. Stereo image pairs were acquired in order to develop accurate three-dimensional profiles of the terrain. Elevation data derived from stereoscopic image pairs were used extensively to determine accessible areas for sample acquisition on the surface.[4] In later phases of the Lander missions, trenches were dug in the surface of Mars to study the physical composition of the Martian soil, and the stereo image pairs were used to determine the depth and shape of the trenches.

The design of the Viking Lander camera systems led to significant computer processing requirements during mission operations. Figure 2-6 indicates that images were scanned from bottom to top and left to right. Most video display systems display image data from left to right and from top to bottom. All image data returned by Viking Lander required a rotation before the imagery could be displayed on conventional video monitors.

The fascimile cameras scanned in equal angle increments in solid angle. The result

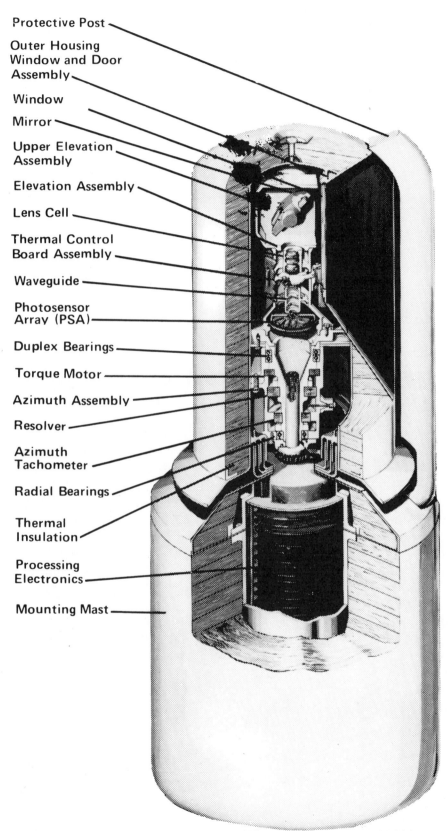

Protective Post

Outer Housing
Window and Door
Assembly

Window

Mirror

Upper Elevation
Assembly

Elevation Assembly

Lens Cell

Thermal Control
Board Assembly

Waveguide

Photosensor
Array (PSA)

Duplex Bearings

Torque Motor

Azimuth Assembly

Resolver

Azimuth
Tachometer

Radial Bearings

Thermal
Insulation

Processing
Electronics

Mounting Mast

Figure 2-5. Cut-away view of the Viking Lander Camera (NASA).

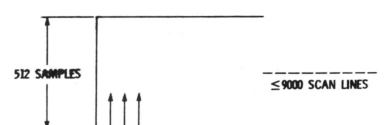

Figure 2-6.   Viking Lander camera digital image format.

of this scanning mechanism was a curvature or warping of object space when the sampled imagery was displayed or recorded on falt surfaces at equal pixel spacings. Extensive software was required to correct the scanned imagery for this effect. Techniques for performing this type of correction are discussed in Chapter 4.

Reference 5 contains a more complete description of the Viking Lander camera system and the imaging mission and includes a large collection of image data acquired during the mission (including a collection of stereo pairs). The Viking Lander example clearly shows the importance of understanding an imaging sensor before

Figure 2-7.   Viking Lander spacecraft mockup, showing surface sample acquisition arm extended between the twin camera systems (NASA).

proceeding to detailed design of a software system for processing image data acquired by that sensor.

Charge Coupled Devices (CCDs)

CCDs are frequently used components in image acquisition sytems. A CCD is a solid-state imaging device. CCDs will be utilized for a variety of remote sensing applications, including the imaging systems in the Hubble Space Telescope project and the Galileo spacecraft that will orbit Jupiter in the 1980s.

A CCD device can be viewed as a fixed array of potential wells on a small square or rectangular solid-state surface. Each well accumulates electrical charge proportional to the incident light intensity at each well position. An image is acquired by exposing the array to a desired scene. The exposure creates a two-dimensional distribution of electric potential stored within each of the potential wells. The digital image is acquired by reading and digitizing the potential stored wihtin each well.

The readout process for CCD systems is illustrated in Figure 2-8. The top line shows the light intensity incident on five of the potential wells within a two-dimensional CCD array. The next line shows the electric potential stored within each well after the image has been exposed. The readout process is performed sequentially, as illustrated on the last two lines of Figure 2-8. The first potential well on each line is read out through an analog-to-digital converter, and the electric potential along each line is shifted by one position. After the potential in the first well has been digitized, all remaining potential wells have transferred their electric potential to their immediate neighbor. This process continues sequentially until all potential wells for each line have been read out and digitized.

CCDs are popular for a variety of reasons. The radiometric response of CCDs is extremely linear, and the devices are quite sensitive to small changes in light intensity. It is thus possible to perform accurate radiometry with these devices, and the systems are so precise that it is not uncommon to digitize individual pixel intensity values to 12 bits of precision. The spectral response of these devices is broader than vidicon or film systems. The fixed position of each potential well provides high geometric precision in the sampled imagery. The devices are small and lightweight

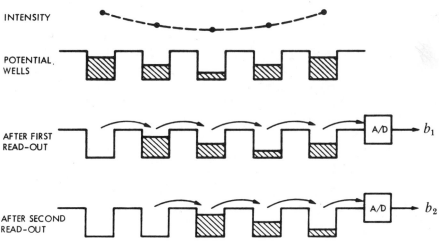

Figure 2-8. Charge coupled device image readout mechanism.

and require no mechanical parts or scanning electron beams. Typical CCD systems providing image sizes of up to 800 by 800 pixels can be produced on chips that are less than two inches on a side. CCD reliability is also quite high, consistent with other solid-state electronic devices.

Scanning Polarimeter Systems

There are a variety of scanning polarimeter systems that are utilized in remote sensing applications. In general, these systems are single-line scanners that are mounted on rotating or spinning spacecraft. Each rotation of the spacecraft provides a single image line, and the spacecraft is precessed slightly between rotations to produce a two-dimensional image. Scanning polarimeter systems were employed for the Pioneer spacecraft and provided multispectral imagery of Jupiter and Saturn from Pioneers 10 and 11. This type of system also is often employed on global weather satellites that monitor weather patterns from synchronous positions in earth orbit.[6] These satellites are placed in geosynchronous earth orbit, ensuring that they remain above the same point on the earth's surface as the earth rotates. They provide repetitive coverage of the earth's weather patterns and often employ scanning polarimeters to acquire imagery.

The LANDSAT Program

The National Aeronautics and Space Administration (NASA) established the Earth Resources Survey Program in 1965. As part of that program, a series of LANDSAT satellites was used to acquire repetitive multispectral imagery of the earths surface, starting in 1972. In the early 1980s, Congress determined that the national interest could best be served by transitioning the LANDSAT program from a government-sponsored program to a commercial activity, operated by the private sector. In 1985, the Department of Commerce released a contract to the Earth Observation Satellite Company (EOSAT). EOSAT is now responsible for developing the sensors, spacecraft, and data processing systems associated with the LANDSAT program, and for the sale and distribution of image data acquired by the LANDSAT satellites. The first LANDSAT spacecraft (initially called the Earth Resources Technology Satellite, or ERTS) was launched in July 1972. LANDSAT 4 was launched in July 1982, and LANDSAT 5 was launched in March, 1984.

Image data products generated from LANDSAT data have been available for purchase by users throughout the world. The United States distributed products through the EROS Data Center located in Sioux Falls, South Dakota while the LANDSAT program was a U.S. Government operation. Data is now available from the LANDSAT program through EOSAT; EOSAT now operates the EROS Data Center. Foreign and domestic ground stations can also receive digital data directly from the spacecraft. Reference 7 contains a history of the early years of the program and an atlas of color imagery from the early LANDSAT spacecraft. Reference 8 contains a more recent description of the spacecraft and imaging systems.

The first three LANDSAT spacecraft operated in circular orbits at an altitude of 920 km (570 miles), with an inclination of 99° relative to a plane passing through the equator. The orbits were designed to be sun-synchronous, so that the spacecraft crossed the equator 14 times per day at approximately 9:30AM local time in each transit and operate at an altitude of 705 km (437 miles), at an inclination of approximately 98°. LANDSATs 4 and 5 provide repetitive coverage of the same area of the earth's surface every 16 days; the first 3 LANDSAT spacecraft operated on an 18 day coverage cycle. Table 2-1 shows the orbital parameters for the LANDSAT systems. Two different LANDSAT spacecraft are shown in Figure 2-9.

The LANDSAT spacecraft provide imaging coverage of a strip of the earth's surface as they travel in their circular orbits. Imaging coverage of the full earths surface is achieved every 18 days for LANDSAT 1 through 3, and every 16 days for LAND-SAT 4 and 5. The time period between coverage of adjacent swaths is different for LANDSATs 4 and 5 than for the 3 earlier spacecraft. For a particular ground swath, LANDSAT 1, 2, and 3 would provide coverage of the next swath to the west on the next day of operation. For LANDSAT 4 and 5, the next adjacent swath to the west will be imaged one week later. The swathing pattern for the two cases is shown in Figures 2-10 and 2-11.

The LANDSAT 1, 2, and 3 spacecraft provided an overlap of approximately 15 percent between adjacent swaths at the equator, with larger overlap near the poles. LANDSATs 4 and 5 provide 7.3 percent overlap at the equator, with larger overlap (over 80 percent) at the poles.

Three types of imaging sensors have been utilized in the LANDSAT series. The first three spacecraft utilized the RBV systems to provide coverage of an area 185 km square in different spectral bands. Because of problems with these imaging systems, there is not a great deal of data available from these sensors.

MSS systems have flown on all 5 LANDSAT spacecraft. The MSS systems acquire imagery in four spectral bands. The spectral range of the four MSS bands is:

MSS BAND	WAVELENGTH, μm	SPECTRAL REGION
4	0.5 to 0.6	"Green"
5	0.6 to 0.7	"Red"
6	0.7 to 0.8	"Near-Infrared"
7	0.8 to 1.1	"Near-Infrared"

Band numbers 1, 2, and 3 were reserved for the RBV spectral bands on the early LANDSAT spacecraft.

TABLE 2-1   LANDSAT ORBITAL PARAMETERS

PARAMETER	LANDSAT 1,2,3	LANDSAT 4,5
Altitude (km)	920	705
Semi-major Axis (km)	7286	7084
Inclination (deg)	99	98
Period (min)	103	99
Coverage Cycle Duration	18 days	16 days
	251 revolutions	233 revolutions
Distance Between Adjacent Ground Tracks at Equator (km)	159	172

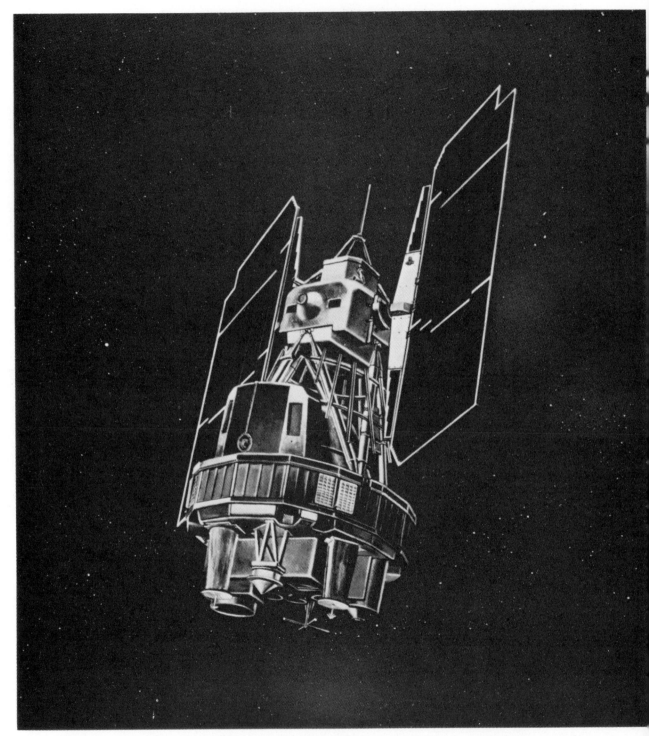

Figure 2-9.   LANDSAT 1 spacecraft, with MSS and RBV image sensors (EROS Data Center).

Figure 2-9 (*continued*).   LANDSAT 4 spacecraft with MSS and TM image sensors (EOSAT).

The TM imaging system has been flown on LANDSAT 4 and LANDSAT 5. The TM provides 7 spectral bands, as follows:

TM BAND	WAVELENGTH, μm	APPLICATION
1	.45 to .52	Coastal water mapping, soil/vegetation differentiation
2	.52 to .60	"Green"
3	.63 to .69	Plant species differentiation
4	.76 to .90	Water body delineation
5	1.55 to 1.75	Snow/cloud differentiation
6	10.4 to 12.5	Thermal mapping
7	2.08 to 2.35	Hydrothermal mapping

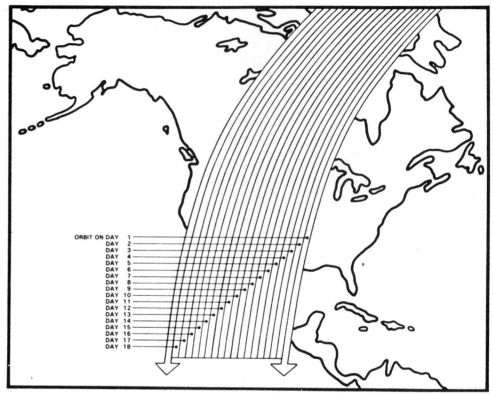

Figure 2-10.   Ground swath pattern for LANDSATs 1, 2, and 3.

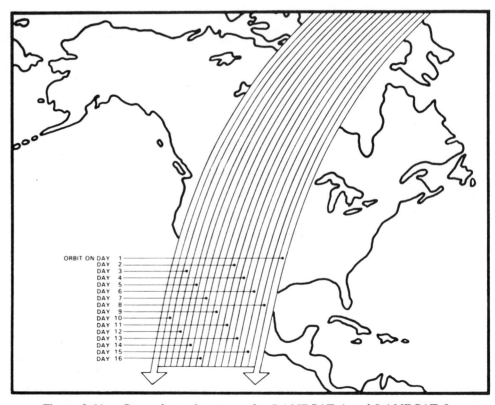

Figure 2-11.   Ground swath pattern for LANDSAT 4 and LANDSAT 5.

The LANDSAT 1, 2, and 3 spacecraft utilized the MSS scanner as the primary image acquisition system. The four spectral bands were designed primarily for agricultural remote sensing applications. The spectral bands of the MSS are useful in monitoring a variety of crops in various stages of growth, and in estimating soil moisture content. The TM spectral bands add the capability to perform geological analysis using remotely sensed data, including mineral exploration.

Figure 2-12 shows all four spectral components of a LANDSAT MSS image of New Orleans. An analysis of several areas in the scene that appear in all four images will provide insight into the variety of spectral response exhibited by the diverse materials on the earth's surface. Note, for example, the low spectral response of

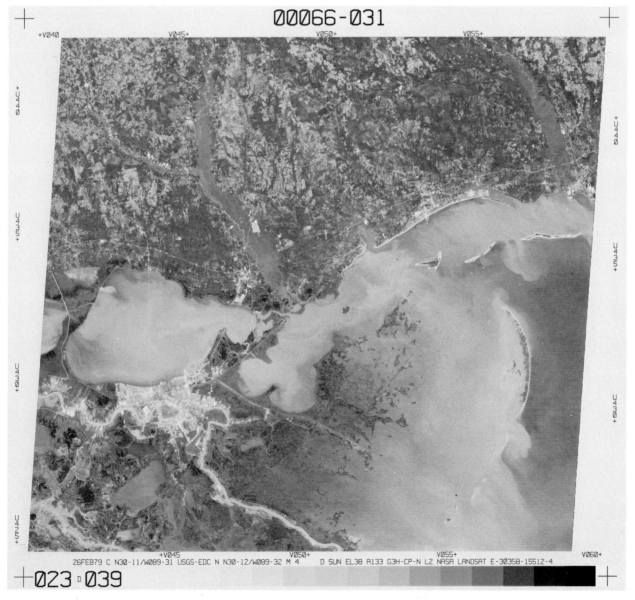

Figure 2-12a.   The four spectral components of a LANDSAT scene of New Orleans. (a) band 4, (b) band 5, (c) band 6, (d) band 7 (EROS Data Center).

Figure 2-12b.

water bodies in the infrared spectral bands, as well as variation in response of vegetation observed in MSS bands 4, 5, and 6.

Figure 2-13 illustrates the manner in which data are acquired by the LANDSAT MSS. The MSS system includes 24 solid-state photosensitive detectors. These detectors represent four sets of six detectors, one for each of the four spectral bands. A scanning mirror is employed to provide imaging coverage from west to east as the spacecraft sweeps across the earth from north to south. Each scan of the mirror provides imaging data from six parallel strips along the ground track to the six detectors in each of the four spectral bands. Data acquired by the 24 detectors are read out and digitized, providing six lines of imaging data in each of the four spectral bands. The mirror then returns to its initial position, and the spacecraft motion ensures that the next mirror scan will acquire imagery of a new set of six parallel

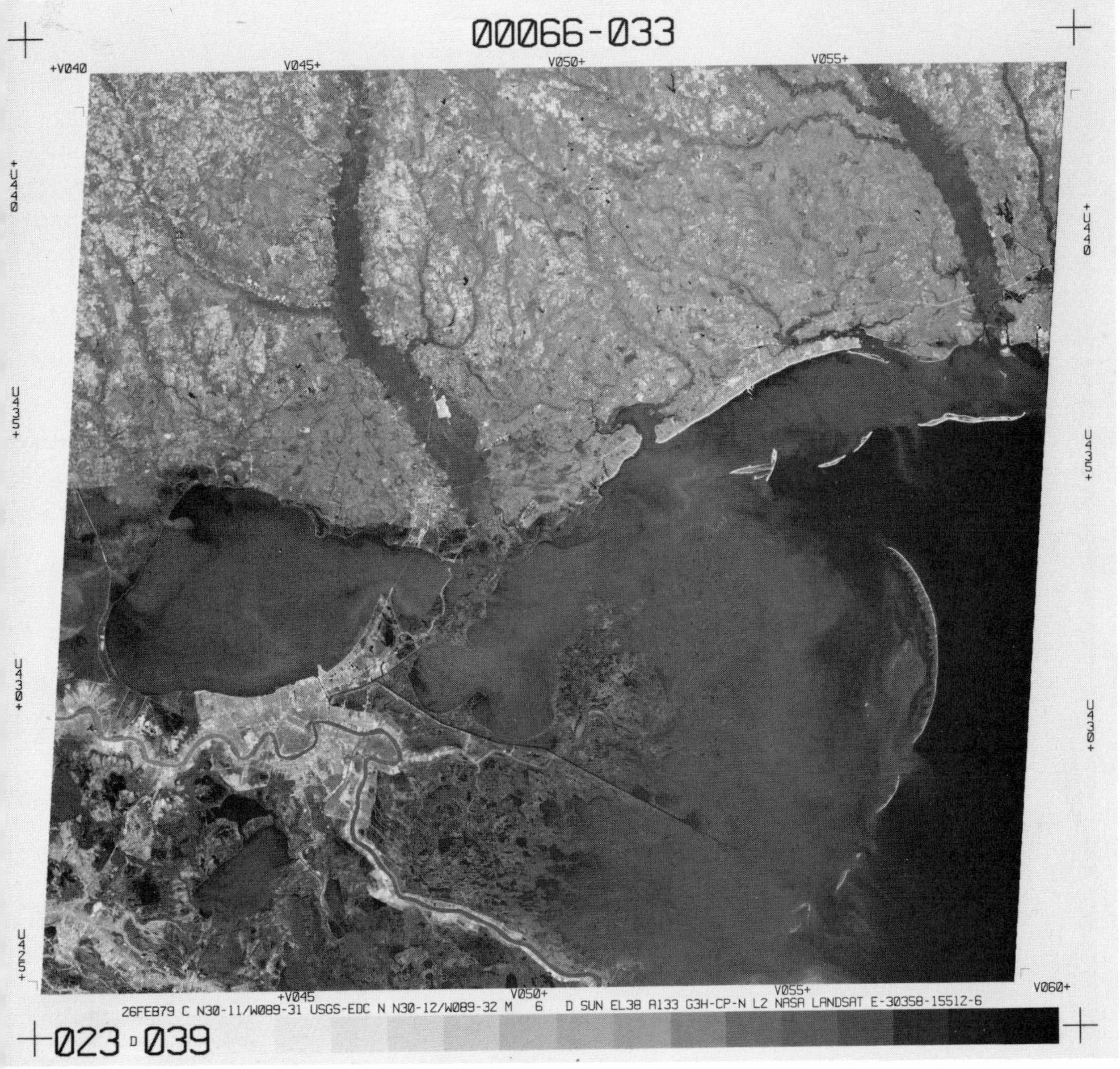

Figure 2-12c.

strips located on the surface immediately below the preceding six swaths acquired on the last mirror scan.

The MSS optics and spacecraft orbit parameters were designed to provide imagery at a resolution of 80 meters per pixel. A full scan of the mirror provides a swath of 185 km (115 miles). The earth rotates under the spacecraft as the scanning occurs from north to south, and this causes a natural skew in all LANDSAT imagery. This skew can be observed in the images shown in Figure 2-12. It is necessary to offset the sequential image lines returned by LANDSAT sensors in order to perform a first-order geometric alignment between the image data and positions of points on the earth's surface.

The Thematic Mapper provides improved spectral and spatial resolution in comparison to the MSS systems. A schematic of the TM is shown in Figure 2-14, and

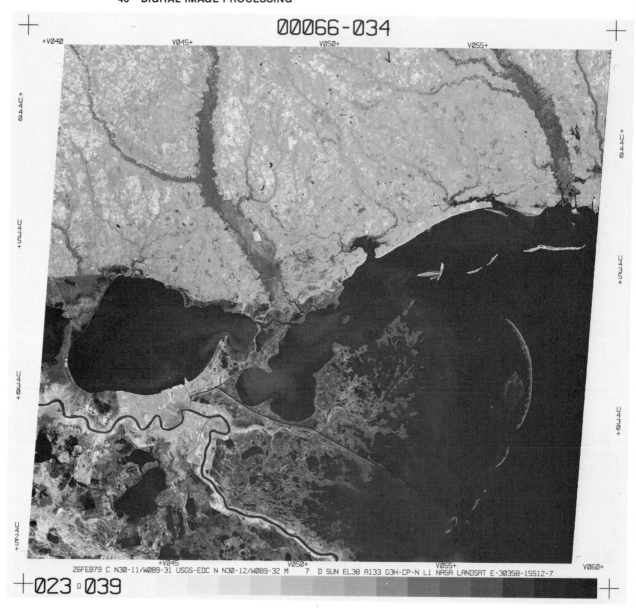

Figure 2-12d.

the assembled system is shown in Figure 2-15. The resolution of all spectral bands except for band 6 is 30 meters/pixel; the resolution of band 6 is 120 meters/pixel. A scanning mirror is utilized to reflect image data across the detector assemblies. Each sweep of the scan mirror generates 16 lines of data for bands 1–5 and 7, and four lines of data for band 6. The TM system was developed to provide improved spatial and spectral resolution for remote sensing applications. One of the first images returned by the TM system on LANDSAT 4 is shown in Figure 2-16.

The SPOT Program

The Satellite Pour l'Observation de la Terre (SPOT) earth observation satellite was launched on February 21, 1986 by the Centre National d'Etudes Spatiales of

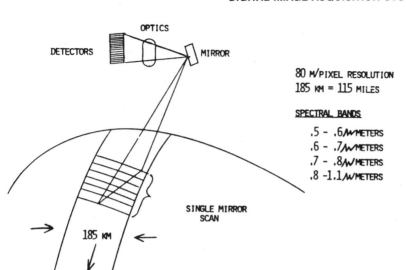

Figure 2-13. LANDSAT MSS image acquisition.

France.[9] Image data from this system is available commercially around the world, and through the SPOT Image Corporation in the United States (see Appendix A1).

The SPOT spacecraft includes twin high-resolution sensors (called HRV systems for "high resolution visible") that acquire either panchromatic imagery in the 0.51 to 0.73 μm wavelength range or multispectral imagery at lower spatial resolution; the sensor viewing angle is adjustable, and imagery can be acquired looking to the

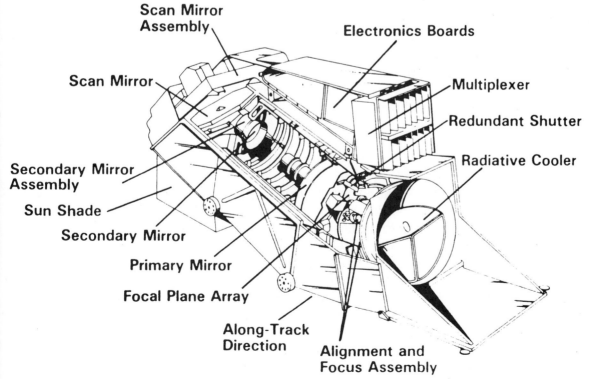

Figure 2-14. LANDSAT Thematic Mapper image system cutaway view.

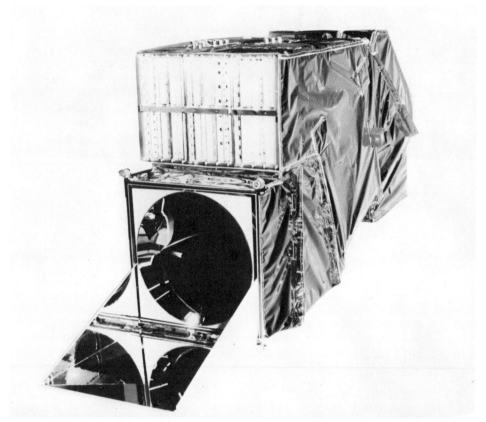

Figure 2-15.   The LANDSAT Thematic Mapper imaging system. This system provides seven spectral bands of image data for earth remote sensing applications (EOSAT).

side along the path of spacecraft travel as well as downward. In this manner, stereo pair imagery can be acquired of selected locations. A schematic diagram of the HRV system is shown in Figure 2-17.

The HRV sensors acquire either panchromatic imagery with a spatial resolution of 10m/pixel or three band multispectral imagery with a spatial resolution of 20 m/pixel. The three band multispectral color imagery is acquired in spectral bands of .5 to .59 μm (green), .61 to .68 μm (red), and .79 to .89 μm (near-infrared).

SPOT travels in a circular sun-synchronous orbit, designed to provide imaging coverage at approximately 10:30AM local time. The spacecraft altitude is 832 km (approximately 500 miles) and the orbital inclination is 98.7°. The orbital parameters were selected to achieve the following characteristics: (a) five days after a particular swath is overflown, the swath immediately to the west is overflown, and (b) approximately 24 hours after a particular track is overflown, the fifth track to the east of it will be overflown, providing two vantage points approximately 500 km apart (at the equator) for stereo pair coverage.

The ground swath width is 60 km for the panchromatic imagery and 117 km for the multispectral imagery. The orbital cycle provides complete earth coverage every 26 days. A SPOT scene will range from 60 km square for a vertical view angle to a 60 km by 80 km maximum at a 27° viewing angle (the maximum viewing angle).

The SPOT HRV sensors utilize the "push broom" scanning technique. A linear CCD array is the active sensor. The camera optics focus the full width of the ground

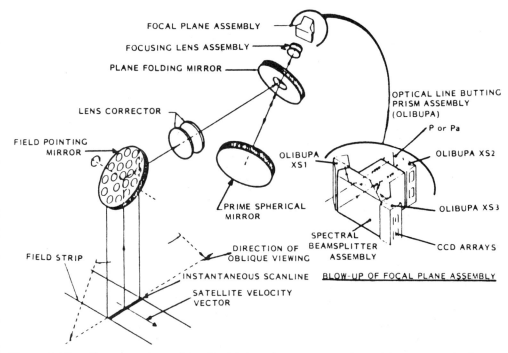

Figure 2-17. Cutaway view of the SPOT imaging system. XS1, XS2, and XS3 indicate the three CCD arrays that provide multispectral imagery.

swath onto the linear CCD array as the spacecraft travels along its orbital path. The CCD array is sampled at a specific frequency to provide sequential lines of image data. Beamsplitters are used to transfer image data to the spectral CCD detectors to acquire multispectral imagery.

A panchromatic SPOT image of the Baltimore area is shown in Figure 2-18 (10 meter resolution). Figure 2-19 shows a color image (20 meter resolution) of the New Orleans, LA, area acquired by the SPOT HRV sensor operating in multispectral mode.

Remote Sensing Ground Data Systems

Digital imaging systems utilized as part of a remote sensing application must often be supported by extensive data processing facilities. The complete remote sensing system must provide capability for command and control of the spacecraft, imaging sensor command and control, telemetry data acquisition, telemetry decommutation, extraction of the digital imagery from the telemetry, formatting and display of the imagery, and delivery of data products of varying format to the user community. The cost of processing digital imaging data and the associated data product generation on the ground for a remote sensing system can often exceed all other costs associated with design, development, and operation of the spacecraft.

The end user is often impacted severely by the design and operation of the system that provides data. As one example, a user data system that is designed to accept image data in a particular format may require extensive modification if the data format provided as input to that system is changed. The simplest example of this type of impact is a change in the physical format of the data tapes provided to the

Figure 2-18.   SPOT panchromatic image of the downtown Baltimore area. The 10 meter resolution provides extremely good detail of physical features (Copyright 1987 CNES, Provided courtesy of SPOT Image Corporation, Reston, VA).

end user. A more complex example would be a user system designed to utilize digital image data that are provided in a standard mapping projection; that system will produce erroneous results if image data are provided in camera system geometry reference coordinates rather than in the expected mapping projection.

This section describes the data processing systems associated with the LANDSAT 3 mission. The LANDSAT 3 system was selected as an example of a complex data system designed to support remote sensing applications. It is also included to provide a basic underting of a data system that produces image data used widely throughout the world for a variety of applications. A review of the changes in process to support LANDSAT 4 and 5 is at the end of this section.

Figure 2-20 illustrates the image data system for LANDSAT 3. Other systems associated with the mission are not shown (e.g., the spacecraft command and control function has not been shown). Telemetry data are acquired at several foreign receiving stations and at one of three NASA receiving stations in the United States. Data received by NASA are relayed to the Goddard Space Flight Center in Maryland via a domestic communications satellite (DOMSAT). DOMSAT is utilized in order to provide high data rate transfer of the large volumes of data acquired by LANDSAT 3.

The LANDSAT 3 data processing system at Goddard utilizes several general-purpose computer systems plus a specially designed digital system that is used to perform particular image correction and rectification functions.[10] At Goddard, the image data are separated from the digital telemetry stream after telemetry decommutation and synchronization. Specially designed computing systems perform corrections to the image data, removing radiometric and geometric distortions introduced into the imagery by the camera system. The corrections are performed on the basis of camera calibration data acquired before launch and during flight operations. Note that end users of the data may require knowledge of the algorithms used to perform these corrections and that errors in performing these corrections within the Goddard facility will be propagated in all data products delivered to the user community.

At Goddard, selected imagery is geometrically transformed into standard cartographic projections, using a specially designed data processing system. The final

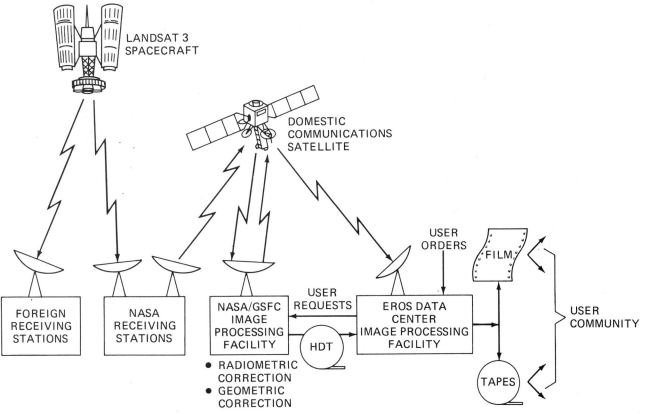

Figure 2-20. LANDSAT 3 image data system.

product produced by Goddard is the *high-density tape* (HDT), which contains the digital imagery along with annotation information and camera-system performance data. These digital tapes are transferred to the EROS Data Center (EDC) in Sioux Falls, South Dakota. Other LANDSAT data are also transmitted to EDC via the DOMSAT satellite. EDC responds to user requests for a variety of image data products.[11] Data products available from EDC include film products (black and white or color prints and transparencies, with or without computer enhancement) and computer-compatible tapes (CCTs), which are produced at standard magnetic tape densities (e.g., 1,600 bits per inch). The HDTs serve as the archival source of LANDSAT data, and EROS utilizes that archive to generate image products in response to user requests.

The EROS data center also creates and maintains a catalog of available LANDSAT data, indexed by geographic coordinates and indicating cloud cover conditions and other relevant parameters for each image available from LANDSAT. An image set is also available on microfiche cards, with indexing by geographic coordinate and cloud cover, for browse and survey purposes.

This system is quite complex. Most users would like to acquire remotely sensed imaging data within a few hours or days of image acquisition. It is more often the case, however, that large remote sensing systems cannot operate at this level, and so delays are introduced that often frustrate the user community. In 1980, for example, the LANDSAT 3 system often introduced delays of up to 120 days between acquisition of digital data on the spacecraft and delivery of data products to users from EDC. A complete system design of a remote sensing system must include early consideration of all the parameters that have an impact on the data reduction facilities that provide the final data products to the user community. Proper design of large and complex systems can often take years, and the design process occurs in an environment characterized by rapid technological developments in the areas of imaging sensors, spacecraft systems, telemetry systems computing hardware and software, and image data display and film recording hardware. Proper design of the computing systems associated with image data processing and product generation is playing an increasingly important role in the development of complex remote sensing systems and is becoming a more challenging task because of the pace at which the associated technology is changing.

Transition to Landsat 4 and 5.   The addition of the TM to the LANDSAT payload caused a significant increase in the quantity of digital data acquired in the LANDSAT program. A new wideband communications package was designed, and an upgrade in data communications systems was required to support the increased number of spectral bands and increased spatial resolution provided by the TM. The TM data are transmitted at 85 megabits/second at X-band frequency, as opposed to MSS data which is transmitted at 15 megabits/second at S-band frequency (consistent with the first three LANDSAT systems). The first three LANDSAT spacecraft carried image data recorders, used for recording of image data prior to digital transmission to ground receiving stations. Data from LANDSAT 4 and LANDSAT 5 can only be acquired via real-time image data acquisition.

The real-time data acquisition operations were to be supported by the Tracking and Data Relay Satellite System (TDRSS), a network of orbiting spacecraft that could support simultaneous TM and MSS data acquisition and retransmission to ground receiving stations. The concept is shown in Figure 2-21. When fully deployed

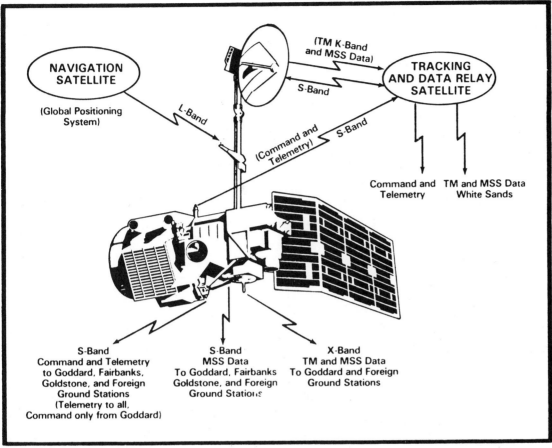

Figure 2-21. Communication link between LANDSAT 4 or LANDSAT 5 spacecraft through the TDRS system, and interface with the Global Positioning Satellite.

in synchronous orbital positions around the world, these spacecraft will provide continuous real-time data acquisition support for the LANDSAT spacecraft. An overview of the fully operational LANDSAT support system is shown in Figure 2-22.

As of this writing, the first TDRS system is operational, in synchronous orbit over the Atlantic Ocean. This system supports near-complete coverage of the Western hemisphere. The second TDRS spacecraft was part of the payload on the tragic Challenger shuttle mission in January 1986, and was lost. Because the LANDSAT 4 and 5 spacecraft support only real-time data acquisition, there are gaps in earth coverage from these systems. These gaps are being filled as additional ground stations are brought on line around the world to support ground data acquisition. Potential users are advised to contact EOSAT regarding available ground coverage from the LANDSAT spacecraft. EOSAT will also provide information regarding data products available and available image processing options.

COMPUTER PERIPHERAL IMAGE ACQUISITION DEVICES

The remote sensing systems discussed in the previous section all produce digital image data directly and are usually operated at large distances from the ultimate users of the image data. Remote sensors usually require large data systems to reduce

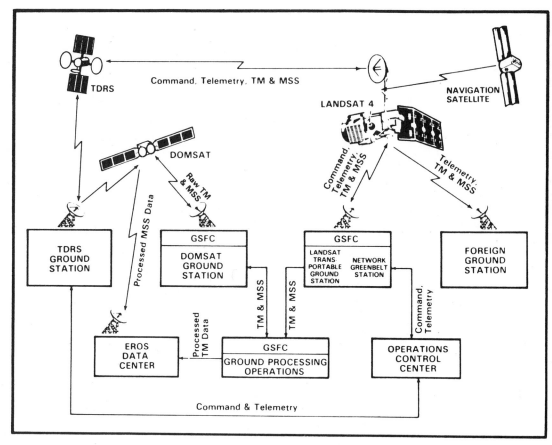

Figure 2-22. Ground support systems for LANDSAT 4 and LANDSAT 5 operations.

and format the imaging data, and there are often delays of days, weeks, or months between acquisition of the data and delivery of data products to final users.

This section describes a variety of systems that are used to convert image data from a variety of media into digital format for computer processing. These devices are normally interfaced directly to computer systems and are operated by users in their local enviornment. Peripheral devices are often interfaced directly to the computer system that will perform the image processing; they operate under computer control, guided by the end user or by a trained operator. This section describes the two major types of peripheral image input devices: film scanners and video digitizers.

Film Scanning Systems

It is often desirable to perform computer processing on imagery that was originally acquired on film. The basic concept of all film scanning systems is the same. All film scanning systems operate by shining a light source through a film transparency and digitizing the transmitted intensity. The transmitted light source is read and digitized at a set of discrete points within the image transparency, producing a two-dimensional digital representation of the image on the transparency. Color film can be scanned in a similar manner. The color components are acquired by scanning the color transparency several times, using spectral filters to separate out the color components.

Flying Spot Scanners.   Flying spot scanners most often employ a cathode ray tube (CRT) as the light source. The CRTs are designed to permit the addressing of individual points within a fixed geometry on the tube. Most CRTs are capable of providing addressable arrays of up to 4,096 points square. A spot of specified brightness can be displayed at each of the addressable locations on the tube. When a transparency is being scanned, each spot on the tube serves as an individual light source, which shines through the film transparency placed next to the CRT (see Figure 2-23). Each spot in the two-dimensional array is illuminated sequentially, and a photosensitive device on the opposite side of the film transparency records the transmitted light intensity. When this type of flying spot CRT is used for film scanning, each spot is programmed to illuminate the transparency with the same intensity.

The transmitted intensity recorded by the photosensitive device is transferred to an analog-to-digital converter, and each spot that illuminates a small portion of the transparency thus produces a digitized value that is proportional to the film density at that position. Most scanners can scan either positive or negative transparencies, and the digital data are either recorded directly or complemented, depending on whether a negative or positive transparency is being scanned.

Flying spot scanners are available that provide a variety of spatial resolutions. Most flying spot scanners utilize spot sizes for individual spots that are at least 25 microns across. Spot sizes smaller than 25 microns can produce very noisy digitized imagery, as a result of the interference of film grain noise. Twenty-five micron spot sizes or larger provide "averaged" intensity values that average out of integrate the effects of the film grain noise within the illuminating spot.

Some flying spot scanners operate with a fixed spot size and fixed spacing between individual spots on the CRT. More expensive devices include the capability of varying the spot size and the horizontal and vertical spacing between adjacent spots.

Laser Or Light-Emitting Diode Scanners.   This type of scanner utilizes a single light source that is moved over the film transparency from position to position sequentially, pixel by pixel. The light sources include laser beams and light-emitting diodes (LEDs). Most devices of this type requires the film to be mounted cylindrically, and the light source is rotated and then moved down the axis of the cylinder to perform the scanning operation. Figure 2-24 shows one example of this type of system.

Laser and LED scanners often provide the capability to scan transparencies at selectable, fixed spot spacings. Here again, a 25-micron spot size is a typical minimum. Scanning of color film is achieved by multiple scans acquired with different

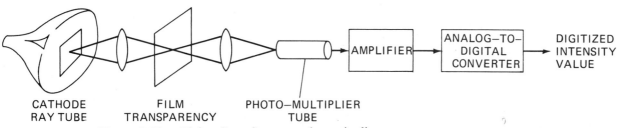

Figure 2-23. Flying Spot Scanner schematic diagram.

Figure 2-24.   Film scanning system. The film is positioned within the cylindrical black drum on the left of the instrument (Optronics Corporation).

spectral filters placed over the photosensitive device that samples the transmitted intensity.

Microdensitometers And Other Flat-Bed Scanners.   There are a variety of devices used for digitizing film transparencies at spot sizes ranging down to one micron and for digitizing astronomical plates. These devices usually require the scanned material to be placed on a flat surface; a single light source is moved across the flat transparency, tracked by a photosensitive device on the opposite side of the transparency. These devices are used to digitize glass astronomical plates and can also be used to digitize film transparencies mounted within glass plate holders. Devices that provide spot sizes as small as one micron are referred to as *microdensitometers*. Film or plate scanning at spot spacing less than 10 to 15 microns usually results in very noisy digitized imagery, since the spot spacing is on the order of the film grain noise at that point. Computer processing is often required to reduce the noise introduced when scanning at very small spot sizes.

Options and Tradeoffs That Affect Selection of Film Scanning Devices.

A variety of factors must be considered when scanning imagery originally recorded on film and when selecting or procuring film scanning equipment for specific applications. The following list can serve as a general outline of the factors that impact selection of particular modes of film scanning.

Spatial Resolution. A spot size larger than the film grain noise is desirable for most applications. The selection of spot size and spot spacing will have an impact on the size of the digitized image, and this will have a major impact on the time required for digital processing of the scanned imagery. A transparency scanned at 100-micron spacing may yield a digitized image that is 1,024 samples square, but the same transparency scanned at 25 microns will yield a digitized image that is 4,096 pixels square. The latter image will have 4 times the spatial resolution but will also produce 16 times the digital data volume.

Film Size. Flying spot CRT systems usually accommodate film sizes of 35 mm, 70 mm, and 105 mm. Laser or LED systems may also accommodate larger film sizes (e.g., 4 by 5 inch or 8 by 10 inch negatives). In many cases, film scanners may accommodate only a single film size.

Geometric Precision. Flying spot CRT systems utilize electron beam technology to position the spot source, and they can introduce geometrical distortion into the scanned imagery becuase of difficulties associated with precisely retaining positional linearity across the full face of the CRT. Laser, LED, and flat-bed scanners usually introduce less distortion, since the geometry is controlled mechanically.

Radiometric Precision. Flying spot CRT systems can introduce errors into the digitized intensities if the light level of each individual spot driven by the CRT is not precisely the same from pixel to pixel. Fluctuations in the laser or LED source can also introduce radiometric errors into the scanned imagery. Some types of photomultiplier tubes are more linear in their response to input light than others, and the analog-to-digital converters used in film scanners can also introduce radiometric distortion. Most CRT scanners are limited to 8 bits of precision in the scanned digital intensity values, whereas some microdensitometers and flat-bed scanners may be capable of up to 12 bits of precision.

Speed. Flying spot CRT or laser scanners can usually digitize more points per second than the other types of scanners. For some high-volume applications, there may be a trade-off between speed of digitizing and desired geometric and radiometric precision.

Cost. The cost of scanning systems varies widely, based on the above factors. A trade-off between cost, speed, and desired precision or accuracy is often involved in selection of a film scanning device.

Video Digitizers

Many applications involve acquisition of analog television signals. In recent years, a variety of devices have been designed to convert conventional television signals from analog to digital format in order to enable computer processing of data acquired by television camera systems.

Television signals are analog signals that are acquired in a fixed format. A video signal is composed of a sequence of images that are transmitted to a viewing monitor at a rate of 30 images (or frames) per second. Each of the component images is composed of a fixed number of lines of analog signal data. In the United States, conventional television data consist of 525 lines of analog video per frame. Other television systems, including closed-circuit television systems and foreign video systems, may utilize a different number of lines. The National Television System Committee (NTSC) is a group established by manufacturers that establishes format conventions and standards for United States broadcast video transmission.

Each line of video data consists of a modulated analog signal, and the standard United States television imagery has a spatial resolution that corresponds to approximately 512 discrete intensity points along each video line. Other systems may provide resolution equivalent to more or less than 512 points per line.

A single standard format, called NTSC video format, is used to transmit standard television signals within the United States. This format accommodates either black and white or color video imagery and is utilized for broadcast television. Chapter 4 contains a description of three components of a color image: hue, saturation, and intensity. NTSC format transmits these three components at the bandwidth of monochrome (black and white) video. The color information is described by the hue and saturation components, and only the intensity component is displayed on black and white monitors.

Image display systems used in conjunction with computer processing often utilize an alternate video format in which the red, green, and blue components of a color image are transmitted as separate black and white video images that are then merged before display on a color monitor. The NTSC format requires compression of the color information so that transmission of the full color image can occur at the bandwidth of monochrome video. Display systems that utilize separate red, green, and blue video signals will preserve more of the true-color information than can be transmitted in NTSC format.

An analog video signal with a frame time of one-thirtieth of a second constitutes a high data rate signal. If a single frame of standard NTSC video data is converted to digital format, a digital image of size 512 samples by 525 lines will be generated. The analog video data is refreshed every one-thirtieth of a second, and this is an effective data rate of approximately 6 Mbytes per second (assuming 1 byte per pixel).

The basic idea of video digitizing involves "freezing" and then digitizing a frame of analog video. Most computing systems cannot process a stream of digitized video pixels acquired at a 6 Mbyte per second data rate, and some form of *rate buffering* is required. Rate buffering is a process through which high rate data are stored in an intermediate storage device as they are acquired at high rate and then read out from the intermediate storage at a lower data rate that can be accommodated by the next device that must access the data.

Figure 2-25 illustrates one method of performing rate buffering during video digitizing. A full video frame is read in analog format during the one-thirtieth of a second refresh time. A high-speed analog-to-digital converter, operating at the full 6 Mbytes per second rate, digitizes the data and enters them into a buffer memory. The buffer memory is large enough to hold at least one digitized video image (512 by 525 pixels for NTSC video). The computer system that is used for subsequent digital processing then reads out the digital frame buffer at a lower data rate (typically 2 Mbytes per second or less for most computer systems). The digitized data are transferred at the lower rate from the digital frame buffer to other auxiliary peripheral storage, where they can be accessed for further computer processing. The

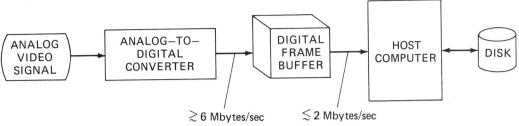

Figure 2-25. Rate buffering during video frame digitizing.

frame buffer is then available to receive another digitized video image. This type of device is often called a *frame grabber*.

Other video digitizing systems perform rate buffering by slowing down the analog-to-digital conversion process to a speed at which several video frames, rather than a single frame, are digitized. As an example, the data rate can be slowed to one-fifth the input analog signal rate by digitizing the first one-fifth of the video lines from the first video frame, then the second one-fifth of the video lines from the next frame, etc. For a 525-line video signal, lines 1 to 105 of the digital image would be derived from the first analog video frame, lines 106 to 210 would be derived from the second video frame, etc.

The video digitizers that operate an input rates less than one-thirtieth of a second per digitized frame all utilize more than one video frame for digitizing. Some perform digitizing of blocks of sequential lines from sequential frames, and others digitize sequential columns of pixels from sequential frames. These slower digitizers are less expensive than frame grabbers but can be used only in applications in which the scene does not change rapidly between successive video frames. A good application for a slow video digitizer would be digitizing an image of a stationary slide viewed through a microscope by a closed-circuit camera system. An example of an application in which slow digitizing may not be adequate would be the tracking of a high-speed object across the camera's field of view.

IMAGING SYSTEM DESIGN CONSIDERATIONS

Several fundamental decisions must be made during the design of image acquisition devices of the type discussed in this chapter. These decisions concern the number of intensity levels to be recorded in each spectral band, the number of spectral bands in which imagery is to be acquired, the spatial resolution that will be preserved in the sampled digital imagery, the size of the output digitized images, etc. Complex trade-off studies are often required before each of these parameters can be established for a particular image acquisition device. Other complex factors involved in these decisions include constraints that may be imposed by communications data rates (either from a spacecraft to the ground for a remote sensing application or between a computer peripheral unit and the central processing unit) or image storage capacity (again either on a remote sensing spacecraft or in a ground-based computer system).

This section presents an overview of the factors involved in making the design trade-offs associated with the development or selection of a particular image acquisition device. The factors that are described are relevant to the full range of acquisition devices described earlier in this chapter, from remote sensing systems operated on spacecraft to the computer peripheral devices used as components in ground-based image analysis systems. The intent of this section is to provide an insight into the decision processes faced by a system designer in selecting or designing image acquisition hardware. The section deals with three main areas in which design decisions are required: radiometric resolution, spatial resolution, and spectral resolution. A few simple examples are used at the end of this section to illustrate the interplay that occurs between these parameters during design trade-off studies.

Radiometric Resolution

All image acquisition devices provide a range of discrete digital intensity levels that correspond to the brightness of the scene sampled by the image acquisition device. The fundamental parameter that determines the radiometric accuracy or precision of digitized intensity values is the number of bits per picture element that is selected to represent the scene brightness in the sampled image. If only 3 bits per picture element are utilized, the sampled imagery will contain only seven discrete levels of brightness. If 8 bits per pixel are quantized, 255 possible digitized intensity values will be provided by the system. Figure 2-26 illustrates the process involved in digitizing an input analog signal. The full dynamic range of the analog signal is displayed as a vertical bar at the left of the figure. If 1 bit is used to digitize the analog signal, a zero or a 1 would be produced by the digitizer; the only intensity information provided by a 1-bit system would be whether the analog signal is above or below the midpoint of the full dynamic range. If 2 bits are used, the analog signal could be determined to a resolution no better than one-fourth the total dynamic range.

Figure 2-26 illustrates the increasing precision to which the analog signal can be represented by digitized intensity values as more bits are used to quantize the input signal. For the input analog signal level V shown in Figure 2-26, a 1-bit digitizer would produce a value of zero, a two-bit digitizer would produce a binary value of 01 (corresponding to a decimal value of 1 within a total possible range from 0 to 3), a 3-bit digitizer would produce a binary value of 010 (decimal 2) within a total possible range from 0 to 7, etc. An 8-bit digitizer would produce a binary value of 010 . . . 0 for the input signal level denoted by V, and 8-bit quantizing would yield a digital range of values extending from 0 to 255.

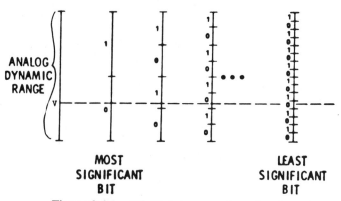

Figure 2-26. Digitizing an analog signal.

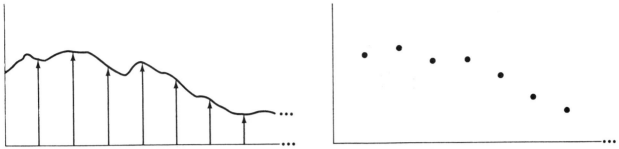

Figure 2-27. Discrete sampling of a continuous analog signal.

The trade-offs involved in determining the number of bits per pixel to be digitized by an image acquisition system involve the radiometric resolution required for the particular application, the communications data rate, and data storage capacity. The larger the number of bits digitized per pixel, the longer the digital transmission of the image data will take, and the more digital storage will be required to store the imagery. It should be noted, however, that 8-bit bytes are standard addressable units of storage in many current digital computer systems, and it is quite common to utilize 8 bits per pixel in digital images, even when the image acquisition system utilizes a sensor that is incapable of resolving 255 brightness levels in the original scene. It should also be noted that more precise image acquisition systems (e.g., systems employing CCDs as the active imaging element) often provide more than 8 bits of precision in intensity readings. Camera systems and scanners providing 12 bits of precision are becoming more common. Finally, note that 8-bit bytes in computer storage can be used to store two 4-bit pixel intensities, and some applications requiring only 4 bits of precision (equivalent to a digitized intensity range from 0 to 15) can utilize computer storage efficiently.

Spatial Resolution

The image acquisition system optics constitute an important component in determining the smallest spatial resolution that can be detected by a particular digital system. A second component is the sampling frequency with which the continuous spatially distributed analog image is sampled. Figure 2-27 illustrates the analog intensity levels present across one line of an image that is being sampled by a digital system. Individual pixel intensity values are read from the analog signal and converted to digital intensities at a discrete set of points along the line. The arrows in Figure 2-27 illustrate one choice of sampling frequency; a digitized pixel intensity value will be acquired at each position indicated by an arrow. The digitized values are shown on the right hand side of Figure 2-27.

The spatial resolution present in a sampled digital image is a function of the frequency at which the analog signal values are sampled. In Figure 2-27, it is clear that the sampling frequency produces digitized sample values that do not adequately represent the higher-frequency components present in the analog signal. The *Nyquist theorem* states that a continuous signal can be reconstructed perfectly up to a particular spatial frequency from a set of discrete samples if the sampling is performed at twice the frequency of interest.

As one example of the use of the Nyquist theorem, consider an image acquisition system with an optics system that provides a net scaling factor from object space to focal plane of 10^4:1. This system will cause an object 100 m across in object space to be reduced to an image of size 1 cm in the focal plane. Suppose that a particular application requires that objects or features of size as small as 2 m must be resolvable in the digitized imagery produced by this system. A 2-m object will be reduced to a size of .02 cm in the focal plane because of the optics scaling factor (.02 cm = 2 m × 1 cm/100 m). The Nyquist theorem indicates that the focal plane must be sampled at twice the desired spatial frequency. In this case, we wish to preserve objects as small as 0.02 cm in the focal plane, and so sampling must occur at twice this frequency, or every 0.01 cm in the focal plane.

The size of output digital images is often determined by the spatial resolution requirements imposed on the imaging system. In the above example, if it were required to scan a 100-m-square area in object space at the 2-m resolution, conversion to the focal plane dimensions indicates that an image of size 100 × 100 pixels will be required. If a resolution of 0.2 m in object space is required, the image size required to scan the same 100-m-square area at the higher spatial resolution would be 1000 × 1000 pixels.

Spectral Resolution

The designer of the imaging system must determine the number of spectral bands in which an image is to be sampled. The selection is a function of the particular application. The LANDSAT TM systems provide seven spectral bands, as discussed previously. The Viking Lander camera provided three color bands, three infrared bands, and several broad-band sensors; each broad-band sensor had a different spatial resolution. The spectral resolution capability of an image acquisition system has a strong influence on system design considerations, since each spectral band added to the system can conceivably add a full-size image component to every multispectral set of image components being acquired.

Examples of Design Trade-offs

In order to illustrate the image acquisition system design trade-offs, consider the variety of image data that can be represented by 8 megabits of digital storage. Eight megabits can, to a first-order approximation, be utilized to accommodate the following variety of image data:

    1000 × 1000 pixel image, 8 bits/pixel, 1 spectral band
    400 × 400 pixel images, 8 bits/pixel, 7 spectral bands
    1000 × 1000 pixel images, 4 bits/pixel, 2 spectral bands

If the same scene in object space is acquired by systems producing each of these three examples, the following can be noted. The first example provides high spatial resolution, with no spectral information. The second system provides a significant amount of spectral resolution, at the expense of spatial resolution. The third system provides some spectral resolution, high spatial resolution, and less radiometric precision than the other systems.

The limitations imposed on selection of the three key parameters discussed in this section can arise from a variety of system design considerations. Trade-offs of the type just described are commonly performed during the design of image acquisition systems.

As a final example of one type of limitation imposed on system design, assume that data transmission speed is critical in a particular application. The following table exhibits the impact on transmission time of two different digital imaging system options, where each system provides images of the same size are in object space.

NUMBER OF BITS/PIXEL	IMAGE SIZE	RELATIVE SPATIAL RESOLUTION	NUMBER OF BITS PER IMAGE	TRANSMISSION TIME AT 16 KB	AT 200 KB
6	100^2	1.0	6×10^4	3.75 sec	0.3 sec
8	1000^2	0.1	8×10^6	500 sec	40 sec

The smaller image, with less spatial resolution and less radiometric precision, can be transmitted over 100 times faster than the more-precise larger image. In certain applications, the telemetry or communications link constraints may preclude acquisition of the optimal imaging data for a particular application.

REFERENCES

1. Wellman, J. P., et al., "The Viking Orbiter Visual Imaging Subsystem," *J Spacecr Rockets* 13, 660–666 (1976).
2. Huck, F. O., et al., "The Viking Mars Lander Camera," *Space Sci Instrum* 1, 189–241 (1975).
3. Mutch, T. A., et al., "The Viking Lander Imaging Investigation," *Icarus* 16, 92–110 (1972).
4. Liebes, S., and A. A. Schwartz, "Viking 1975 Mars Lander Interactive Computerized Video Stereophotogrammetry," *J Geophys Res* 82, 28, p. 4421 (1977).
5. *The Martian Landscape,* NASA SP-425, U.S. Government Printing Office Stock Number 033-000-00716-7, 1978.
6. Allison, L. J. and A. Schnapf, et al., "Meteorological Satellites," in *Manual of Remote Sensing, 2nd Edition,* Chapter 14. Falls Church, VA, American Society of Photogrammetry, 1983.
7. *Mission to Earth–LANDSAT Views the World,* NASA SP-360, U.S. Government Printing Office Stock Number 033-000-00659-4, 1976.
8. Freden, S. C. and F. Gordon, Jr., "Landsat Satellites," in *Manual of Remote Sensing, 2nd Edition,* Chapter 12. Falls Church, VA, American Society of Photogrammetry, 1983.
9. Courtois, M. and G. Weill, "The SPOT Satellite System," in *Monitoring Earth's Ocean, Land and Atmosphere from Space—Sensors, Systems and Applications,* Progress in Astronautics and Aeronautics Volume 97, New York, American Institute of Aeronautics and Astronautics, 1985.
10. Schoene, L. P., "Image Processing on the Master Data Processor," *Information Technology–JCIT3 Preprints,* New York, North-Holland Publishing Company, 1978, p. 633.
11. Horsted, W. B., "Image Processing of LANDSAT 3 Data at the EROS Data Center," *Information Technology–JCIT3 Preprints,* New York, North-Holland Publishing Company, 1978.

3
Subjective Image Processing Techniques

INTRODUCTION

Most digital image processing techniques fall into one of two broad categories: subjective and quantitative. Subjective image processing is designed to improve human visual interpretation of an image. Subjective processing, often called *image enhancement,* is usually performed in an adaptive, interactive, and iterative manner. It is a trial and error process, and success is based on the ability of the observer to detect information of interest to him or her in the final enhanced or processed image. The techniques employed in subjective image processing are often simple and are readily implemented with the hardware provided with most currently available image display systems. The changes achieved in the "before" and "after" versions of images processed subjectively are often quite dramatic, despite the relative computational simplicity of many of the subjective techniques.

Quantitative image processing is usually performed on imagery in a nonadaptive, noninteractive manner. Quantitative processing is based on predefined mathematical algorithms, and success in processing is based on the correctness of the mathematical model. Examples of quantitative processing include correction for camera system-induced geometric distortion or computation of a two-dimensional Fourier transform of an image.

This chapter describes the most commonly utilized techniques for subjective image processing. Chapter 4 summarizes the basic techniques of quantitative image processing.

Several texts[1-4] contain detailed presentations of the techniques presented here as well as material not summarized in these two chapters. The intent of Chapters 3 and 4 is to provide an introduction to the analytic methods employed in digital image processing for those attempting to perform system design. The reader is provided references to other sources for detailed description of the techniques summarized here and references to sources providing important supplementary information.

IMAGE HISTOGRAM

A basic tool utilized in performing subjective enhancement and image analysis is the *image histogram*. The histogram reveals the distribution of digitized intensity within an image; it is represented graphically as a plot of the number of picture elements at a given intensity, $N(b)$, plotted versus intensity, b. Three examples of image histograms are shown in Figure 3-1.

The histogram in Figure 3-1a represents a well-exposed image, with most of the pixel intensities falling around midscale or midgray. The histogram in Figure 3-1b

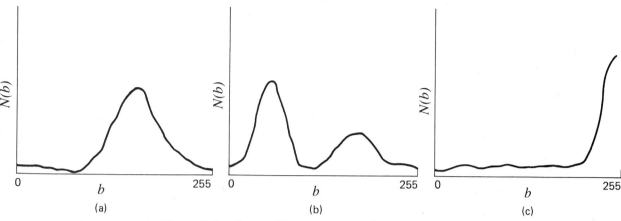

Figure 3-1. Image Histograms.

is a bimodal histogram with two distinct peaks. This indicates that the image could be a high-contrast image with many dark and many bright regions. An image of a scene at sunset, with a bright sky and dark surface, could produce this type of histogram. An image of an ice field with cracks in the ice through which dark water is visible could also produce this type of histogram.

Figure 3-1c shows a histogram of an overexposed image. The majority of the pixels have been saturated at or near full white. There can be several reasons for this phenomenon. If the image was acquired by a remote sensing system, the exposure controls for the camera system could have been improperly computed or transmitted to the imaging system. If the digitizing system was a film scanner, the operator could have set the dynamic range of the scanner improperly before digitizing.

It is possible to perform contrast manipulation of the images that produced the histograms shown in Figures 3-1a and b, using techniques described in this chapter, in order to produce an optimal display of the information content. It is impossible to recover the situation shown in Figure 3-1c, however. The only way to correct the problem shown in Figure 3-1c is to reacquire the image at correct exposure. In the case of a film scanning system, that may be a simple process. In the case of an earth-orbiting spacecraft or a spacecraft in deep space that flies past a planet only once, the reimaging procedure may be impossible.

It is often quite useful to compute the relative percentage of pixels within an image at each intensity. If an image is L lines by S samples, the percentage of pixels at each itensity b_i can be computed from

$$p(b_i) = 100 \ N(b_i) \ / \ (L \cdot S) \qquad (3\text{-}1)$$

The *cumulative distribution function* is also useful. It represents the percentage of pixels with intensities at or below a particular intensity, b_i, and is computed from

$$C(b_i) = \sum_{k=1}^{i} p(b_k) \qquad (3\text{-}2)$$

CONTRAST ENHANCEMENT

Most digital imaging systems can resolve more levels of intensity than can be presented on display devices. Intensity levels ranging from 0 to 255 are typical, produced by camera systems, film scanners, or video digitizers that quantize the observed brightness range using 8 bits of resolution. The human eye is able to resolve approximately 32 distinct shades of gray. The digital imaging system therefore provides more intensity information than the human eye can resolve.

Volatile image display devices typically utilize cathode ray tubes (CRT's) as the display element. CRT's are typically limited to between 32 and 64 resolvable shades of gray. Film recorders used to generate film renditions of digital imagery are also limited in the number of resolvable shades of gray that can be written to the film medium. Most film renditions of black and white digital imagery will also be limited to a resolution of between 32 and 64 shades of gray. The actual value is also dependent on film type.

When an image is recorded onto film or displayed on a volatile display system, the full intensity range of the imaging system is displayed so that black corresponds to the minimum quantized intensity and white corresponds to the maximum quantized intensity. For an 8-bit system, black thus represents $b = 0$ and white represents $b = 255$. When an 8-bit image is displayed on film or display, the 255 shades of gray available within the image data are subsampled at a ratio of approximately 255:32, or around 8:1.

If a digital image has an intensity distribution such that the majority of pixels fall within a subset of the digitized intensity value range, straightforward display of the unprocessed image will yield a very low-contrast result that does not fully display the information actually available in the digitized image.

In the histogram shown in Figure 3-1*a,* the majority of the pixels in the image are at intensity values clustered about the midgray point of the histogram. If the image is recorded on black and white film without modification of the digital data, the film product will be almost all gray; at best, variations of only one or two gray shades about midgray will occur.

Figure 3-2 shows a Mariner 9 image of the Martian surface and its associated histogram. The image has been processed so that it represents a radiometrically correct view of the low-contrast surface of the planet. The Mariner 9 camera system quantized 9 bits of intensity data so that values of b ranging from 0 to 511 were produced by the system. The histogram reveals that the majority of the pixel values in the image lie between approximately 96 and 136. The two gray step wedges immediately above and below the image reveal the limitations in dynamic range of the film recording process. Each step in the ascending and descending gray wedges corresponds to a difference of 32 gray levels on a 9 bits per pixel basis. It is difficult to discern the difference between adjacent gray steps within the gray scales shown in the figure. The gray wedge indicates the difficulty of detecting a variation of 32 intensity levels in the output photographic product, and shows why it is difficult to discern the variation within the image in the displayed product, since the actual digital data variation (examine the histogram of the actual data) falls within only 40 digital intensity levels. The variation in the image shown in Figure 3-2 of approximately 40 digital intensity levels is portrayed within two or three gray shades on the film product. For this reason, the image shown in Figure 3-2 reveals little of the actual intensity variation that occurs within the image.

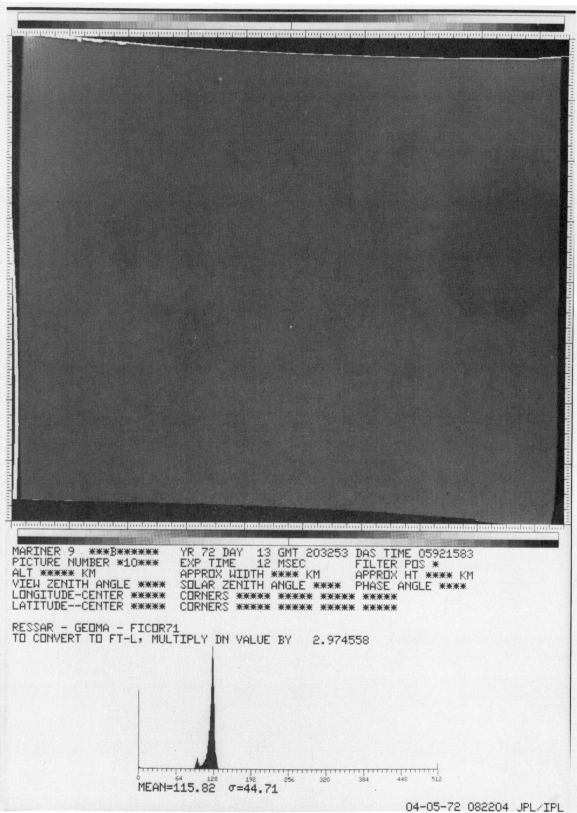

Figure 3-2. Radiometrically corrected Mariner 9 image of Mars (Jet Propulsion Laboratory).

Linear Contrast Enhancement

It is necessary to transform the intensity values in the unprocessed image in order to display the subtle intensity variation present within the image. One commonly utilized technique is *linear contrast enhancement*. The objective is to utilize the full dynamic range of the output display medium to reveal the intensity variation present within an image. This technique is most often applied when the intensity variation within an image occurs within a very limited range of intensity values. The technique is based on transforming each pixel intensity level in the input image into a new value in the output image for display.

In order to perform a linear contrast enhancement, the analyst examines the image histogram and determines the intensity range containing the large majority of the input pixels. The range is defined by limiting values b_{hi} and b_{low}. An output image is constructed in the following manner:

1. For each pixel with intensity at or below b_{low}, the intensity value is reassigned to black ($b = 0$).
2. For each pixel with intensity at or above b_{hi}, the intensity value is reassigned to full white ($b = 255$).
3. For all pixels with input intensity values between b_{low} and b_{hi}, an output intensity is assigned that represents a linear transformation between b_{low} and b_{hi}.

This description has been based on an 8-bit imaging system with a digital intensity range of zero to 255. The units should be changed appropriately for systems with other than 8-bit intensity resolution.

The algorithm can be represented mathematically by the following equations:

$$b_{out} = \begin{cases} 0, & b_{in} \le b_{low} \\ \dfrac{b_{in} - b_{low}}{b_{hi} - b_{low}} \cdot 255, & b_{low} < b_{in} < b_{hi} \\ 255, & b_{in} \ge b_{hi} \end{cases} \qquad (3\text{-}3)$$

where b_{in} is the input intensity value of a particular pixel and an 8-bit system is assumed. Figure 3-3 presents a graphical representation of the transformation defined above.

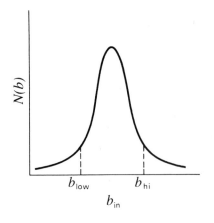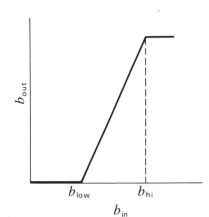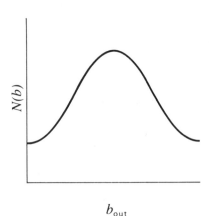

Figure 3-3. Linear contrast enhancement.

Figure 3-4 shows the results of applying a linear contrast enhancement to the Mariner 9 image of Figure 3-2. A linear contrast enhancement preserves relative brightness relationships within the image but has the effect of redisplaying the information content by utilizing the full available dynamic range of the output display medium. A linear enhancement with $b_{low} = 103$ and $b_{hi} = 134$ was used to produce the enhanced result shown in Figure 3-4.

This type of enhancement is often called *contrast stretch,* since the image histogram is "stretched" to fill the full dynamic range of the output display medium. Linear contrast enhancement is particulaly well suited to image with Gaussian or near-Gaussian histograms, where all the intensity values fall generally within a single narrow subset of the intensity range available within a particular imaging system.

Piecewise Linear Contrast Enhancement

Image histograms are not always on the near-Gaussian type, and other, more general techniques are often used for contrast manipulation. A linear contrast enhancement is not the most desirable type of contrast manipulation for images characterized by bimodal histograms, for example. It would be difficult to assign the limits of a linear contrast enhancement to the histogram depicted in Figure 3-1*b*. In this case, it would be advisable to perform a *piecewise linear stretch* of the type shown in Figure 3-5. The analyst determines a series of linear enhancement steps designed to expand the intensity ranges in which the data fall to fill the full dynamic range of the display madia. Mathematically, this corresponds to setting up a series of values of b_{low} and b_{hi} and using equations of the form of Equation 3-3 within each region, depending on the input intensity value of each pixel.

Automated Contrast Enhancement

It is often desirable to perform contrast enhancements based on computer analysis of the input image histogram. The *automated ends-in search* contrast enhancement technique allows the analyst to specify that a certain percentage of the pixels in the output image must be saturated either full black or full white. A program is then written that analyzes the input histogram and utilizes the cumulative distribution function to identify the intensity values at which the appropriate percentages will saturate when a linear contrast enhancement is performed. In the notation defined by Equations 3-1 and 3-2, the analyst will specify that p_{low} percentage of the output pixels be saturated black (b_{out} set to 0) and p_{hi} percentage of the output pixels be saturated white (b_{out} set to 255 in an 8-bit system). The program uses this information to select the end points of a linear contrast enhancement.

The image histogram and cumulative distribution function are used to locate the value of b_{low} such that

$$b_{low} = b_k \text{ where } C(b_k) \geq p_{low} \qquad (3\text{-}4)$$

where the search starts at $k = 1$ and proceeds through increasing values of k.

In a similar manner, the high end of the histogram is searched to select b_{hi}:

$$b_{hi} = b_k \text{ where } [1 - C(b_k)] > p_{hi} \qquad (3\text{-}5)$$

where the search starts at $k = k_{max}$ (255 in an 8-bit system) and proceeds downward in k.

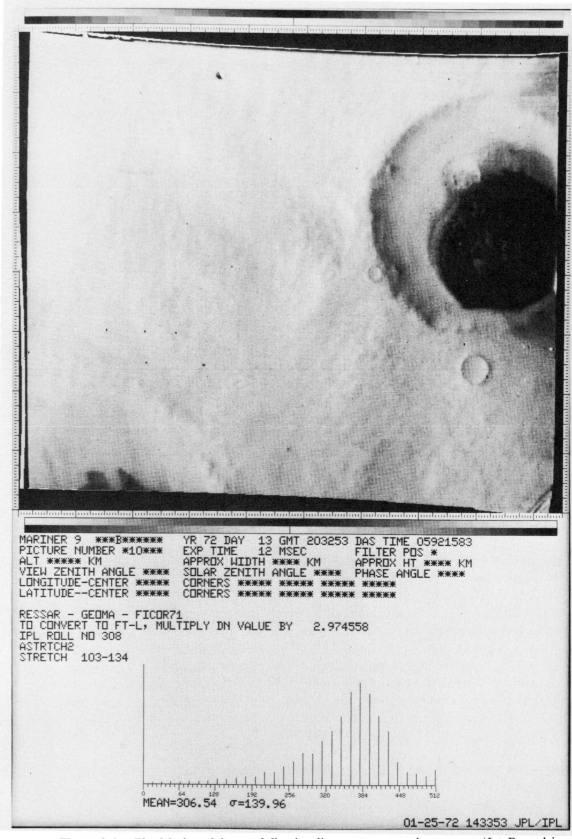

Figure 3-4. The Mariner 9 image following linear contrast enhancement (Jet Propulsion Laboratory).

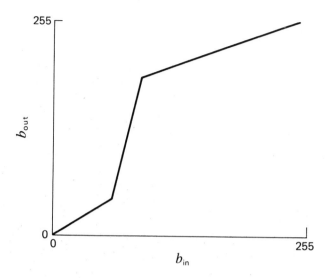

Figure 3-5. Piecewise linear contrast enhancement.

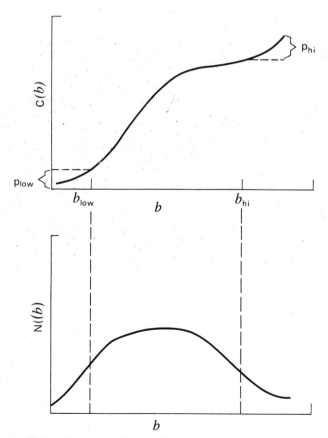

Figure 3-6. Automated ends-in search contrast enhancement.

A linear contrast stretch is then performed, using the values of b_{low} and b_{hi} as selected above. This technique is illustrated in Figure 3-6.

Many other automated contrast enhancement techniques have been developed, and all are based on histogram analysis. Each of the automated techniques utilizes the cumulative distribution function and a definition of the desired output intensity histogram to define the enhancement performed on each individual image.

Arbitrary Contrast Enhancement

The contrast enhancement techniques discussed so far all utilize one or more linear functions to define the intensity transformation between input and output images. The most general form of contrast enhancement involves mapping each individual intensity value into a specified output value, where the transformation of each input intensity value is individually determined, based on the particular application.

Any artibrary contrast enhancement transformation can thus be defined by establishing a set of table look-up values, storing one value of output intensity for each possible input intensity value:

$$b_{out} = T(b_{in}) \tag{3-6}$$

If a contrast enhancement is implemented via a table look-up, a wide variety of contrast transformations are possible. Typical nonlinear transformations that are implemented via table look-up include transformations to a Gaussian histogram and transformation to an output histogram in which all output intensity levels are as equally populated as possible within quantization constraints. The latter transformation is often referred to as a *ramp CDF stretch*, since the cumulative distribution of an equally populated histogram is a linearly increasing function (a ramp). Several techniques for contrast manipulation based on histogram analysis and table look-up implementation are described in reference 5.

Figures 3-7 and 3-8 show two enhanced versions of a LANDSAT MSS image. In Figure 3-7 the output histogram is a Gaussian function, and in Figure 3-8 a ramp CDF stretch has been performed. Each of these enhancements is implemented via table look-up. Reference 1 contains a few detailed examples of table look-up enhancement, including numerical examples illustrating selection of table values to achieve specific desired output histograms.

Digital display systems now available commercially include table look-up hardware. With these systems, it is possible to define a contrast enhancement function that is implemented by storing a set of values into the table memory in the display system. The stored digital values are processed through the table look-up hardware before conversion to analog signal values for video display. It is possible with most systems to achieve storage of a full set of new table values within the time it takes to read the full image and convert it to analog for display; the video refresh time is one-thirtieth of a second. It is thus possible to manipulate the contrast of an image stored within the display memory and to observe the contrast-enhanced image directly on a volatile display very rapidly. With these systems, once the input digital image is stored with local display memory, it is possible to select an optimal contrast enhancement for a given image within a few minutes of an interactive contrast manipulation session.

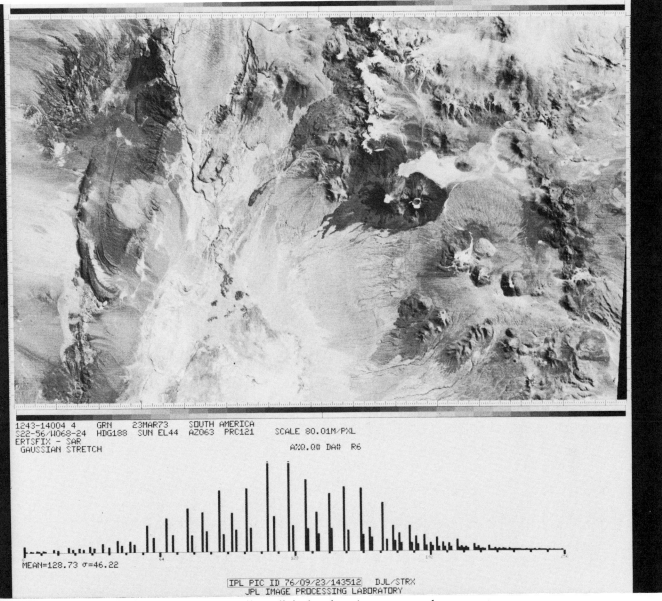

Figure 3-7. LANDSAT MSS scene of the Chile-Bolivia border. A contrast enhancement that maps the output intensity distribution to a Gaussian has been applied (Jet Propulsion Laboratory).

Implementation Note

Each of the contrast manipulation techniques discussed so far can be implemented in computer software or hardware via the table look-up procedure. For each contrast enhancement, the full set of possible output intensity values, b_{out}, is computed and paired with each possible input value, b_{in}. The result is a stored table of the type described in Equation 3-6. When the enhancement is actually performed, the table look-up procedure is used, thus avoiding expensive mathematical computations for each pixel that is processed.

As an example, the linear contrast enhancement described in Equation 3-3 can

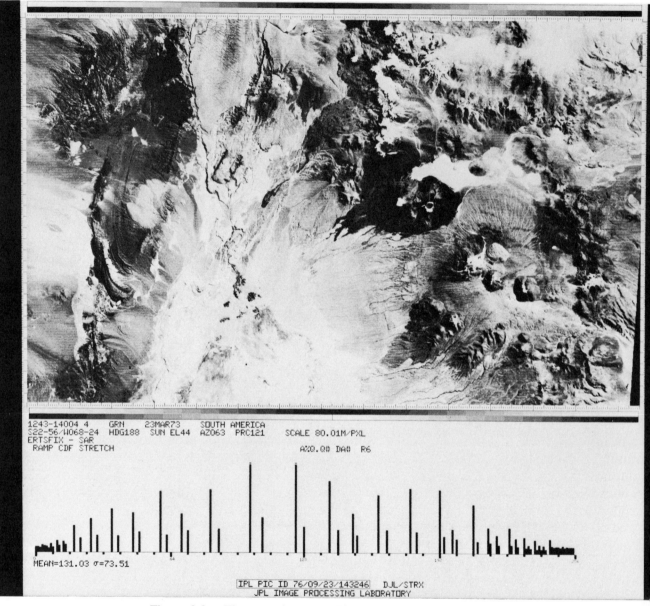

Figure 3-8.   The same image as Fig. 3-7, but with a "ramp CDF" contrast enhancement applied (Jet Propulsion Laboratory).

actually be performed by using table look-up implementation. Once b_{low} and b_{hi} are specified, pairs of values of b_{in} and b_{out} are stored in a table, using Equation 3-3 to compute the values of b_{out} for each possible value of b_{in}; in an 8-bit system, the table is generated by allowing b_{in} to vary from 0 to 255, and 255 corresponding values of b_{out} computed from Equation 3-3 are stored as the 255 table entries.

Once the table has been computed and stored, the enhancement described by Equation 3-3 is performed via a table look-up (Equation 3-6) rather than by performing the mathematical computations at each pixel.

IMAGE CONTOURING

There are several available techniques for displaying contours of equal intensity within a digital image. These techniques are useful in radiometric analysis, where determination of surface albedo is important. Contouring is also an important tool for analyzing the radiometric shading introduced by a particular camera system or film scanner, and determining the degree of brightness shading that may be present in a film scanning system.

One of the most popular methods used to perform image contouring is *bit-clipping*. When this technique is used, the analyst specifies that a certain number of the most significant bits (MSBs) of each digitized pixel intensity value will be "clipped," or set to zero. This has the effect of breaking up a region of gradual full black-to-white transition into several subregions within which the intensity cycles from black through white several times. As an example of the effect introduced by this technique, suppose that the leftmost 2 bits of each 8-bit picture element intensity value are to be clipped (i.e., we will set to zero the 2 MSBs of each pixel intensity value). The following table illustrates the effect:

b_{in} RANGE	b_{out} RANGE
0 through 63	0 through 63
64 through 127	0 through 63
128 through 192	0 through 63
192 through 255	0 through 63

The intensity range from zero through 255 will be displayed as four subintervals, and the intensity values in the output image will be reset to values between zero and 63 within each subinterval. Figure 3-9 shows the relationship between input and output intensity values achieved in this example.

A linear contrast stretch between zero and 63 would be performed on the resulting bit-clipped image so that the intensity values in the output image would be transformed to fill the full dynamic range of the output display medium.

Figure 3-10 shows two different bit-clipped versions of the same digital image. The image was a calibration image taken before launch of the Mariner 9 vidicon camera system and was one of a series of images recorded to characterize the radio-

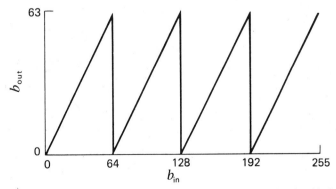

Figure 3-9.   Intensity transformation corresponding to "clipping" the 2 MSBs.

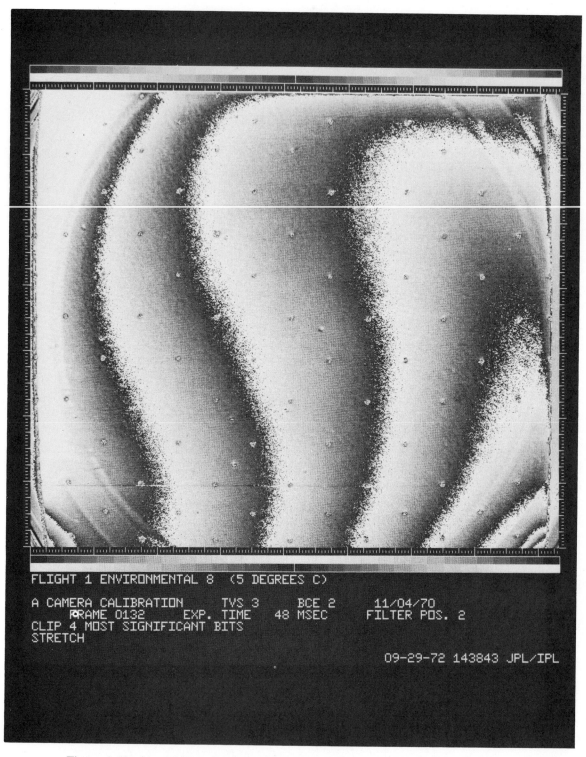

Figure 3-10. (a) Vidicon camera calibration image with 4 MSB's clipped; **(b)** same image with 6 MSB's clipped (Jet Propulsion Laboratory).

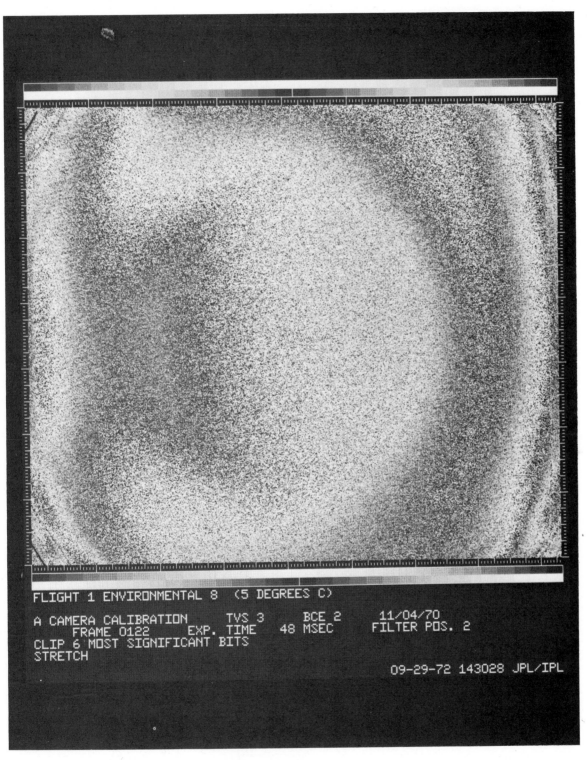

FLIGHT 1 ENVIRONMENTAL 8 (5 DEGREES C)

A CAMERA CALIBRATION   TVS 3   BCE 2   11/04/70
      FRAME 0122   EXP. TIME   48 MSEC   FILTER POS. 2
CLIP 6 MOST SIGNIFICANT BITS
STRETCH

                              09-29-72 143028 JPL/IPL

Figure 3-10 (b).

metric performance of the camera system. The original image was taken with the camera field of view uniformly illuminated; the same light intensity fell on each area of the vidicon's active imaging surface. If the camera system were perfect, every pixel in the sampled image would have the same digital intensity value. The Mariner 9 vidicon camera was not a perfect instrument, and each of the vidicons used on the Mariner 9 spacecraft introduced intensity shading into every image taken with the cameras. The bit-clipped images were used to analyze the degree of shading in each camera. Figure 3-10a was produced by clipping 4 MSBs of the original 9-bit intensity levels in the recorded image. Contour lines of equal intensity are clearly visible. In addition, since 4 bits of the 9-bit intensity values were set to zero, each black-to-white transition represents a transition of 31 in digital intensity.

Figure 3-10a presents the same image after clipping the 6 MSBs of each pixel. The number of MSBs that is clipped depends strongly on the intensity distribution within the image being contoured. These two images clearly indicate that a 4-MSB clip provides much more information relative to the degree of vidicon shading than a 6-MSB clipped version for the particular input image involved in this analysis.

A second popular method of image contouring involves setting particular input intensity values in the input image to black ($b = 0$) or white ($b = 255$ in an 8-bit system). This method can be used, for example, to superimpose contours on an image at intervals of 32 or 64 in digital intensity. This technique has the advantage of retaining the majority of the input image data visible in the output image, since only those pixels at the contour values are modified. Bit-clipping often renders the image detail unrecognizable in the output image. However, the random noise present in most digital systems will not guarantee that continuous contour lines will be generated. A graphical illustration of this type of transformation is shown in Figure 3-11.

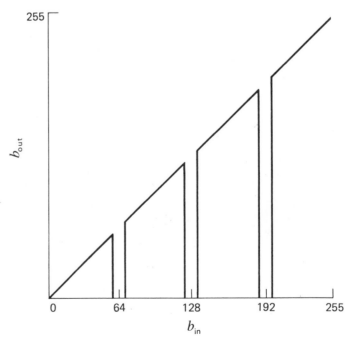

Figure 3-11. Iso-intensity contouring.

In mathematical terms, we establish k contouring levels b_{c1}, b_{c2}, b_{c3}, . . . b_{ck}. The transformation becomes

$$b_{out} = 0 \text{ if } b_{in} = b_{c1} \text{ OR } b_{c2} \text{ OR } \ldots \text{ OR } b_{ck}$$
$$b_{out} = b_{in} \text{ otherwise}$$

$$(3\text{-}7)$$

Implementation Note

Either of these two contouring techniques can be implemented via a table stretch. Both methods can be viewed as intensity transformation techniques, and a table of output intensity values can be stored as a function of the input intensity values once a particular contouring technique is selected. The processing is then performed via table look-up, instead of performing expensive bit masking or logical decision analysis for each input pixel to determine the appropriate output value.

Image contouring options are often included in software modules used to perform contrast manipulation because of the similarity in implementation. The same software module, based on table look-up processing, is then used to perform a variety of contrast manipulation or image contouring functions, based on options specified by the user.

SPATIAL FILTERING

An image will contain information at a wide range of spatial frequencies. Overall gradual transitions from light to dark within an image can be interpreted as low-frequency components. Rapid, local variations in contrast represent information at a higher frequency. Local texture is an example of image information that is high-frequency information.

It is possible to perform an analysis of the spatial frequencies present in digital image, utilizing Fourier transform techniques. The topic of image filtering deals with various techniques designed to isolate the various spatial components present within an image. One- or two-dimensional Fourier transforms of an image will reveal a large low-frequency component, corresponding to the gradual intensity variation within the scene, and a variety of high-frequency "spikes" may be present in the transform, indicating periodic structure or periodic scene detail present within the image.

The topic of image filtering can become quite complex and is dealt with extensively in other sources; reference 3 provides a good introduction to this topic. In this section, a rather simple technique often used in image enhancement will be described. This technique is called *high pass filtering,* and it is performed on an image to remove the slowly varying components and retain only the high-frequency local variations in the processed image.

This technique is used for analysis of surface structure and local image detail. It is quite useful in cartography, when a mapmaker wishes to depict the local topographic detail and surface structure and has no interest in gradual changes of surface albedo.

Computationally, high pass filtering is performed with an efficient algorithm that subtracts a local moving average from each individual pixel intensity value. A rectangular window of height H lines and width W samples in centered on a pixel located at line l, sample s. In line and sample space, the window runs from lines l_1 to l_2, where

$$\ell_1 = \ell - H/2$$
$$\ell_2 = \ell + H/2 \qquad (3\text{-}8)$$

and from samples s_1 to s_2, where

$$s_1 = s - W/2$$
$$s_2 = s + W/2 \qquad (3\text{-}9)$$

The filter is achieved by subtracting a local moving average intensity value from each pixel in turn and then adjusting the output intensity values to lie about the midpoint of the digital gray scale. For an 8-bit system (intensities ranging from 0 to 255).

$$(b_{\text{out}})_{\ell s} = 128 + (b_{\text{in}})_{\ell s} - \sum_{j=\ell_1}^{\ell_2} \cdot \sum_{k=s_1}^{s_2} (b_{\text{in}})_{jk}/(HW) \qquad (3\text{-}10)$$

An efficient implementation of this algorithm will take advantage of the fact that the entire moving average need not be computed at each pixel. If the algorithm proceeds sequentially through the image, only the pixel values that enter and leave the moving window need be involved in computation.

A variey of techniques can be used to deal with computation of the moving average at the edges of the digital image. These techniques include (1) artifically extending the image beyond the actual image border by repeating the border pixel values into an artificial set of extended lines and samples, and (2) extrapolating the image intensity near the borders, based on the image behavior within a few pixels of the border.

A linear contrast enhancement is often applied to a high pass filtered image before film recording or display. A high pass filter basically computes the deviations from a moving local mean within the image. Pixel intensities tend to be highly correlated with their immediate neighbors. The high pass filtered image will thus have a very narrow intensity histogram, similar to the Guassian histograms discussed earlier in this chapter. For that reason, the information remaining after a high pass filter has been applied can be viewed effectively only by applying a contrast enhancement technique. Most high pass filtering software modules have a built in option that enables the analyst to invoke an automated or specified contrast enhancement.

A graphical representation of the effect of the high pass filter algorithm is shown in Figure 3-12. Figure 3-12a depicts a plot of the digital intensity across one line of an image before application of a high pass filter. Figure 3-12b shows an artist's rendition of a plot of the intensity across the same line of the image after application of a high pass filter. Note that the gradual transition from bright to dark and back to bright again that is visible in Figure 3-12a does not appear in Figure 3-12b. Figure 3-12b illustrates the retention of only the high-frequency or rapidly varying intensity fluctuations that occur on the line of interest.

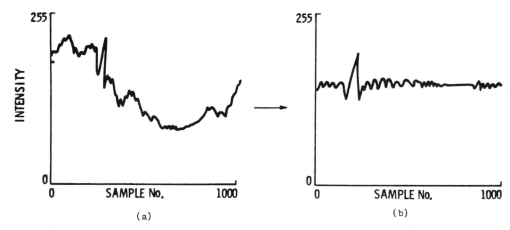

Figure 3-12. Graphical representation of the effects of high pass filtering.

The size of the filter rectangle and its shape can be modified to achieve different bandpass filters and to perform filtering that retains or eliminates image detail that may be aligned with the image raster in the line or sample direction. A very narrow, very long filter will remove features that are nearly vertical in the image, for example. Additional details regarding the frequency response properties of this type of filter can be found in reference 6, along with a more detailed description of the algorithm. Reference 7 also describes this algorithm as applied to the Mariner 9 images of Mars. A scene-dependent high pass filter (one that varies the filter performance as a function of the degree of local scene detail) is described in reference 8. Several filters that can be applied in the spatial domain are also described in reference 9.

Figures 3-13 and 3-14 show the results of applying this filter to a LANDSAT MSS image of the Altyn Tagh region of China. Figure 3-13 is a linearly contrast-enhanced version of one spectral component of the LANDST MSS scene. The contrast enhancement has saturated some of the pixels either black or white within specific areas of interest in the scene. This image was used in a study of earthquake fault structure, and a particularly significant fault that runs nearly diagonally from upper right to lower left through the image was not displayed optimally for geological interpretation in the contrast-enhanced version.

Figure 3-14 shows the same image after high pass filtering and contrast enhancement. The fault of interest is now clearly visible, as is other local structural detail that is not visible in the contrast-enhanced version.

Figure 3-15 shows the results of applying the high pass algorithm to the Mariner 9 crater image considered previously (Figures 3-2 and 3-4). The linearly contrast-enhanced version in Figure 3-4 preserved the relative brightness relationships within the scene. It is clear in Figure 3-4 that the center of the crater is much darker than the surface surrounding the crater. In the high pass filtered version, the overall large-scale brightness variations within the scene have been lost, but the local structural variation within the scene is clearly visible. Note especially the detail visible in the crater center that was not visible in the contrast-enhanced version. The high pass filtered version is quite useful in geological interpretation and for cartographic pur-

Figure 3-13.   LANDSAT MSS scene of the Altyn Tagh region of China, with linear contrast enhancement applied (Jet Propulsion Laboratory).

poses. The contrast-enhanced version is quite useful for studying the radiometric properties of the Martian surface.

BIT-SLICING

Bit-slicing is a technique designed to isolate particular intensity intervals within an image. The technique involves generation of an output image with all pixels black ($b = 0$), except for those pixels in the input image whose intensities fall within a particular region of interest.

Two types of bit slicing are illustrated in Figure 3-16. In Figure 3-16*a,* the output image will be generated with white pixels wherever the input image intensity falls within a particular band of interest. Figure 3-16*b* illustrates an intensity transformation in which all pixels with intensities above a particular value will be transformed to white in the output image, and all pixels with intensities below that value will be displayed as black in the output image.

Figure 3-17 shows a mosaic of a series of synthetic-aperture radar (SAR) images of an ice field.[10] The mosaic has been high pass filtered, and the resultant image displays the ice field with the breaks within the ice clearly visible. These breaks are called leads. The SAR imagery was acquired as part of a study concerned with behavior of the ice leads as a function of time, and one quantity of interest was the directional properties of the leads. In particular, it was felt that the leads would

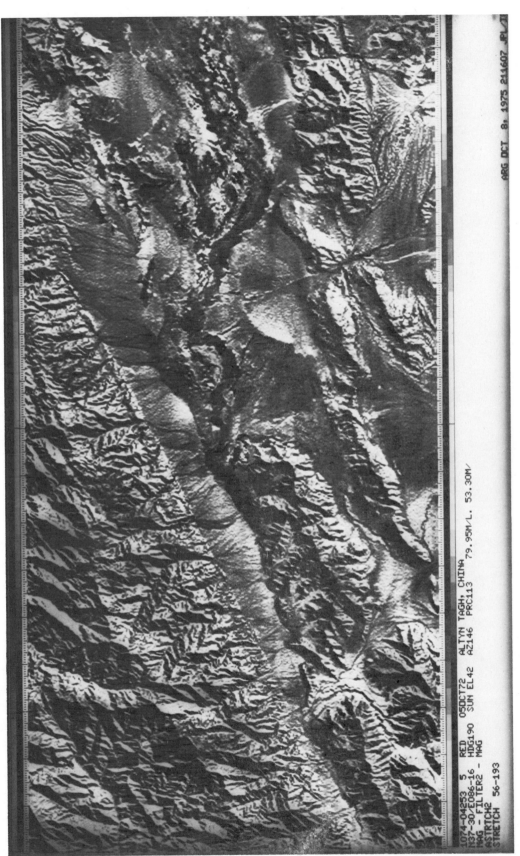

Figure 3-14. Same LANDSAT MSS scene as Fig. 3-13, but after application of a high pass filter and linear contrast enhancement (Jet Propulsion Laboratory).

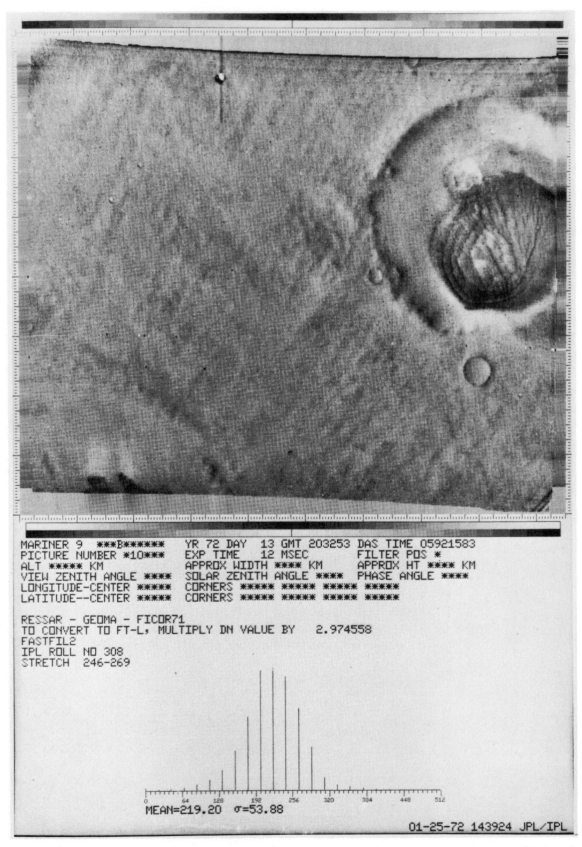

Figure 3-15.   The Mariner 9 Mars crater image, after application of a high pass filter and linear contrast enhancement (Jet Propulsion Laboratory).

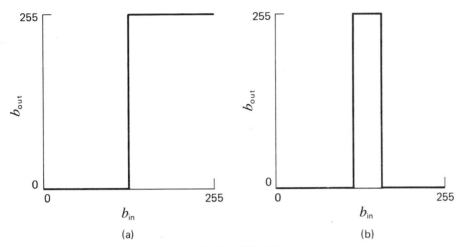

Figure 3-16.   Bit slicing.

exhibit a preference in their orientation. In order to isolate the leads from the surrounding ice material, a bit slice was performed using the type of transformation shown in Figure 3-16a. Figure 3-18 shows the result. The bit slice has separated the leads from the ice as desired. The leads are visible as the black objects in the bit-sliced image, whereas the ice and the surrounding background are all saturated white.

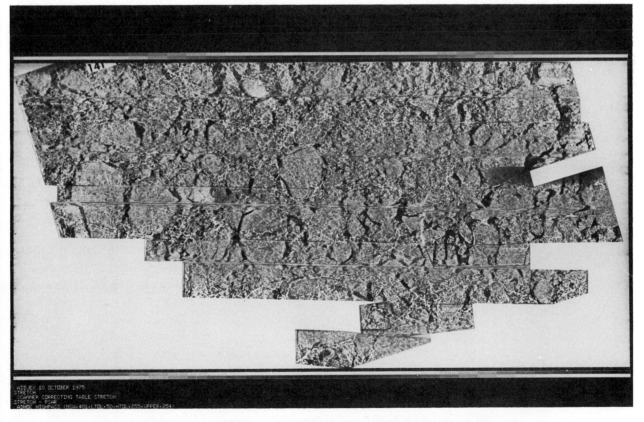

Figure 3-17.   Mosaic of SAR images of an ice field. The leads are the dark regions between the ice blocks (Jet Propulsion Laboratory).

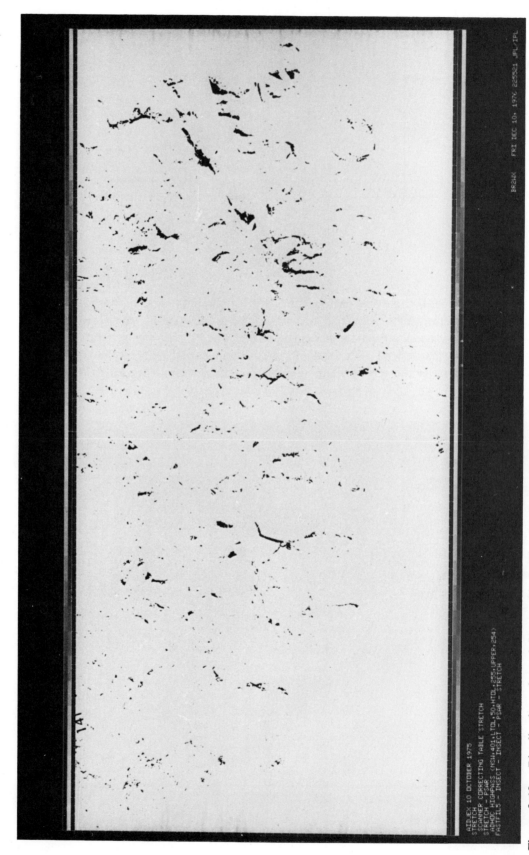

Figure 3-18. Bit sliced version of the mosaic in Fig. 3-17. The leads have been separated from the ice and the background (Jet Propulsion Laboratory).

COLOR ENHANCEMENT TECHNIQUES

False Color

The eye is limited in terms of the number of discrete shades of gray that it can resolve. In general, the eye can distinguish only about 32 discrete gray shades. The eye is less limited in color discrimination and is capable of distinguishing up to several hundred discrete color shades. For this reason, color is an important tool in image enhancement.

Color often is useful in interpreting a single image that would normally be displayed in black and white into a full-color image. When this is done, color is added as a mechanism to aid the human interpreter in data analysis. A full 8-bit image containing intensities from zero to 255 can be transformed into a color image, and the eye can discriminate almost the full intensity range in color rendition. The color image produced by translating a monocolor image into a color presentation is called a *false-color* image. This is no relation between the color produced in a false-color image and the true color of the object that was imaged.

False-color images are produced by intensity transformations that are similar to contrast enhancements. The input intensity range of the digitized image is transformed into three separate output intensity ranges: one for red, one for green, and one for the blue components of a color output composit image. From a single input image, three output images are produced.

One example of a transformation that will produce a false-color image is shown in Figure 3-19. Low-intensity values will be depicted in the blue shades, with high intensities portrayed in red, and intermediate intensities depicted in green shades. The transformation shown will mix varying amounts of the primary colors together to create a continuous range of color variation from blue to red that corresponds to the original range of monocolor intensity present in the input image. The three separate images produced from the single input image are then combined in a film recorder or volatile color display system to produce an output full-color image.

This technique is often used to display three-dimensional data that are not inherently imaging in nature. A sensor can record temperature as a function of spatial coordinates, and the resulting data can be displayed as a false-color image; it would be natural to depict low temperatures as blue and high temperature as red in this type of presentation.

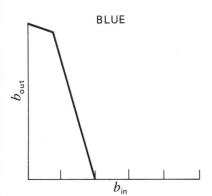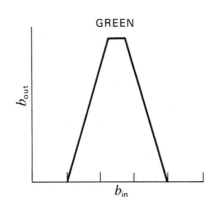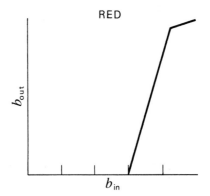

Figure 3-19.   Transformation to false color.

Color Compositing

Color enhancement and display techniques are most commonly used in applications in which images of a particular region have been acquiried in more than one spectral band and a single display of all the available data is desirable. Color can also be used to display data of different types that are available over the same region. For example, a combination of gravity field data, magnetic data, and elevation data can be displayed as a color composite image, with a separate color (red, green, or blue) used to represent each of the three component data types.

Color compositing involves the merger of three separate images into a single-color image. Three separate images are created, and a separate color is assigned to each. Once the color assignment is made, the three components are input to a digital film recorder or a volatile display system, where they are merged into a single-color representation.

Figure 3-20 is a color composite image of an area in Australia. This image was recorded in four spectral bands by the LANDSAT multispectral scanner. Three of the four components were selected to generate this color composite. Each of the three component images was separately enhanced, and then the three enhanced images were input to a color film recording device. The process is shown in Figure 3-21.

Separate enhancement of each of the three component images will vary the nature of the color composite product. Separate manipulation of each of the component images is often performed interactively in order to optimize the display of desired information in the color composite product. This technique is commonly employed for LANDSAT MSS imagery and other multispectral imagery. The techniques used to generate the color composite imagery on film and in volatile display systems are discussed in Chapter 6.

LANDSAT MSS color composite construction often involves enhancement processing which is performed in a standard manner, so that the photo interpreter can perform image analysis on a large image data set, using his or her knowledge of the

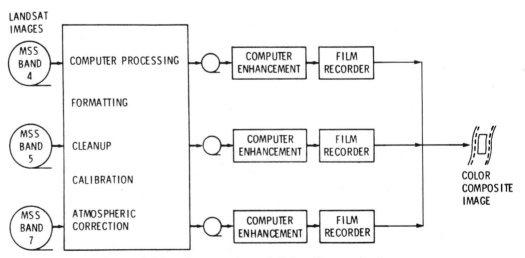

Figure 3-21. Construction of Color Composite Imagery.

standard color presentation normally employed. In most LANDSAT MSS processing, red is used to display the infrared component of the multispectral imagery, and vegetation usually appears as red in LANDSAT MSS color imagery.

One example of the utility of extreme contrast exaggeration in one component of a color image is shown in Figure 3-22. This is a color composite generated from three spectral component images of one of the Jovian satellites, Io, obtained by the Voyager 1 spacecraft. Three separate images have been spatially registered, and each of the three components has undergone contrast manipulation. The enhancement was designed to emphasize the ultraviolet component of the image. The untraviolet filter was incorporated in the Voyager imaging system to aid in atmospheric analysis. One of the discoveries of the Voyager mission was the presence of active volcanoes on Io. The color composite clearly reveals the presence of one of the volcanoes, and the presentation of the ultraviolet image as the blue component yields a vivid presentation of the atmospheric disturbance that surrounds the volcano. The color enhancement has been designed to allow measurement of the extent of the material venting from the volcano (using the blue component) while saturating the surface detail in the green and red components.

Color Ratioing

Another color technique often used to reveal subtle variations that exist between the individual spectral components of a multispectral image is *image ratioing*. Intensity variations often are highly correlated between different spectral components of the same scene. Color, when used in conjunction with ratio imagery, can be used as a discriminant to isolate small variations between spectral components.

The color ratioing process is shown schematically in Figure 3-23. A ratio image is constructed from two input images by taking the ratio of digital intensity values at each pixel location:

$$r_{\ell s} = \frac{(b_{\ell s}) \text{ IMAGE 1}}{(b_{\ell s}) \text{ IMAGE 2}} \cdot \gamma \qquad (3\text{-}11)$$

where r_{ls} is the ratio value at line l sample s in the ratio image and y is a scaling factor used to expand the computed ratio values to fill the dynamic range of the pixel intensity values. For example, if values of r can range up to 1.5, assigning a value of $\gamma = 170$ will ensure that the intensities in the ratio image will lie below 255 (assuming an 8-bit system).

The process shown in Figure 3-23 involves utilization for all four spectral bands of information provided by the LANDSAT multispectral scanner. For this application, ratioing has an advantage over color composite generation, in which only three of the four available spectral components are utilized. Enhancement of each of the component ratio images is also employed to optimize the display of desired information.

Figure 3-24 shows a color ratio composite image produced from the same LANDSAT MSS scene shown in standard color composite form in Figure 3-20. Comparison of the two figures indicates the improvement in visibility of subtle detail in the color ratio version.

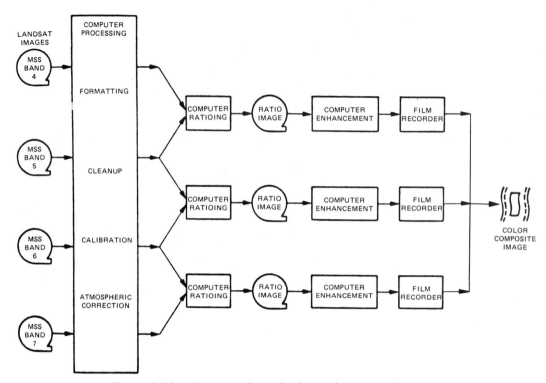

Figure 3-23. Construction of color ratio composite imagery.

Neither color representation of the LANDSAT MSS image is a true representation of the actual surface coloration in the region of Australia depicted in the LANDSAT MSS scene. Color is being used as a tool to aid in interpretation and to provide a dramatic means of discriminating spectral differences that may in fact be quite subtle. The use of color as an aid in interpretation represents a growing technology, and these two image products dramatically illustrate the power of color representation in aiding image analysis. They also serve as excellent examples of subjective image enhancement, since several versions of each product were produced before the final versions were selected; the criteria for selection were based on the ability of the human observer to discriminate the desired detail in the output products.

REFERENCES

1. Gonzalez, R., and P. Wintz, *Digital Image Processing*, New York, Addison-Wesley, 1977.
2. Rosenfeld, A. and A. Kak, *Digital Picture Processing* (2 volumes), New York, Academic Press, 1982.
3. Pratt, W. K., *Digital Image Processing,* New York, Wiley, 1978.
4. Castleman, K. R., *Digital Image Processing,* New York, Prentice-Hall, 1979.
5. Schwartz, A. A., "New Techniques for Digital Image Enhancement," *Proceedings of the Caltech/ JPL Conference on Image Processing Technology, Data Sources and Software for Commercial and Scientific Applications,* Jet Propulsion Laboratory Report SP 43-30, November 1976.
6. Seidman, J., "Some Practical Applications of Digital Filtering in Image Processing," *Proceedings of the Symposium of Computer Image Processing and Recognition,* Vol. 2, Dept. of Electrical Engineering, University of Missouri, Columbia, 1972.
7. Green, W. B., et al. "Removal of Instrument Signature from Mariner 9 Images of Mars." *Appl Opt* 14, 105 (1975).

8. Schwartz, A. A., and J. M. Soha, "Variable Threshold Zonal Filtering," *Appl Opt* 16, 1779 (1977).
9. Lee, J., "Digital Image Enhancement and Noise Filtering by Use of Local Statistics," *IEEE Trans. on Pattern Analysis and Machine Intelligence,* Vol. PAMI-2, 2, pp. 165–168 (March 1980).
10. Bryan, M. L., W. D. Stromberg, and T. G. Farr, "Computer Processing of SAR L-Band Imagery," *Photogramm Engr & Remote Sensing* 43, 10, pp 1283–1294 (Oct. 1977).

4
Quantitative Image Processing Techniques

INTRODUCTION

This chapter describes image processing techniques that are applied to one or more images in a noninteractive, nonadaptive manner. The techniques are based on an underlying mathematical model, and the results of processing imagery with these techniques are acceptable if the mathematical model is correct. For that reason, these techniques are called *quantitative* rather than *subjective,* since subjective processing normally involves a trial and error process and a subjective evaluation of the final product by an analyst; quantitative techniques are usually applied to one or more images without analyst intervention.

One example of quantitative processing is removal of radiometric distortion introduced into images by a sensor system. A film scanner may have a fixed shading pattern, and all images digitized with that scanner will have that shading pattern introduced into the digitized imagery. This pattern is undesirable and should be removed before any analysis of the digitized image. The scanner shading characteristics are modeled, and a program is written to remove the shading artifact from every scanned image. Once the shading pattern has been measured and the program that removes that pattern has been checked out, the process is applied routinely to every image scanned by that system. Success in processing is based on the degree to which the scanner shading has been correctly modeled mathematically, not on subjective evaluation of every processed image by an analyst.

A second example of quantitative processing is cartographic projection of remotely sensed imagery. It may be desirable to display every image acquired by a remote sensing imaging device in a standard mapping projection. The parameters defining the projection include the spacecraft position and orientation, the camera's viewing geometry, and the desired cartographic projection. The computation can proceed once these parameters are specified to a program designed to perform the projection. Here again, once the mathematics is specified and the program is checked out, the process would be performed with no analyst intervention.

This chapter describes the basic techniques of quantitative image processing, including geometric transformation, cartographic projection, image registration, radiometric distortion correction, multispectral classification, color manipulation, and convolutional filtering. The chapter serves as an introduction to these topics; references are provided to more detailed sources for each topic.

GEOMETRIC TRANSFORMATION

Introduction

All the operations described in the previous chapter do not modify the size or shape of the image. Contrast enhancement, high pass filtering, and other operations described in Chapter 3 all modify the intensity value of a particular pixel in place; the location of the pixel does not change as a result of the processing. In general, the processes described so far do not modify the size or shape of the imagery, and the intensity modification of each pixel dictated by the particular algorithm is usually performed by processing the image sequentially, line by line and sample by sample within each line.

The class of image processing operations in which the size and shape of the image may be modified are called *geometric transformations*. These operations can modify the image's size and shape and can alter the spatial relationships between pixels.

One simple example of a geometric transformation is magnification by an integer factor. Figure 4-1 shows the result of magnifying a 4-sample by 2-line image segment by a factor of 2. The magnification is achieved by replicating each input pixel 4 times in the output image. An 8-sample by 4-line output image segment is thus created, with 4 times the number of pixels present in the input image.

This may appear to be a trivial example, but there are circumstances in which this type of magnification is useful. A film recorder may have a fixed sample spacing so that input pixel intensities are recorded onto a film negative at a single fixed separation distance. It may be necessary to produce large prints from the negatives recorded on this type of device, and the restriction to a single pixel spacing on the negative may cause the appearance of esthetically undesirable distractions in the output image products (e.g., the pixels may appear as single spots widely separated by black background in the enlargements). A more pleasing enlargement would result if the image pixels were replicated on the original negative before the enlargement process, and the simple magnification achieved by replicating pixels may be quite useful in this application. Many of the film recorders discussed in Chapter 5 incorporate pixel replication options, enabling playback of image data at magnification ratios of 1:1, 2:1, and 4:1.

Geometric manipulation usually involves more than simple magnification of the image. A more complex example of geometric transformation is cartographic projection of an image that is taken at an oblique viewing angle relative to the surface normal at the center of the field of view of the camera system. In this case, the image must be realigned by changing the spatial relationships between the pixels so that the final image product presents the pixels in a standard cartographic projection (e.g., Mercator).

The projection of a rectangular image raster of a camera system onto a spherical surface (such as a planet) is nonlinear, and cartographic projection requires a varying degree of realignment within the image raster. The degree of relocation of the pixels within the raster is a function of their location within the field of view of the camera system. In some regions of the field view, pixels must move more than in

14	27	9	15		14	14	27	27	9	9	15	15
				X2 →	14	14	27	27	9	9	15	15
26	28	8	19									
					26	26	28	28	8	8	19	19
					26	26	28	28	8	8	19	19

Figure 4-1. Magnification of image segment a factor of 2.

other areas in order to achieve correct cartographically projected pixel positions. This effect is illustrated in Figure 4-2.

Two basic definitions are required in order to perform a geometric projection:

1. The geometric relationship between the pixels in the input and output images must be defined; this definition establishes the geometric transformation that is being performed. For each pixel in the output image, the location within the input image from which the pixel will be extracted must be defined.
2. In the most general case of geometric transformation, the pixel locations in the input image from which the output pixels are drawn do not fall on exact raster positions within the input image. A mechanism for determining the intensity values assigned to the new pixels in the output image must be established. This mechanism normally involves some method for intensity interpolation.

These two definitions were easily established for the simple case of magnification by 2 of a small image segment (Figure 4-1). The factor of magnification, 2, established the spatial positioning, and the intensity assignment was based on replication of the intensity values for each pixel in the input image. The more general transformation applications become significantly more complex, however.

Spatial Interpolation

The technique generally used for geometric transformation of digital images involves a definition of the spatial relocation of the pixels through the use of *tiepoints*. Tiepoints are pixels for which the displacement between the input and output images can be defined precisely. For each tiepoint, the location in line and sample coordinates in the input and output images is known precisely.

Tiepoint relationships can be derived in a variety of ways. For a simple magnification, the four corner pixels of the input image serve as tiepoints, and the degree of magnification determines the location of those pixels in the output image (and the size of the output image). Magnification of a 3-line by 3-sample image by a factor

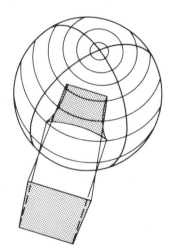

Figure 4-2. Projection of rectangular camera system focal plane image onto spherical planet.

of 2 will yield a 6 by 6 output image, and the transformation of the four corner tiepoints is defined by the following table:

TIEPOINT NUMBER	INPUT IMAGE (LINE, SAMPLE)	OUTPUT IMAGE (LINE, SAMPLE)
1	(1,1)	(1,1)
2	(1,3)	(1,6)
3	(3,1)	(6,1)
4	(3,3)	(6,6)

In the more general case, a geometric transformation is defined by dividing the input image into a series of quadrilaterals; the four corner points of each quadrilateral serve as a set of tiepoints defining the transformation for that quadrilateral. This procedure is illustrated in Figure 4-3. For a given quadrilateral, the line and sample coordinates of the four tiepoints in the input and output images is known:

TIEPOINT NUMBER	INPUT IMAGE (LINE, SAMPLE)	OUTPUT IMAGE (LINE, SAMPLE)
1	(ℓ'_1 , s'_1)	(ℓ_1 , s_1)
2	(ℓ'_2 , s'_2)	(ℓ_2 , s_2)
3	(ℓ'_3 , s'_3)	(ℓ_3 , s_3)
4	(ℓ'_4 , s'_4)	(ℓ_4 , s_4)

The output image is created by stepping sequentially through the output image line by line and sample by sample. At each line and sample coordinate of the output image, (ℓ, s), the location in the input image from which the output pixel will be extracted is computed, using bilinear interpolation:

$$\ell' = a_1\ell + a_2 s + a_3 \ell s + a_4$$
$$s' = a_5\ell + a_6 s + a_7 \ell s + a_8$$

(4-1)

where the eight coefficients $a_1, a_2, \ldots, a_8$ are obtained by solving the eight equations in eight unknowns that exist from the definition of the known values of (ℓ, s) and (ℓ', s') at the four tiepoints for each quadrilateral.

INPUT IMAGE   OUTPUT IMAGE

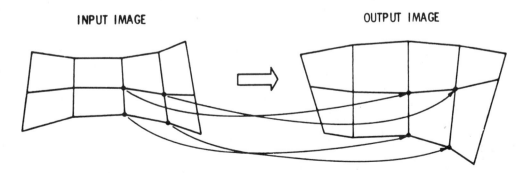

Figure 4-3.   Definition of geometric transformation through tiepoint definition.

Intensity Interpolation

The coordinates of the pixel location in the input image, (ℓ',s'), computed from Equation 4-1 will normally not fall on discrete raster locations in the input image. In general, (ℓ',s') will fall between four pixels in the input image, as shown in Figure 4-4. A technique must be developed for determining the pixel intensity value to be assigned to the "new" pixel in the output image located at position (ℓ,s).

The simplest interpolation technique is *nearest neighbor*. The intensity of the pixel in the output image is assigned the intensity value of the pixel closest to (ℓ',s') in the input image:

$$b_{\ell,s} = b_{\text{pixel closest to } (\ell',s')} \tag{4-2}$$

This interpolation can be implemented by using the rounding features of integer arithmetic in most digital computer systems.

Bilinear interpolation is a technique that utilizes the intensity values of the four immediate neighbor pixels. The intensity of the output pixel at position (ℓ,s) is computed using

$$b_{\ell,s} = c_1\ell' + c_2 s' + c_3\ell's' + c_4. \tag{4-3}$$

where the coefficients $c_1, \ldots, c_4$ are determined from the four equations in four unknowns that can be written, based on the fact that the intensity of the four neighboring pixels in the input image and their line-sample coordinates are known. Details of the spatial relationships between the four nearest neighbors and the location of coordinates (ℓ',s') are shown in Figure 4-5.

There are other, more sophisticated techniques for intensity transformation. *Cubic convolution* interpolation[1] uses the 16 nearest neighbor pixel intensities in interpolating the intensity value of the pixels in the output image. It is based on modeling the resolution degradation that occurs when sampled digital imagery is created; that degradation is of the sin x/x type, and cubic convolution interpolation is based on fitting a sin x/x function to the 16 nearest neighbors to position (ℓ',s'). The intensity value at (ℓ',s') is then determined on the basis of that surface fit. Cubic convolution thus attempts to model the intensity distribution as it existed in object space, before

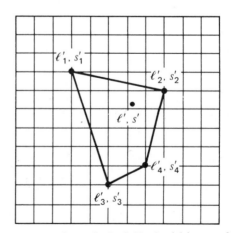

Figure 4-4. Location of pixel ℓ',s' within quadrilateral.

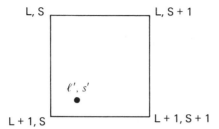

Figure 4-5. Relation of ℓ',s' to the four neighbor pixels.

digital sampling, in order to determine precisely the correct intensity values to assign to interpolated pixels. The precision of cubic convolution requiries significantly more computer resources than either bilinear or nearest-neighbor interpolation techniques.

Examples

Figure 4-6 shows an image of a uniformly ruled grid target taken with the Mariner 9 camera system before the launch. This image exhibits the "barrel" distortion found in many vidicon-based camera systems. The straight lines of the grid target are severly curved in the sampled image, particularly near the corners of the image. This distortion is present in every image taken with this system, although the degree of distortion varies from image to image. The degree of distortion varies significantly throughout the field of view of the camera. Note especially that the target lines are nearly linear in the center of the image and that the degree of distortion increases significantly near the edges of the image.

It is impossible to model this distortion with a single quadrilateral that defines the degree of distortion throughout the entire image. Instead, the image is broken into a series of quadrilaterals, and the distortion is determined for each quadrilateral within the image. The black spots visible in Figure 4-6 correspond to small metallic squares called *reseau marks* that are scribed on the front surface of the vidicon system. Calibration tests were designed to model the distortion of the camera system, and the distortion model was based on mapping the pixel coordinates of these reseau marks to their correct positions; the correct positions for the reseau marks are those which project the image into proper geometric coordinates in object space.

Each of the reseau marks was used as a tiepoint, since the observed distorted locations of each reseau mark could be determined within each sampled image, and a set of "correct" locations for each reseau mark has been determined from calibration testing. Each digitized image was broken into a set of quadrilaterals, using the reseau marks as the tiepoints of the quadrilaterals. Mapping the reseau marks to their correct locations defined the geometric transformation required to remove the system-induced distortion.[2]

Figure 4-7 shows the results of applying a geometric transformation to remove the camera system-induced distortion. The degree to which the image had to be "stretched" in the corners is clearly evident. Geometric transformations are often called *rubber sheet transformations,* since the effect is similar to printing a photograph on a piece of rubber and then stretching and manipulating the image into its proper geometric reference frame.

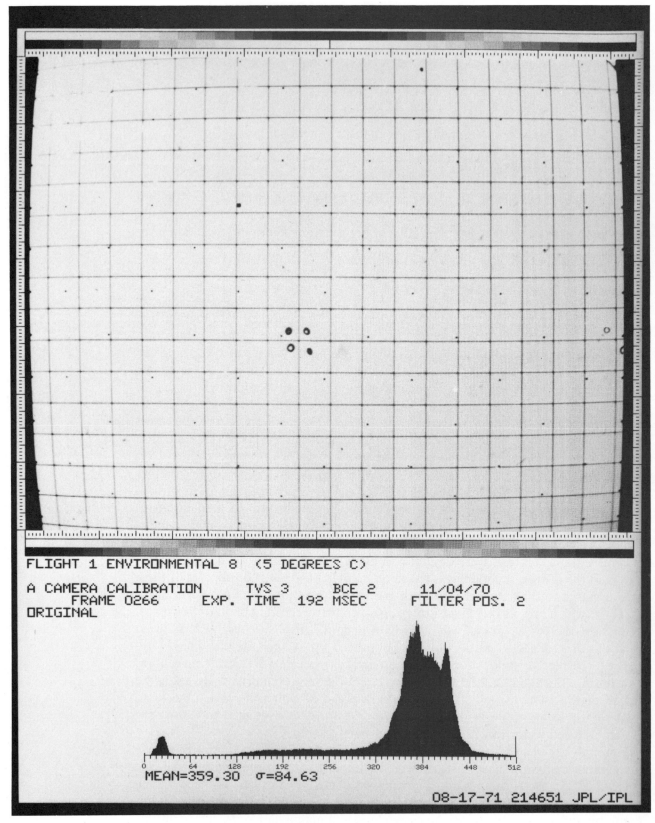

Figure 4-6.   Image of Mariner 9 geometric calibration test target (Jet Propulsion Laboratory).

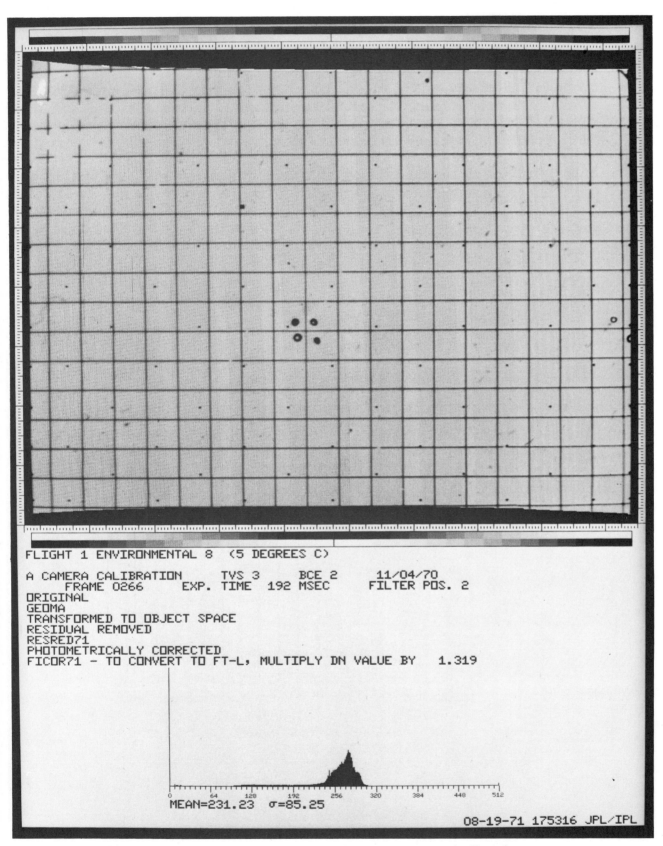

Figure 4-7. Mariner 9 test target image after correction for camera geometric distortion (Jet Propulsion Laboratory).

Figure 4-8 is an image taken of a grid test target during pre-flight calibration of the Viking Lander facsimile camera system. The Lander camera sampled object space in equal steps of solid angle. The effect of this sampling is to distort the scene so that linear features in object space appear curved when the sampled image is displayed on a flat surface. A projection is required that places the pixels in the correct geometric relationships to be viewed on a flat surface (such as a page of this book).

There were no reseau marks or other aids within the Viking Lander camera system that could be used to determine a transformation of each image to correct for the sampling distortion. Instead, the camera system was extensively modeled, using ray-tracing techniques, before flight.[3] The solid-angle distortion was determined for each camera system throughout the full field of view of the camera. The distortion function was modeled as a function of the azimuth and elevation coordinates of each pixel within the field of view. Each image was then corrected by applying this model, with quadrilaterals defined on the basis of the azimuth and elevation coordinates of each individual image. A corrected grid target image is shown in Figure 4-9.

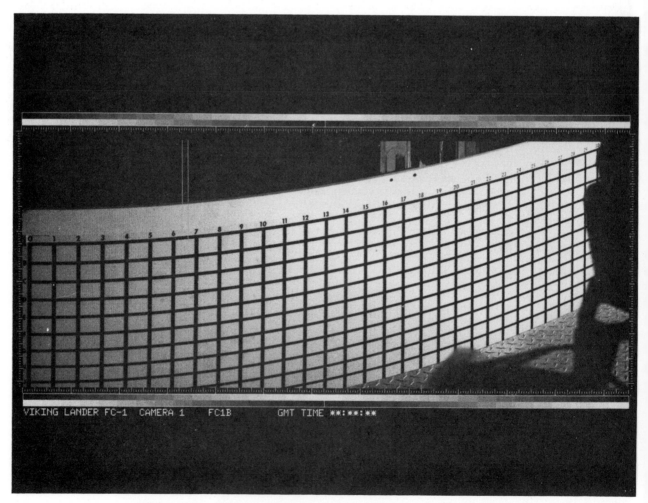

Figure 4-8. Viking Lander geometric calibration image (Jet Propulsion Laboratory).

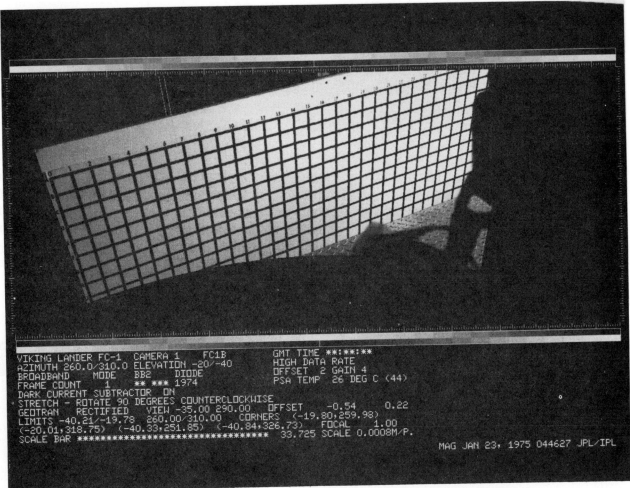

Figure 4-9. Viking Lander grid target image after distortion correction (Jet Propulsion Laboratory).

Figures 4-10 and 4-11 depict another geometric transformation with tiepoints derived in another, completely different manner. Figure 4-10 shows the second image recorded after touchdown of the Viking Lander 2 spacecraft on the surface of Mars in September 1976. The Lander 2 spacecraft landed in such a manner that the spacecraft was tilted downward approximately 8° relative to the horizon. The facsimile camera, which scans the level horizon in a cylindrical scan, produced a "tilt" distor-

Figure 4-10. Viking Lander 2 image of Utopia Planitia on September 3, 1976 (NASA/Jet Propulsion Laboratory).

Figure 4-11. Utopia Planitia image after correction for distortion caused by spacecraft orientation (NASA/Jet Propulsion Laboratory).

tion into the imagery; scanning a level horizon with a cylindrical scanner tilted downward produces a sinusoidal horizon, as is evident in Figure 4-10.

Figure 4-11 shows the same image after application of a transformation designed to remove the "tilt" distortion. Here again, information external to the camera system has been utilized to correct the imagery.

Cartographic Projection

Geometric transformation is widely used to perform cartographic projection. The objective is to transform the image into a standard mapping projection. This is desirable because a variety of nonimaging geographically referenced data bases are often used in conjunction with remotely sensed imagery. Transforming a digital image into a standard cartographic projection enables the analyst to deal with the image data in a standard, well-known coordinate frame of reference.

It is possible to align a remotely sensed image with standard available map products once the image is transformed into a cartographic projection. In addition, it becomes easier to align other geographically registered data bases with the remotely sensed imagery. For example, a data base containing elevation data or magnetic field data may be available for a given area; these data bases may be referenced or indexed by longitude-latitude coordinates, and it would be difficult to utilize imaging data to supplement the elevation and magnetic field data without first aligning the image data within a standard geographical coordinate system.

There are a variety of standard mapping projections currently in common use. They include orthographic, Lambert conformal conic, Mercator, and polar stereographic projection. The mathematical details of each of these projections are dealt with extensively in reference 4 and summarized in reference 5.

Figures 4-12 and 4-13 illustrate one particular projection, the orthographic projection. Figure 4-12 shows an image of Mars taken by the Viking Orbiter 1 spacecraft at an oblique viewing angle relative to the surface. The large volcanic crater appears to be elliptical because of the oblique viewing geometry. Figure 4-13 shows the same image after transformation to an orthographic projection. The orthographic projection transforms the image to a viewing geometry in which the observation point is directly above the center of the field of view. The shape of the crater has been corrected by the cartographic projection.

There are two mapping projections that have been developed specifically for LANDSAT imagery. The *Hotine Oblique Mercator* (HOM) projection divides the earth into five zones of latitude. Witin each zone, oblique strips corresponding to individual LANDSAT paths are projected onto a plane so that the axis of the projec-

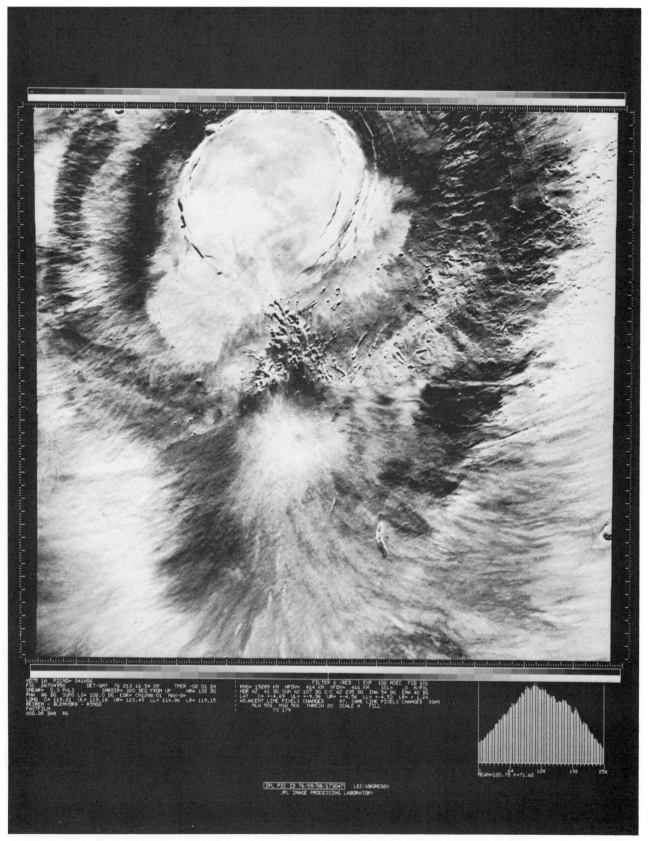

Figure 4-12.   Viking Orbiter image taken at an oblique viewing angle (Jet Propulsion Laboratory).

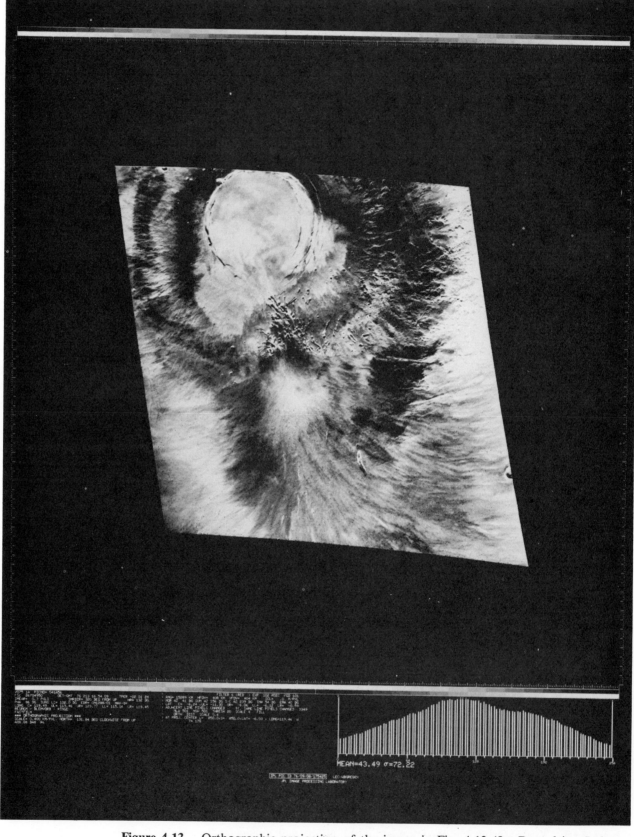

Figure 4-13. Orthographic projection of the image in Fig. 4-12 (Jet Propulsion Laboratory).

tion corresponds approximately to the path of the scene centers. The *Space Oblique Mercator* (SOM) projection is modeled on the dynamics of the LANDSAT spacecraft motion. A continuous projection of the area viewed in the LANDSAT scene is performed, incorporation the time-dependent values of the satellite platform motion, the sensor motion, and the earth's motion. Details of these projections can be obtained in references 6 through 8. The factors involved in the SOM projection are shown in Figure 4-14.

Geometric Transformation Implementation Notes

Geometric transformation can require significant computing resources and can involve large amounts of input/output time when it is implemented on a digital computer. There are several factors to be considered when developing software for performing geometric transformation.

It is often desirable to write software specifically designed for performing the more elementary geometric manipulations. Funtions such as zoom (expand an image by a given factor), shrink (reduce an image size by a given factor), and 90° rotation should be implemented in special-purpose software or hardware that is optimized to perform those operations. This will save a large amount of computing time that would be consumed if these operations were performed using the full bilinear interpolation techniques described in this section.

When an image is either shrunk or magnified by an integer factor, it is often advisable to create an output image with an odd number of lines and samples. In this manner, it is possible to preserve the intensity values of the input pixels, avoiding interpolation and resulting loss in spatial resolution. If a 1,000 by 1,000 image is to

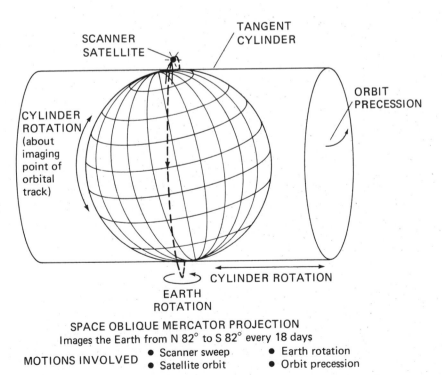

SPACE OBLIQUE MERCATOR PROJECTION
Images the Earth from N 82° to S 82° every 18 days

MOTIONS INVOLVED
- Scanner sweep
- Satellite orbit
- Earth rotation
- Orbit precession

Figure 4-14.   Parameters involved in SOM projection (EROS Data Center).

be magnified by a factor of 2, write the software so that the output image size will be 1,999 by 1,999. In this manner, every pixel in the input image will map into every other pixel in the output image, with its intensity value preserved (i.e., not interpolated). Figure 4-15 illustrates this effect. In practice, it would be advisable to create a 2,000 by 2,000 image in order to avoid awkward image sizes of 1,999 by 1,999 but the algorithm should enable generation of the output image using the every-other-pixel mapping; the addition of the 2,000th line and 2,000th sample can be performed artificially (e.g., replication of the last pixel in each line and repetition of the last image line).

The general geometric transformation process requires a significant amount of input/output access on most computing systems. It is generally not possible to store the full input and output images in computer memory, and so the output image normally is developed on peripheral disk storage units; the input image is also normally located on disk storage, and the program must bring into memory the lines of the input image in the order in which they are accessed as the output pixel intensities are computed. A review of the before-and-after examples in this section will reveal that computation of the pixel intensities along an individual line in the output image will require access to more than a single line in the input image. In the worst case, a 90° rotation, each single line in the output image will draw from every line in the input image. The number of lines of the input image that must be stored in memory in order to compute pixel intensities in a single line of the output image depends critically on the angle of rotation between the input and output image.

Geometric transformation should be performed with software that maximizes the amount of buffer space in real (not virtual) memory so that the number of times a single line in the input image is reread is minimized. It may be necessary to develop several versions of the general-purpose geometric transformation software module, selecting one of the versions at execution time on the basis of the severity of the displacement between input and output images for the particular transformation. It may be desirable to utilize additional disk storage buffer space containing blocks of image lines, reading the primary input (the input image) and secondary input (buffered sets of input image lines) sequentially from disk to memory to avoid excessive computation times.

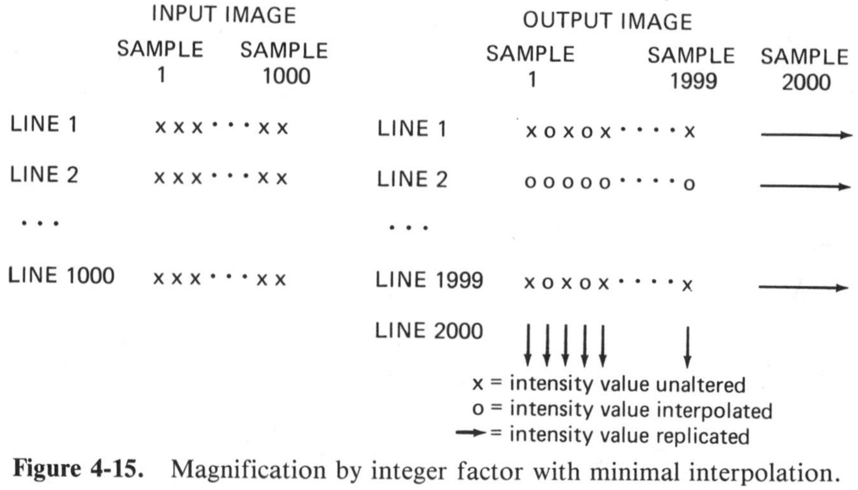

Figure 4-15. Magnification by integer factor with minimal interpolation.

Finally, any geometric transformation that involves intensity interpolation will degrade the spatial resolution of the image. The intensity interpolation process inevitably will cause a reduction in spatial resolution, and the interpolation process can be viewed as a blurring filter that will cause loss in high-frequency resolution. It may often be desirable to produce two versions of image product: one with no geometric transformation performed (preserving the spatial resolution at the cost of retaining geometric distortion) and a second, transformed product. It is also desirable to merge several required geometric transformations into a single transformation rather than performing several geometric transformations sequentially, in order to reduce the resolution degradation in the final product. If a geometric distortion correction and a cartographic projection are required, it is advisable to merge both transformations into a single overall transformation that can be performed once, as an example.

IMAGE REGISTRATION

A variety of applications, including image differencing and image registration, may require an ability to geometrically align more than a single image to the same spatial reference grid. It may be of interest to difference two images taken of the same area over a period of time in order to detect changes that have occurred. If the two images were not taken under the same precise viewing geometry, they must be aligned spatially before differencing. If they are not aligned correctly, the difference image will reveal the misalignment between the two images and will not depict the changes that have occurred.

Mosaicking is another application that requires an ability to align more than one image within a fixed geometric reference space. It may be desirable to digitally mosaic a series of images that may have been taken with different view angles. This can be done only if the images are all aligned or registered to the same geometric control grid.

There are several techniques used for image registration.[9] The selection of the proper registration technique for a particular application depends on the accuracy or precision required in registration.

Cartographic projection is a technique that can be applied for image registration purposes. All images that are to be registered are cartographically projected to the same mapping projection. Each transformed image is thus projected to the same geometric coordinate reference frame. The transformed images can then be differenced or mosaicked together if the geometric precision is adequate for the application.

Figure 4-16 shows a mosaic of the state of Arizona constructed from a series of LANDSAT MSS images acquired from two passes of the LANDSAT satellite over Arizona that were widely separated in time. Each LANDSAT MSS scene was cartographically projected, and the individual projected components were merged into a single digital mosaic of the entire state. The accuracy of the projection was adequate for this application, since registration of the multiple imagery to less than 1-pixel precision was not required to produce the mosaic.

It may be necessary to perform more precise registration when the precision with which the camera's viewing geometry or the spacecraft's position is not adequate to perform cartographic projection to less than 1-pixel precision. The most precise registration techniques involve detailed correlation of common features in multiple

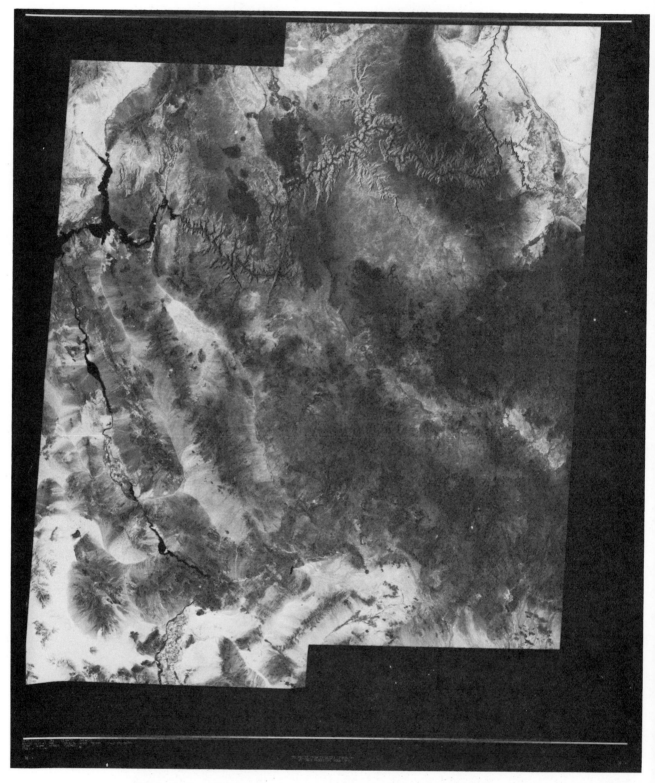

Figure 4-16.   Computer generated digital image mosaic of the state of Arizona (Jet Propulsion Laboratory).

images in order to define the detailed offset of common features located in more than one image. When correlation techniques are employed, common features can be identified in more than one image, and these features serve as tiepoints for a geometric transformation that maps one image onto a second image, as shown in Figure 4-17. Correlation measurements are used to define the relative geometric offset between the location of the same feature in two images.

The correlation process is performed in the following manner. A moving window of size W samples by H lines is established (H and W must be odd numbers). The window is centered on a particular feature in the first image (denoted as image 1). The upper-left corner of the window will be at line ℓ_1 sample s_1. The approximate location of the same feature in the second image (image 2) is determined. A second window, also of size W and H, is centered on that point; the upper-left corner of the window in the second image is then located at line ℓ_2, sample s_2, in image 2. A correlation coefficient of the form

$$C_{\ell_2, s_2} = \sum_{\ell=0}^{H-1} \sum_{s=0}^{W-1} \frac{(b_{\ell_1+\ell, s_1+s} - b_{\ell_2+\ell, s_2+s})^2}{W \, H} \qquad (4\text{-}4)$$

is computed. This coefficient is saved, and the window in image 2 is then moved to a new location by incrementing ℓ_2 and/or s_2; a new value of the correlation coefficient is then computed and stored. The process continues through several selections of window location in image 2, remaining in the neighborhood of the first point selected. The point at which there is maximum correlation between image 1 and image 2 is then determined. The maximum can be determined by interpolation techniques, which will provide subpixel precision in determining the location of the highest correlation between the two images in the region containing the feature selected for correlation.

The point of maximum correlation determines the relative offset in lines and samples between the location of the same feature in both images. It thus can serve as a tiepoint for defining a geometric transformation that aligns image 1 with image 2. The transformation is performed as soon as enough tiepoints within the image pair have been selected. This technique results in precise subpixel alignment of two or more images.

Figure 4-18 shows the results of an image-differencing computation performed with a pair of Mariner 9 images of Mars. The Mariner 9 spacecraft in orbit around

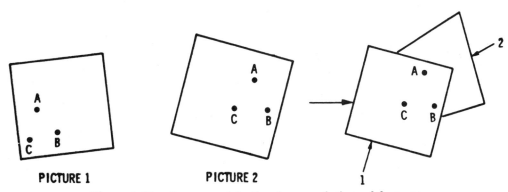

Figure 4-17. Image registration by correlation of features.

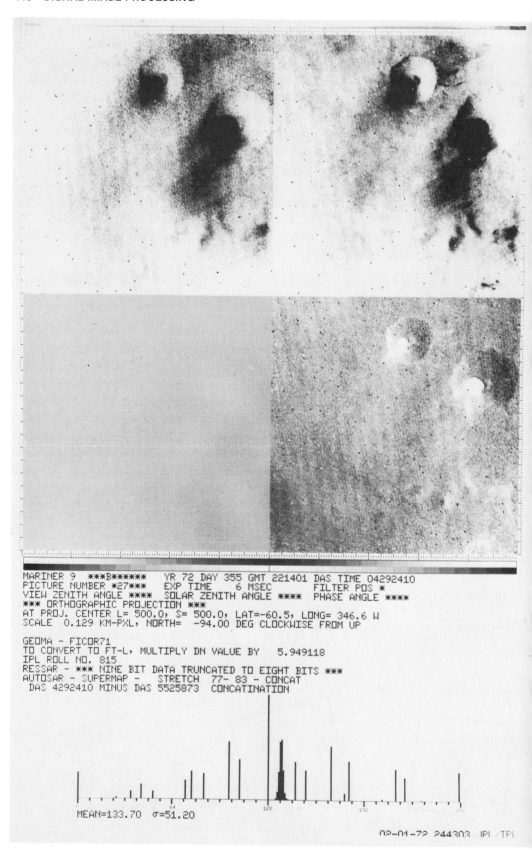

Figure 4-18.   Image differencing example (Jet Propulsion Laboratory).

the planet recorded two images of the same region of the surface over an interval of approximately two weeks. Contrast-enhanced versions of segments of the two images are shown at the top of Figure 4-18. These segments were first cartographically projected, and then precision registration was performed, using correlation techniques based on identification of common features. The two images are thus aligned to a precision of less than one picture element.

The lower-left image shows the enhanced difference image, which is obtained by subtracting the pixel intensity in one image from the pixel intensity at the corresponding location in the second image. An unenhanced difference image obviously reveals very little, since the change between the two scenes is quite small, and Mars is inherently a low-contrast planet. Contrast enhancement of the difference image, shown in the lower right of Figure 4-18, reveals difference in intensity between the two image segments as either white or black (the difference image is computed so that zero difference falls at midgray in the intensity range).

The two images were obtained in a two-week period during which a widespread dust storm was slowly abating. Analysis of the two image segments by eye reveals that the crater edges became more distinct during that two-week period as a result of the reduction in the amount of particulate matter suspended in the atmosphere during the time interval. This change is seen clearly in the difference image, in which the crater rims appear white. The unaided eye cannot discern some of the more subtle intensity changes that have occurred. Only the use of the image differencing technique can reveal the change in albedo (surface brightness) that has occurred in the centers of the two craters (note the two white spots in the enhanced difference image). The differencing process is also the only way that the albedo changes on the surface below the right-hand crater can be detected visually.

These two image segments must be aligned precisely in order for the image differencing process to succeed. If the craters had not been aligned, for example, the difference image would reveal the misregistration of the image pair, and it would be difficult to isolate the real surface changes within a difference image that would be very confusing in appearance.

GEOGRAPHIC CORRELATION WITHOUT CARTOGRAPHIC PROJECTION

There are several situations in which it is desirable to correlate remotely sensed imagery with geographic coordinate systems but impossible or undesirable to perform cartographic projection of the digital image. Reasons for avoiding geometric transformation include the following: (1) The resolution degradation that accompanies the transformation may hinder further analysis of the imagery. (2) Precision correlation may be impossible because of lack of identifiable geographic or cultural tiepoints that can be used to control the transformation.

An example of this situation is the use of weather satellite imagery. It is often impossible to identify ground features in weather imagery because of low spatial resolution and cloud obscuration of surface detail. Weather imagery is also extremely time-critical, and the delays involved in digitally transforming the imagery may be unacceptable. It is still important to know the geographic location of the weather patterns and cloud structures that are being analyzed.

In these cases, it may be desirable to leave the digital image in the sensor viewing geometric reference frame and to warp or distort the geographic data to fit or overlay the digital image. This type of processing usually requires substantially less computing resources than image rectification, and the registration of geographic data to image data can often be performed to accuracies of a few pixels.

One example of warping geographic information onto an image data base is shown in Figure 4-19. A graphical representation of the borders of the southwestern states has been overlaid on a GOES weather satellite image. The graphic overlay is based on a fixed spacecraft viewing geometry (the GOES satellite is a geosynchronous spacecraft and remains roughly fixed over the same point on the earth's surface). The registration between the graphics overlay and the image data may not be correct to better than a few pixels. However, the fixed overlay is quite adequate for general weather analysis and forecasting needs, and the required correlation between image data and geographic reference coordinates has been achieved at a minimal expenditure of computing resources.

RADIOMETRIC DISTORTION CORRECTION

Many camera systems and film scanners introduce a radiometric distortion into the digital imagery that they can produce. There are usually two contributing factors to this distortion. A perfect camera system will respond to light within a particular intensity range and will produce digital intensity values that are linearly related to the light intensity in object space. Many imaging systems or scanners respond nonlinearly, however, and this is the first major cause of radiometric distortion.

The second type of artifact that can be introduced by a digital imaging system results from a lack of spatial uniformity in the system's response to light levels; different regions within the camera's field of view respond differently to the same input light intensity.

These two effects are illustrated in Figure 4-20. The two curves show the digitized intensity values that result from imaging a linearly increasing light intensity for a vidicon system. The two curves are for two different locations within the camera field of view; point A is at the upper-left-hand corner, and point B is at the lower-right corner of the field of view. There can be many reasons for this nonlinearity and for the spatial variation in response to input intensity. Vidicon systems typically

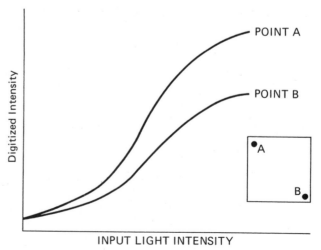

Figure 4-20.   Radiometric response function at two locations in the system field of view.

PLATE I

Figure 1-12. Geometrically projected view of the Los Angeles basin produced by exaggerating topographic detail within a LANDSAT Thematic Mapper multispectral image based on an elevation data set of the same area (Jet Propulsion Laboratory).

Figure 1-15. Two different LANDSAT Thematic Mapper images of the Hubbard Glacier area in Alaska, showing the closure of Russell Fiord between August 1985 and September 1986 (Earth Observation Satellite Company).

PLATE II

Figure 1-14. Color ratio enhancement of a LANDSAT scene of the Coconino plateau (Jet Propulsion Laboratory).

PLATE III

Figure 1-18. GOES satellite image with wind bars. The wind speed and direction has been determined from multiple image analysis (Unisys Defense Systems).

PLATE IV

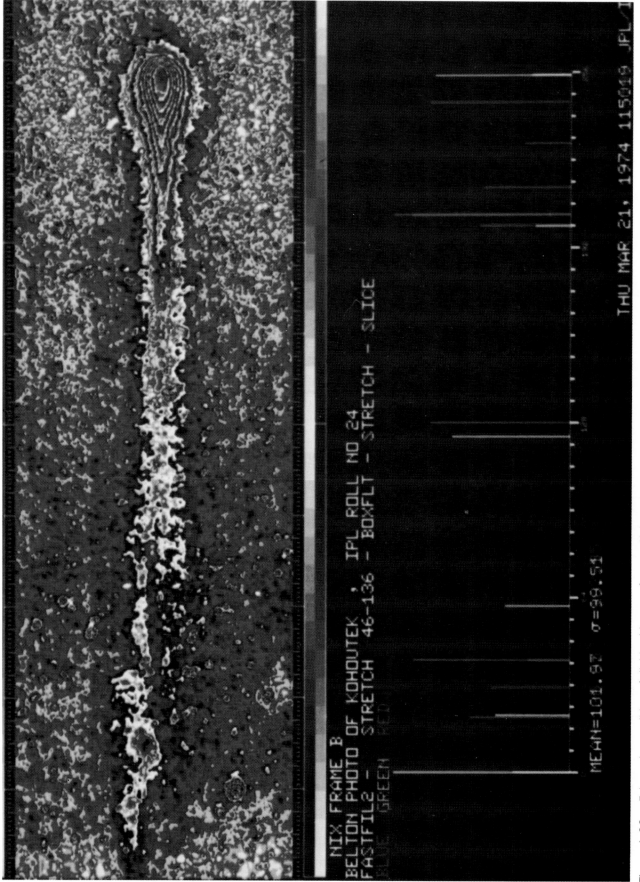

Figure 1-23. False color rendition of digitized image of comet Kohoutek (Jet Propulsion Laboratory).

PLATE V

02NOV82 C N38-52/W076-46 USGS-EDC N N38-53/W076-47 T1 3⁴   SUN EL31 A152 S S CP N   NASA LANDSAT E-40109-15140-3

Figure 2-16. LANDSAT 4 Thematic Mapper image of the Washington, D.C. metropolitan area. The color image has been produced by combining three of the seven spectral bands. This image represents an area approximately 100 miles square at 30 meter resolution (EOSAT).

Figure 2-19. SPOT color image of the New Orleans metropolitan area (Copyright 1987 CNES, Provided courtesy of SPOT Image Corporation, Reston, VA).

PLATE VI

Figure 3-20. Color composite rendition of LANDSAT scene of East Pilbara region of Australia (Jet Propulsion Laboratory).

PLATE VII

Figure 3-22. Color composite enhanced image of the limb of Io, one of the satellites of Jupiter. The ultraviolet component is portrayed as blue (Jet Propulsion Laboratory).

PLATE VIII

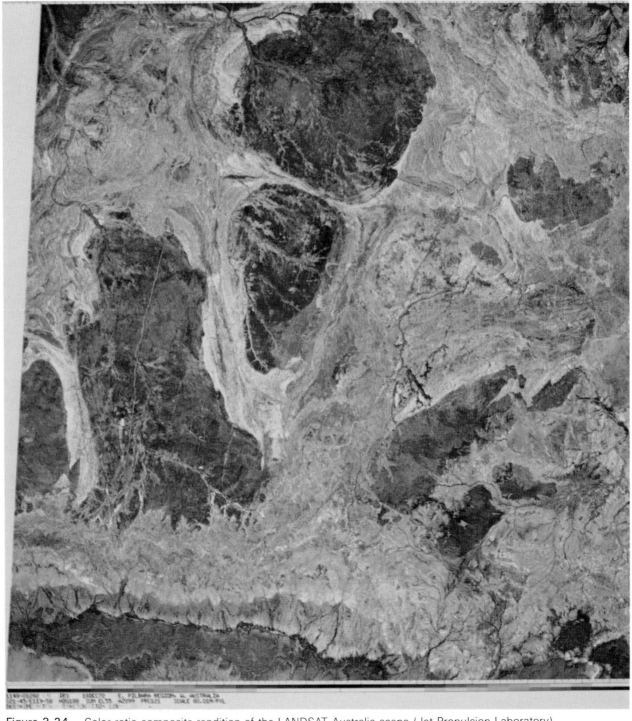

Figure 3-24. Color ratio composite rendition of the LANDSAT Australia scene (Jet Propulsion Laboratory).

PLATE IX

Figure 4-19. GOES satellite image with geographical boundary overlay (Unisys Defense Systems).

PLATE X

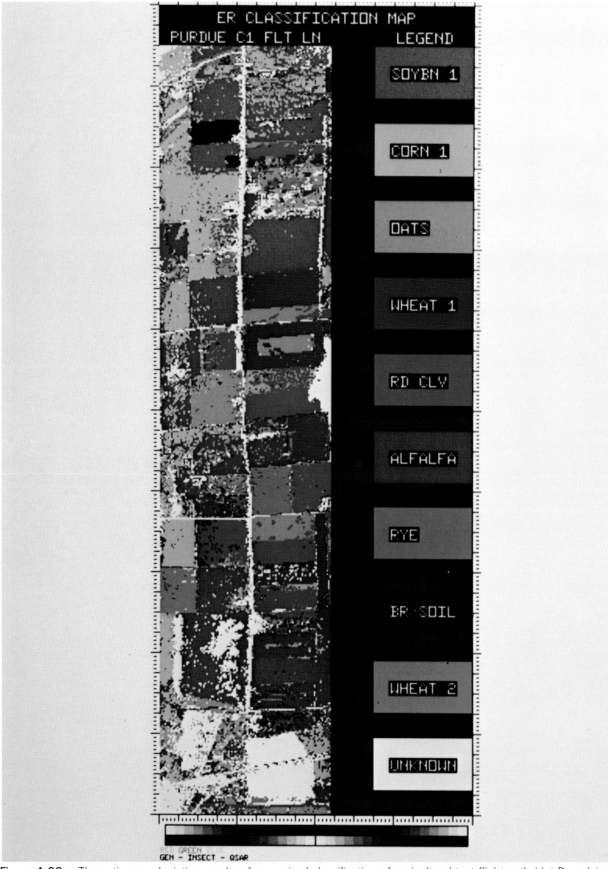

Figure 4-28. Thematic map depicting results of supervised classification of agricultural test flight path (Jet Propulsion Laboratory).

PLATE XI

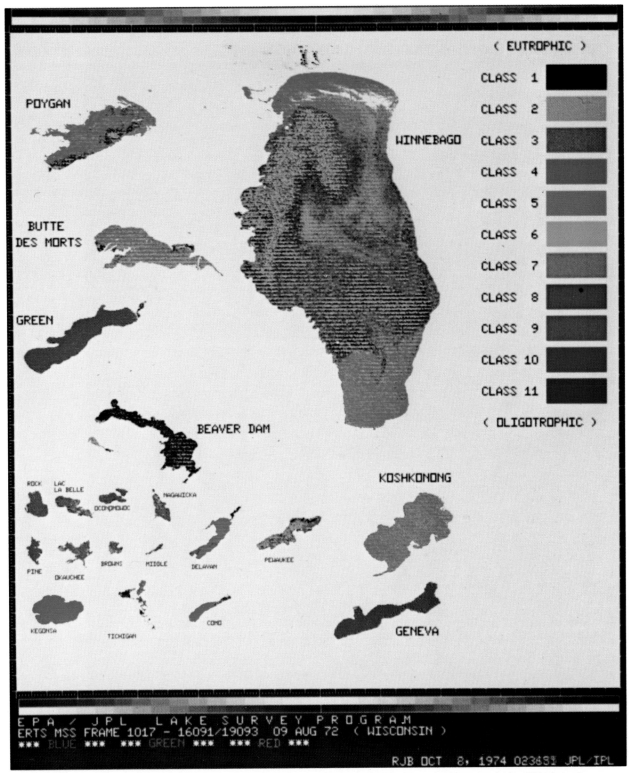

Figure 4-29. Classification of degrees of Wisconsin lake eutrophication based on multispectral classification of LANDSAT imagery (Environmental Protection Agency/Jet Propulsion Laboratory).

PLATE XII

Figure 4-32. Color composite image of Mars constructed from a series of Viking Orbiter images (Jet Propulsion Laboratory).

PLATE XIII

Figure 4-33. Hue/saturation enhancement of the color composite Mars image (Jet Propulsion Laboratory).

PLATE XIV

Figure 5-12. Example of use of region-of-interest. This image is a color representation of a merger of a synthetic aperture radar image acquired by the Shuttle-borne Shuttle Imaging Radar (SIR-B) system with a digital terrain data base. The region-of-interest display capability has been used to identify an area of the merged image in which only the topographic data has been displayed (Unisys Defense Systems).

Figure 9-12. Four screens driven by commercially available PC-based image processing software. The displays illustrate use of menus for the selection of operations to be performed, graphics overlay, histogram and frequency spectrum computation and graphical display, selection of the region of interest for specific processing, and other operations (Data Translation Inc.).

PLATE XV

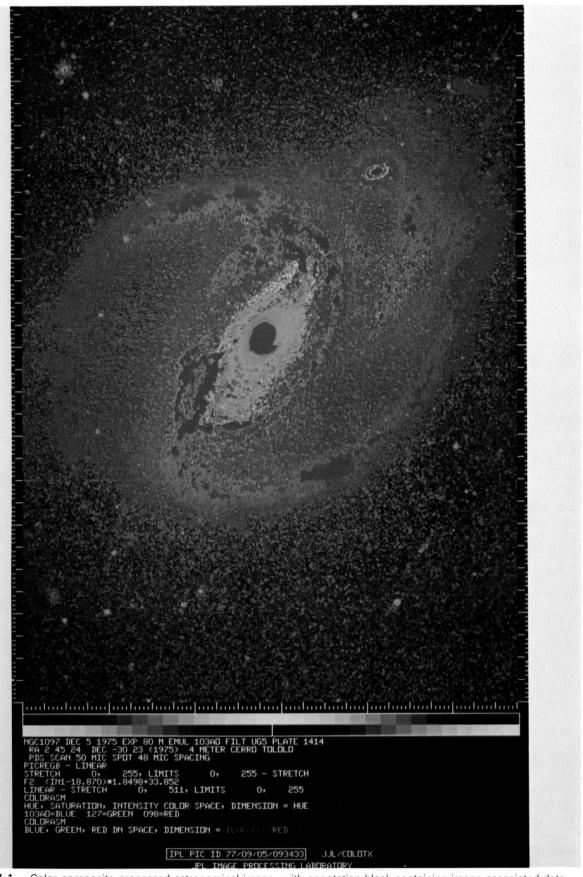

Figure 7-1. Color composite processed astronomical image, with annotation block containing image associated data (Jet Propulsion Laboratory).

PLATE XVI

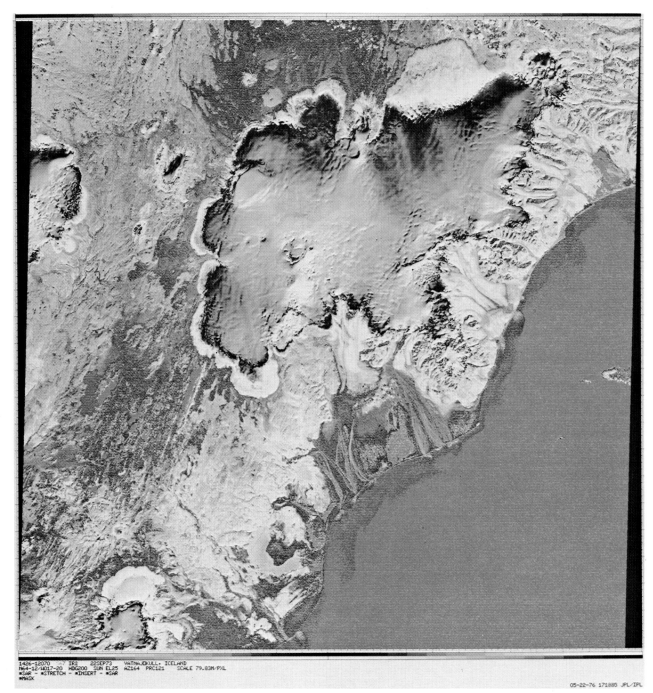

1426-12070 · ⁂7 IR1 22SEP73 VATNAJOKULL, ICELAND
N64-12/W017-20 HDG200 SUN EL25 AZ164 PRC121 SCALE 79.83M/PXL
*SAR - *STRETCH - *INSERT - *SAR
*MASK

05-22-76 171880 JPL/IPL

Figure 7-2. Color composite LANDSAT-1 image of Iceland, with annotation block (Jet Propulsion Laboratory).

produce this type of distortion, although the severity has been exaggerated in Figure 4-20. Film scanners typically exhibit both nonlinearity and spatial variation in response.

It is necessary to remove this type of distortion before performing image analysis for most applications. If the data source for a given analysis task is digitized imagery produced by a film scanner, for example, it is necessary to apply a correction for the scanner shading before performing any other digital processing if the scanner introduces a degree of shading into every scanned image that will hinder subsequent image analysis.

There are several types of mathematical models that are used to characterize these distortions. The models vary in complexity, precision, and required computing resources for implementation. All the models provide a mechanism for removal of radiometric distortion from digital imagery.

The simplest correction technique involves the use of a single template correction applied to every image. A gross characterization of the spatial shading is obtained by recording a single image of uniform input intensity at a light level near midscale of the imaging system's dynamic range. The single digitized frame then serves as a template for shading removal. The average digitized brightness for the full image is computed, and the pixel intensity value at each point is ratioed to the average value. The ratio values are then inverted and multiplied by the pixel values in corresponding positions in other digitized imagery produced by the same system.

The single template correction is often not adequate to restore radiometric precision. If the response is truly nonlinear, as depicted in Figure 4-20, a single point correction near midscale of the system's response range will not be adequate.

A more complex radiometric response model can be developed by recording a series of images at increasing values of light intensity. The images are taken with the field of view uniformly illuminated at each intensity step. The result of this process is a table of values of digitized brightness versus input intensity for each pixel location in the system. If a sequence of seven or nine images is recorded in this manner, a table can be developed with seven or nine entries for each pixel, relating digitized intensity to true input intensity. A variety of interpolation techniques can then be applied, depending on the desired precision of the correction, to remove the radiometric distortion effects from the digitized imagery. The interpolation will produce modified digital intensity values at each pixel that are linearly related to radiometric intensity units.

Interpolation Techniques

There are several interpolation techniques used to perform radiometric correction. The choice of the particular technique is dependent on a trade-off between the desired precision of the correction and the computational cost of performing the correction.

One of the simplest correction techniques is based on fitting a best-fit straight line to the radiometric response curve at each pixel or at a subset of pixels. Characterization of every image pixel will be considered first.

The set of digitized intensity values obtained by acquiring a series of images at increasing intensities will be characterized using the notation $b_{I,\ell s}$. $b_{I,\ell s}$ is the digitized intensity for a pixel at line ℓ, sample s when an intensity I is imaged. The straight-line or linear correction involves fitting a straight line to the response function, as shown in Figure 4-21. The straight line has slope $m_{\ell s}$ and offset $b_{o,\ell s}$, where both b and m vary with pixel location. The straight-line fit is

$$b_{I,\ell s} = m_{\ell s}\, I \, + \, b_{0,\ell s} \tag{4-5}$$

The full set of $m_{\ell s}$ and $b_{0,\ell s}$ is obtained for each pixel and stored as a *radiometric calibration file* for the imaging or scanning system. When an image is acquired, Equation 4-5 is used to compute the correct intensity value in the following manner. Acquisition of an image can be viewed as acquisition of a set of digitized pixel intensity values $b_{I,\ell s}$; these digital values are related to the true intensity in object space by the relationship in Equation 4-5, and the true (or corrected) intensity values for that pixel can be computed from

$$I_{\ell s} = (b_{I,\ell s} \, - \, b_{0,\ell s}) \cdot \omega \, / \, m_{\ell s} \tag{4-6}$$

ω is a scaling factor introduced to ensure that the corrected intensity values are scaled to fall within the desired number of bits of precision. As an example, suppose that a film scanner digitizes 8 bits of intensity information, and it is desired that the corrected intensity values also have 8 bits of precision. If the true intensity range in which the scanner will operate corresponds to a real brightness range from zero to 1,500 ft-Lamberts, values of $I_{\ell s}$ will exceed the 8-bit range if Equation 4-5 is applied without introduction of the scaling factor. In this example, a value of $\omega = 1/6$ will guarantee that corrected intensity values fall within the range of zero to 255 (8-bit representation).

Figure 4-22 shows a typical radiometric shading pattern for a vidicon system; film scanners can also introduce similar shading. The image has been linearly contrast-enhanced to show the shading pattern more clearly. The image was taken of a uniformly illuminated radiometric target designed so that the light intensity was uniform throughout the camera system's field of view. The left side of the camera vidicon is obviously more sensitive to light than the right side of the vidicon, and

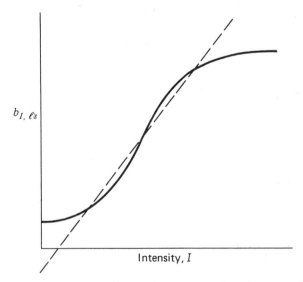

Figure 4-21. Linear fit to radiometric response function at a single pixel.

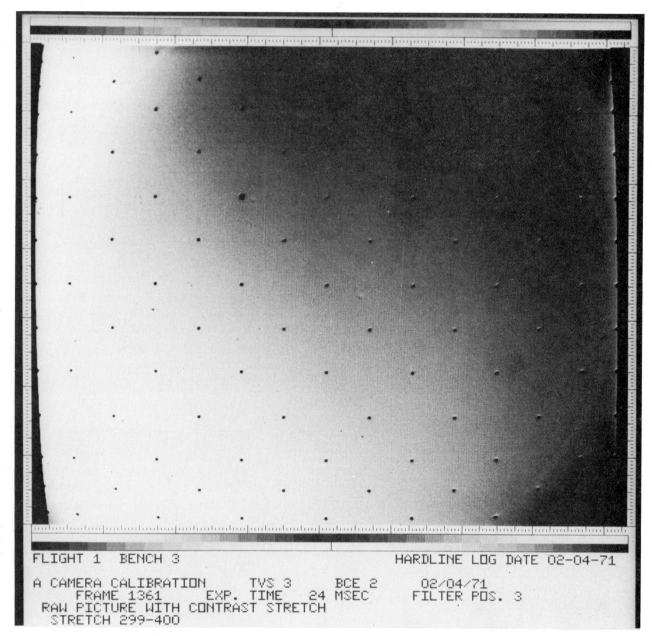

FLIGHT 1   BENCH 3   HARDLINE LOG DATE 02-04-71

A CAMERA CALIBRATION   TVS 3   BCE 2   02/04/71
     FRAME 1361   EXP. TIME   24 MSEC   FILTER POS. 3
  RAW PICTURE WITH CONTRAST STRETCH
     STRETCH 299-400

Figure 4-22. Contrast enhanced version of a uniformly illuminated calibration image (Jet Propulsion Laboratory).

this shading distortion must be removed or it will interfere with proper analysis of all images taken with this camera system.

A more subtle artifact also visible in Figure 4-22 is the ring at the lower-right corner of the image. This ring is caused by electron interaction with a metal ring present in the system, and it will be present in all images at the same position within the field of view. This type of spatial radiometric distortion should also be removed from all images taken with this sensor.

Figure 4-23 shows the results of applying a linear shading correction to this image. The image is now radiometrically corrected witin the accuracy limitations of the

FLIGHT 1   BENCH 3   HARDLINE LOG DATE 02-04-71

A CAMERA CALIBRATION   TVS 3   BCE 2   02/04/71
     FRAME 1361   EXP. TIME   24 MSEC   FILTER POS. 3
INTERP
  FIRST ORDER SHADING CORRECTION

Figure 4-23. The calibration image of Fig. 4-22 after linear shading correction and contrast enhancement (Jet Propulsion Laboratory).

linear correction. The corrected image now appears to be illuminated uniformly, and the ring artifact has also been removed by this processing. (Recall that the black marks within the image are the reseau marks that are used to perform geometric distortion correction.)

The linear correction was particularly effective on the image shown in Figure 4-22 because it was taken at an intensity near midscale in the camera's dynamic range. At this light intensity, the vidicon response is nearly linear, and a linear correction is a good selection. However, as Figure 4-20 shows, the linear correction is a poor choice at near-black or near-white intensities for systems characterized by the typical "s-shape" radiometric distortion curve. Scanners and some imaging systems tend to saturate at either end of the intensity range, and the response can become highly nonlinear in those regions.

A more precise (and more complex) correction that provides more precision throughout the full range of intensity variation is *piecewise linear radiometric correction*. Figure 4-24 depicts the representation of the radiometric response curve by a series of linear segments. The segments are usually determined by the intensity values selected for the sequence of uniformly exposed images used to calibrate the system. For each pixel, a table of values is stored, containing digitized intensity $b_{I_k, \ell s}$ versus intensity I_k. The process of radiometric correction involves an interpolation within the appropriate intensity range for each pixel. If the table values of digitized intensity are $b_{I_k, \ell s}$, for each input pixel with digitized itensity $b_{I, \ell s}$, the point is found such that

$$b_{I_{k-1}, \ell s} \leq b_{I, \ell s} \leq b_{I_k, \ell s} \qquad (4\text{-}7)$$

The corrected intensity for that pixel is then computed by using linear interpolation:

$$I_{\ell s} = \omega \cdot \left[\frac{(b_{I, \ell s} - b_{I_{k-1}, \ell s})}{(b_{I_k, \ell s} - b_{I_{k-1}, \ell s})} (I_k - I_{k-1}) + I_{k-1} \right] \qquad (4\text{-}8)$$

This is a more expensive correction procedure than the straight-line fit procedure, since it involves an interpolation at each pixel. It is more precise than the linear correction, however, and it may be worth the additional computation cost, depending on the specific application.

Spatial Interpolation

The radiometric correction techniques discussed up to this point have dealt with storage of either point-slope information or tabular information for each pixel. The

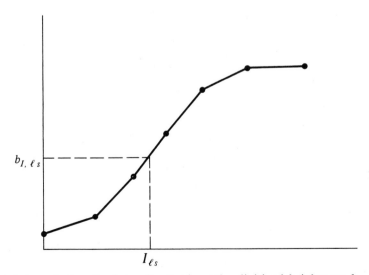

Figure 4-24. Interpolation for intensity $I_{\ell s}$ given the digitized brightness $b_{I, \ell s}$, using piecewise linear fit to the radiometric respose function.

number of data points required to store correction data for each pixel can become very large or even prohibitive. Two million data points must be stored in order to provide slope and offset information for each pixel in a 1,000 by 1,000 size image acquired with a two-dimensional array scanning system (not a linear array). Seven million data points must be stored in the calibration file to provide a piecewise linear correction capability, using seven entries of digitized brightness versus intensity.

Radiometric response is usually slowly varying as a function of position within the image (note the slow spatial variation in shading exhibited in Figure 4-22). Thus, it is often possible to store the required information at a subset of pixels and to perform a spatial interpolation for the required correction factors at each pixel position. A design trade-off must be performed before making the decision to use spatial interpolation. The trade-off is usually between the amount of storage required to store the calibration file and the computational cost of performing spatial interpolation at each pixel position.

Figure 4-25 illustrates one technique for dividing the image field of view into squares, where the correction factors used in a linear radiometric correction are stored for the vertexes of the squares. Those factors could be the slope and offset values used for linear radiometric correction, or they could be the full set of table values used for piecewise linear interpolation. For this discussion the variable g represents any of the factors that are used in a particular radiometric correction algorithm. g thus represents one of a set of values that are used in a radiometric correction file, stored at a series of vertexes within the image. The spacing at which parameters are stored is a function of the degree of variation in the shading and the precision desired in the radiometric correction.

Radiometric correction is performed by considering each pixel in turn, line by line and sample by sample. At pixel location line l, sample s, the square within which (ℓ,s) falls is determined. This square will have four vertexes, denoted by (l_1,s_1), ..., (ℓ_4,s_4). If the pixel spacing between vertexes is Δ, the value of the parameter g at position (ℓ,s) is determined by using bilinear interpolation

$$g_{\ell s} = d_1\ell s + d_2\ell + d_3 s + d_4 \tag{4-9}$$

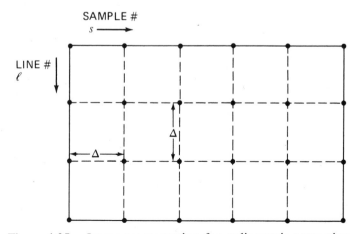

Figure 4-25. Image segmentation for radiometric correction.

where

$$d_1 = Q/\Delta^2$$

$$d_2 = (g_2 - g_1)/\Delta - s_1 Q/\Delta^2$$

$$d_3 = (g_3 - g_1)/\Delta - \ell_1 Q/\Delta^2 \tag{4-10}$$

$$d_4 = g_1 - \ell_1(g_2 - g_1) + s_1(g_3 - g_1) / \Delta + \ell_1 s_1 Q/\Delta^2$$

and where

$$Q = g_1 - g_2 - g_3 + g_4$$

$$g_1 = g(\ell_1, s_1), \; g_2 = g(\ell_2, s_2), \text{ etc.} \tag{4-11}$$

$$\Delta = \text{length of one side of the square in pixels}$$

This interpolation procedure can be used to determine slope/offset values for a linear radiometric correction or the table look-up values for a piecewise linear correction.

Implementation Note

Equation 4-9 can be rewritten as follows:

$$g_{\ell s} = s(d_1 \ell + d_3) + (d_2 \ell + d_4) \tag{4-12}$$

The quantity $(d_1 \ell + d_3)$ can be computed once for each line, for each square, and stored, as can the value of the quantity $(d_2 \ell + d_4)$. The interpolation required for each increasing value of sample, s, can thus be performed using only a single multiply and add computation, particularly if the nonvarying quantities are correctly indexed by relating sample number to square number. In this manner, the interpolation can be performed quite rapidly.

MULTISPECTRAL CLASSIFICATION

Multispectral imagery refers to acquisition of image data of the same area in different spectral bands. It is possible to perform a variety of information-extraction processes if image date are available in more than one spectral component. Most of the information-extraction techniques rely on analysis of the spectral reflectance properties of the image and employ special algorithms designed to perform various types of spectral analysis.

Multispectral classification is a widely used analysis technique. It is used to classify the material in the original scene based on analysis of the relative spectral properties of the various materials in the scene. It has become widely used in analysis of the LANDSAT and SPOT multispectral imagery for agricultural, geological, and land-use applications as well as for other earth-resources applications. The techniques are also broadly applicable to other types of analysis (e.g., astronomy). This section will provide a brief overview of techniques used for multispectral classification. More details regarding these techniques are available in references 10 and 11.

Figure 4-26 contains an illustration of the relative spectral properties of four surface materials that are commonly observed in remotely sensed images of the earth's surface. The relative spectral radiance of the four materials in normal sunlight and at a particular viewing angle is shown. Loam has a relatively low radiance in the wavelength region that is illustrated, and the spectral radiance of loam is almost a constant low value throughout that region. Alfalfa, on the other hand, exhibits low radiance up to approximately 0.65 μm and then exhibits a sharp rise to high values beyond 0.65 μm. It is thus possible to distinguish between these two materials by examining their relative radiance properties.

The four spectral bands of the LANDSAT multispectral scanning system (MSS) imaging system are shown below Figure 4-26. The LANDSAT MSS provides the equivalent of four images of the same area, which each image represents the average relative radiance in one of the four wavelength bands. A single pixel in a LANDSAT MSS image can be represented as a vector of four values, where each of the four values is a digital intensity derived from one of the four spectral component images. An analysis of the relative digital intensities across the four bands can be used to identify the particular material that has been imaged at a specific pixel location. Thus, it is possible to *classify* the image data into various classes by analyzing the spectral behavior of each individual pixel. If the spectral properties of a variety of materials of interest are known, automated analysis of the multispectral image can be used to classify each pixel as belonging to one of the materials or to an "unknown" category.

As an example of classification, assume that only LANDSAT MSS bands 5 and 6 will be used to discriminate between the four materials shown in Figure 4-26. We

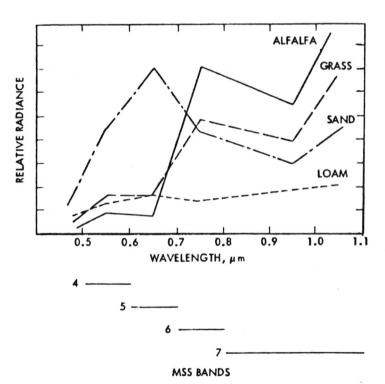

Figure 4-26. Relative radiance of four materials, and the spectral limits of response of the four LANDSAT MSS bands.

can plot the centroid of the relative radiance within each of the two bands for all four materials, as is done in Figure 4-27. Loam, as noted previously, has relatively low and almost constant reflectivity in the band 5-band 6 region of the spectrum. If the centroid of radiance in band 5 is plotted against the same parameter in band 6 for loam, a point near the lower-left corner of Figure 4-27 results. Alfalfa, however, has a low radiance in the band 5 region and high radiance in the band 6 region; the plot of the centroid locations results in a point plotted relatively far out on the band 6 axis of Figure 4-27. The four centroid points are plotted in Figure 4-27 for all four materials, and it is clear that the materials can be easily discriminated, based on their spectral properties.

A multispectral classification of an image is performed by analyzing each pixel in turn and then determining whether the spectral response exhibited by that pixel corresponds to the spectral response of a predetermined set of response characteristics for known materials. In Figure 4-27, decision boundaries have been drawn that delineate the regions between the materials. The boundaries have been drawn by scribing normals to the vectors connecting the centroid points. Any pixel whose spectral response produces a point within the lower-left section of Figure 4-27 would be classified as loam. If only bands 5 and 6 were being employed to perform the classification, the digital intensity from the band 5 component would be plotted against the digital intensity from the band 6 component, and the pixel would then be classified on the basis of its location relative to the regions defined in Figure 4-27. Pixels that resulted in points plotted far from any of the established regions would be classified as "unknown."

In practice, the process is performed in multidimensional space. For the LAND-

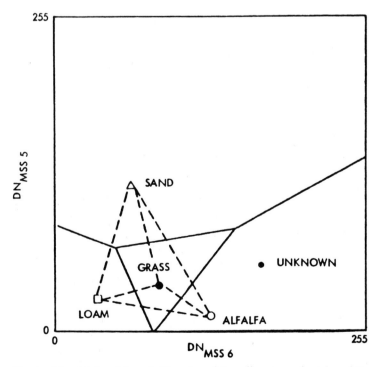

Figure 4-27. Centroids obtained by plotting band 5 radiance against band 6 radiance, and classification decision boundaries.

SAT MSS, four spectral components are used to perform classification, although it may be possible to perform a significant amount of discrimination on the basis of fewer than four components. Conceptually, additional data (e.g., elevation, magnetic field data, etc.) can be combined with multispectral imagery as an aid in discrimination.

Two types of multispectral classification are commonly performed. *Supervised classification* refers to classification performed as described above. A set of preestablished spectral properties is used as a data base against which each pixel's spectral response is compared; classification into one of the known materials or the single "unknown" class is performed.

The spectral data base for comparison is often created by using *training sites*. The analyst determines regions in the scene for which he or she knows the *ground truth;* i.e., the analyst identifies areas in the scene for which he or she knows the material on the surface. The analyst then identifies those regions and labels each region with the material name. The algorithm then is used to compute the relative spectral respponse for that subarea of the image and stores it within the data base. When the analyst has identified all possible training areas, the classifier then proceeds to classify all pixels in the scene. Classification accuracy is often evaluated by establising training sites and then performing classification on an area known to contain the same material as the training sites. The number of misclassified pixels can be used as an evaluation of the precision of the classification.

Unsupervised classification is performed by running a classification algorithm without any predefinition of the spectral classes of interest. The data are *clustered* in multidimensional space, and the analyst then determines the significance of each of the clusters that occurs.

A variety of techniques are used to perform clustering in both supervised and unsupervised classifications. Most techniques involve utilization of a surface fit that encompasses clustered data in multidimensional space.

The centroid-based decision space shown in Figure 4-27 is an oversimplification of techniques that are currently in common use. If a training site is established within a multispectral image, the collection of pixels within that training site will form a cluster of data points when plotted in multidimensional space. It is possible to fit an ellipsoid to the clustered points and to define the ellipsoid by the standard measures (eccentricity, lengths of major and minor axes, etc.). When classification is performed, pixels will be assigned to classes on the basis of the degree to which they fall into the regions defined by the ellipsoids. It is often necessary to refine or readjust the classification scheme by modifying the parameters of the ellipsoids generated in multidimensional space.

Classifiers operate by using a variety of criteria for assigning a pixel to a particular class. Typical classifiers utilize ellipsoid fits, classification based on minimum distance from class centroids, or other techniques.

Thematic Maps

The results obtained from multispectral classification algorithms are often displayed in the form of *thermatic maps*. A thematic map is produced by color-coding each individual pixel to represent the class into which it has been assigned by the classification algorithm.

One common device involves displaying water as blue, agricultural crops as a variety of green or brown shades, residential or urban areas as other shades, etc. The thematic map is thus an artificial image produced in geometric registration to the original multispectral image data base from which it is derived. The thematic map is a useful way to present the information extracted by the classification process.

Examples

Figure 4-28 is an illustration of classification of a variety of agricultural crops and of the difficulty inherent in performing precise multispectral classification. The original multispectral image was acquired by an airborne scanner flying over a test strip planted with a variety of crops in various growth stages. This test situation enabled detailed testing of the accuracy of classification algorithms, since "ground truth" was available at every location along the flight path.

The thematic map shown in Figure 4-28 indicates the results of a supervised computer classification. Each pixel was analyzed to determine the best match between stored reflectance properties of the various crops and the reflectance properties of the pixel in the input multispectral image. A thematic map was produced, indicating the classification assigned to each pixel by color-coding as shown. Note the misclassification that occasionally occurs, illustrated by the appearance of single picture element that are the wrong color scattered within some of the field boundaries. Note also the degree of confusion near the field boundaries.

Figure 4-29 sumarizes the results of an experiment that used LANDSAT MSS imagery to determine the degree of organic material buildup within a body of lakes in the state of Wisconsin. A lake with a high percentage of algae and other organic materials is called *eutrophic,* and a lake that is relatively free from organisms is called *oligotrophic.* The computer processing began with the separation of all water bodies from all land bodies, using a single pair of LANDSAT MSS spectral bands to distinguish land from water. A series of training sites for the classification was extracted from the imagery that corresponded to regions of selected lakes where water samples had been acquired and classified into degrees of trophic content ranging from oligotrophic to eutrophic, using standard chemical techniques. The training sites were then used as a basis for supervised classification, and a thematic map was prepared of the extracted lake portions of the imagery. Additional details regarding evaluation of water quality by means of LANDSAT MSS data can be found in references 12 and 13.

COLOR MANIPULATION

The use of color for subjective image interpretation was discussed in Chapter 3. In this section, the quantitative representation of color will be described, and one technique used to manipulate color imagery will be presented. Additional discussion of this topic can be found in references 14 and 15.

The three components of a color image are the red, green, and blue components. The *CIE coordinate system,* defined by the Commission Internationale de l'Eclairage, defines a set of units in which the relative strengths of the three components are normalized so that the total of the three components is always equal to 1.0:

$$r + g + b = 1.0 \qquad (4\text{-}12)$$

A pixel that is all red, for example, would be represented by values of $r = 1.0$, $g = 0.0$, $b = 0.0$.

The *achromatic point* is defined in this system as the point at which the relative intensities of the three components is equal, i.e.,

$$r = g = b = 1/3 \qquad (4\text{-}13)$$

The achromatic point represents a color shade of neutral gray.

This coordinate system can be used to represent all possible mixtures of the three primary colors. The *CIE curve* is often used to indicate the relationship between color coordinates defined in this manner. The CIE curve is shown in Figure 4-30; one of the color components is plotted against a second component, with the third component value then implied by the relationship of Equation 4-12. In Figure 4-30, green is plotted against red, with blue implied. Any color in the CIE coordinate system is expressed as a single point in the plot shown in Figure 4-30.

The outer boundary of the CIE curve expresses the variation in color range through the wavelength range from blue to green to red. This variation is called *hue.* Within the interior, the distance at which a point is located relative to the outer boundary indicates the degree of pastel present in the particular color; this is often called *saturation.* The achromatic point is shown in the interior of the curve in Figure 4-30.

It is often quite desirable to manipulate the color properties of a digital image directly in hue and saturation space, avoiding the need to separately manipulate each of the three component images used to generate a color composite image. A technique has been developed that enables a mathematical transformation between the r, g, b component intensities and the hue-saturation-intensity (HSI) parameters. For a given point in the CIE color system, it is possible to transform the values of r, g, b directly to values of hue, h, saturation, s, and intensity, i. The transformation is achieved by defining an HSI coordinate system, as shown in Figure 4-31.

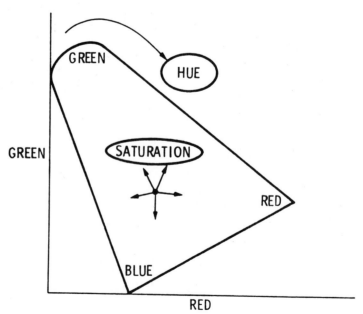

Figure 4-30. The CIE curve.

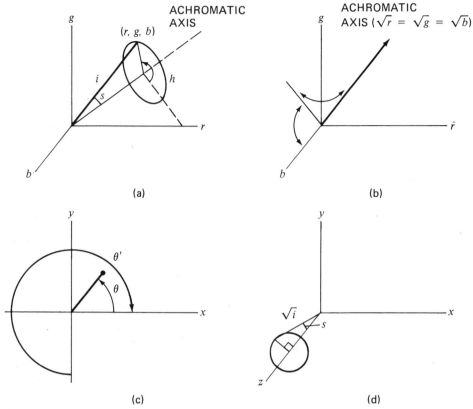

Figure 4-31. Relationship between (r,g,b) coordinate system and (hue, saturation, intensity) coordinates.

The r, g, b coordinate system is shown in Figure 4-31 as a set of orthogonal axes. A vector is drawn from the origin through the achromatic point ($r = g = b = 1/3$). An arbitrary point in color space (r, g, b) is shown in Figure 4-31a. The hue coordinate, h, of this point is defined proportional to the degree of rotation about the achromatic point as shown. The saturation, s, is defined in proportion to the length of a vector from the achromatic point to the point (r, g, b), and the intensity, i is proportional to the vector length from the origin.

The transformation is performed by defining a new set of orthogonal axes, one of which is the achromatic vector. This is done by rotating the achromatic axis into the blue axis, forming a new z axis (Figure 4-31b):

$$\begin{bmatrix} x \\ y \\ z \end{bmatrix} = \begin{bmatrix} 1 & 0 & 0 \\ 0 & \sqrt{2}/\sqrt{3} & -1/\sqrt{3} \\ 0 & 1/\sqrt{3} & \sqrt{2}/\sqrt{3} \end{bmatrix} \begin{bmatrix} 1/\sqrt{2} & 0 & -1/\sqrt{2} \\ 0 & 1 & 0 \\ 1/\sqrt{2} & 0 & 1/\sqrt{2} \end{bmatrix} \begin{bmatrix} \sqrt{r} \\ \sqrt{g} \\ \sqrt{b} \end{bmatrix} \qquad (4\text{-}14)$$

(it is convenient to work with the square roots of the original color coordinate values). The hue, saturation and intensity values can then be computed as shown in Figures 4-31c and 4-31d:

$$i = r + g + b$$
$$s = \cos^{-1}(z/\sqrt{i})$$
$$h = 3\pi/2 - \Phi$$

(4-15)

where $\Phi = \tan^{-1}(y/z)$.[16]

This transformation is applied to a color image pixel by pixel. Each pixel of the input image is assumed to correspond to one point in color space, and the pixel intensities within the three component images at that location determine the r, g, b values. h, s, and i are then computed for each pixel. The result is a set of three new images: a hue image, a saturation image, and an intensity image. The hue and saturation images can then be manipulated directly, using subjective contrast manipulation techniques, to modify the color properties of the image. It is possible, for example, to perform a hue exaggeration by processing the hue image with a linear contrast stretch algorithm. A linear contrast stretch of the hue image can be used to expand the range of color space presented within a digital image and is analogous to the linear contrast stretch described in Chapter 3 for black and white images that expands available image intensity data into the full black-to-white range of the display device. The saturation component can also be modified to adjust the degree of pastel present in the output product. A conversion back to r, g, b coordinates is performed after manipulation of the HSI components, yielding three component color images (red, green, and blue) that can be utilized as input for color volatile display or film recording devices.

The advantage of manipulation of color imagery in HSI space is that it provides direct control of color manipulation through utilization of the CIE coordinate system. An individual color is represented as a single point rather than a set of three points that must be interpreted carefully to determine a resultant color value.

Figures 4-32 and 4-33 illustrate manipulation of a color image by using HSI techniques. Figure 4-32 is a color composite image of Mars taken during the final approach of the Viking Orbiter 2 spacecraft. The color composite has been constructed by the following process: (1) The three images that were exposed separately through three separate filters as the spacecraft moved toward the planet were geometrically registered to each other, using correlation techiques. (2) Radiometric correction of the three images was performed to remove camera-system radiometric nonlinearities. (3) The color mixture was extrapolated to yield red, green, and blue components because the spectral filters used on Viking Orbiter did not correspond directly to red, green, and blue bandwiths for color film recording.

Figure 4-32 is the best true-color rendition of the planet that can be achieved within the limitations of the Orbiter vidicon camera radiometric precision and the particular spectral filters that were selected for the camera system. The three histograms below the image are used to depict the color information within the image. The top row of three histograms shows the intensity distribution within the three component images and corresponds to the red, green, and blue intensity distributions. The second row of three depicts, from left to right, the histograms of the hue image, the saturation image, and the intensity image.

Analysis of the hue and saturation histograms shows that the hue and saturation data are confined to a small portion of the total range of hue and saturation. This means that there is relatively little color variation within the image, and this is a quantitative verification of the visual appearance of the image. The bottom three histograms correspond to the hue, saturation, and intensity histograms of the image actually shown; they are identical to the second row in Figure 4-32, since these parameters have not been modified before film recording of this version of the image.

Figure 4-33 is an enhanced version of the image shown in Figure 4-32. This version was produced by performing a moderate contrast stretch of the hue and saturation images. The enhancement was designed to maintain the same mean hue and saturation as the true-color version, and the hue/saturation enhancement is thus a gradual expansion of the color range of the image around the neighborhood in color space of the original image. This enhancement reflects a decision to maintain the overall hue and saturation rendition of the image and not to expand the hue properties of the enhanced version throughout the extent of color space. A product that differs significantly from the original image could have been produced by performing a ramp CDF stretch. A ramp CDF stretch of the hue and saturation images would produce an enhanced product with color ranges based on an attempt to equally populate all available color space within the CIE curve boundaries.

HSI techniques can also be used to merge disparate data types for display. In some cases, image data at a variety of spatial resolutions may be available. A synthetic-aperture radar image at high resolution may be available for an area for which LANDSAT data are also available. A color composite image of the LANDSAT scene could be generated, using three spectral components as the red-green-blue components of the color reconstruction. The LANDSAT scene could then be converted to HSI representation, and the higher-resolution SAR image and the LANDSAT scene could be registered geometrically. The SAR image could then be used as the intensity component, along with the hue and saturation images derived from the LANDSAT multispectral image. The resulting HSI product could then be transformed back to RGB representation for display or film playback. This type of processing corresponds to ''coloring in'' the higher spatial resolution monocolor SAR imagery with the color information derived from the LANDSAT multispectral imagery. The HSI process can thus be used as a compact method of displaying a large amount of information derived from several sources.

CONVOLUTIONAL FILTERING

In Chapter 3, an example of a high pass enhancement filter was presented. The high pass filter illustrated in Chapter 3 was an example of a filter applied in the spatial domain to perform a particular manipulation of the frequencies within the image. This section described the general application of convolutional filters in the spatial domain for frequency filtering of digital imagery.

A convolutional filter applied to imagery is represented generally by a set of filter weights arrayed within a matrix of dimension H lines by W samples. The individual filter weights are adjusted to represent a specific frequency filter when applied to the imagery. The filter weights can be represented as:

$$
\begin{array}{cccc}
f_{11} & f_{12} & f_{13} \ldots & f_{1W} \\
f_{21} & f_{22} & f_{23} \ldots & f_{2W} \\
 & \ldots & & \\
f_{H1} & f_{H2} & \ldots & f_{HW}
\end{array}
$$

The filter is applied by centering the filter over each pixel in turn within the image, and convolving the image data with the filter:

$$(b_{out})_{\ell s} = \sum_{j=1}^{H} \sum_{k=1}^{W} f_{jk}(b_{in})_{\ell - H/2 + j - 1, s - W/2 + k - 1} \tag{4-16}$$

The larger the values of H and W, the closer the convolutional filter will match the desired frequency response of the filter. H and W are selected to be odd integers so that the convolutional filter can be centered about each pixel in turn. Values for H/2 and W/2 are rounded down when computed.

An equivalent to the high pass enhancement filter described in Chapter 3 would utilize a set of convolutional filter weights (in a 3 × 3 convolution filter example) of:

$$\begin{bmatrix} -1 & -1 & -1 \\ -1 & 8 & -1 \\ -1 & -1 & -1 \end{bmatrix}$$

A low pass or smoothing filter that corresponds to computing a local average around each pixel in the image is achieved by applying the following set of filter weights (again, a 3 × 3 filter example):

$$\begin{bmatrix} 1 & 1 & 1 \\ 1 & 1 & 1 \\ 1 & 1 & 1 \end{bmatrix}$$

An enhancement filter emphasizing vertical edges in an image would utilize weights like:

$$\begin{bmatrix} -1 & 0 & 1 \\ -1 & 0 & 1 \\ -1 & 0 & 1 \end{bmatrix}$$

A commonly utilized edge detector is the *Sobel edge detector*. Two convolutional filters are applied to the input image:

$$F_1 = \begin{bmatrix} -1 & -2 & -1 \\ 0 & 0 & 0 \\ 1 & 2 & 2 \end{bmatrix}$$

$$F_2 = \begin{bmatrix} -1 & 0 & 1 \\ -2 & 0 & 2 \\ -1 & 0 & 1 \end{bmatrix}$$

If $(f_1)_{jk}$ represents the filter weights in filter F_1 and $(f_2)_{jk}$ represents the filter weights in filter F_2 then the output pixel intensity value is computed from:

$$(b_{out})_{\ell s} = a \left[(b_{1,out})_{\ell s} + (b_{2,out})_{\ell s} \right] + b \tag{4-17}$$

(b)

(d)

UPPER LEFT   ORIGINAL IMAGE
UPPER RIGHT 11X11 HIGH FREQUENCY BOOST
LOWER LEFT   5X5 LOW PASS FILTER
LOWER RIGHT SOBEL EDGE DETECTOR

SYSTEM
DEVELOPMENT
CORPORATION
13:42:44 8-APR-87 A BURROUGHS COMPANY

Figure 4-34. Effects of convolutional filtering. (a) Top left, original image with contrast enhancement. (b) Top right, same image after application of high pass filter. (c) Bottom left, same image after application of a low pass filter. (d) Lower right, same image after application of Sobel edge detector (Unisys Defense Systems).

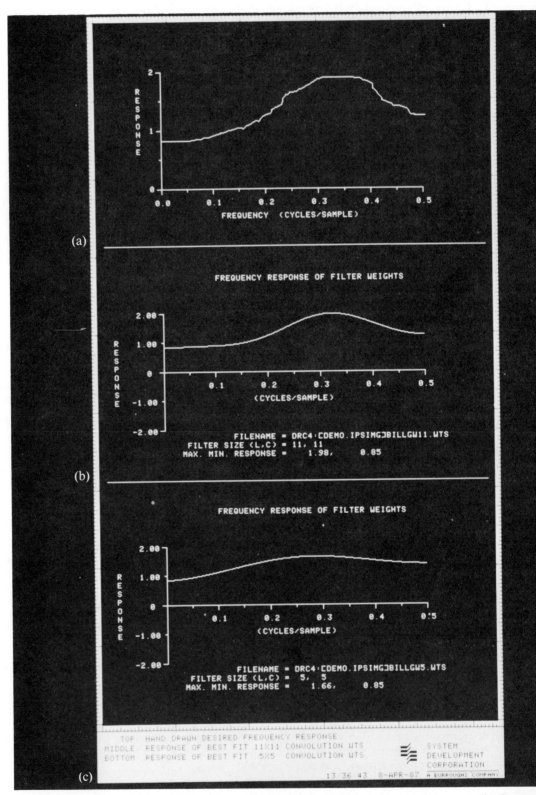

Figure 4-35. (a) Top, frequency response of filter desired by the user. (b) Center, frequency response of an 11 × 11 convolutional filter with weights adjusted to give best fit to frequency response in (a). (c) Bottom, frequency response of a 5 × 5 convolutional filter with weights adjusted to match frequency response in (a). The 11 × 11 filter provides a much closer fit to the frequency response of the desired filter.

where a and b are scaling constants and

$$(b_{1,out})_{\ell s} = \sum_{j=1}^{H} \sum_{k=1}^{W} (f_1)_{jk}(b_{in})_{\ell - H/2 + j - 1, s - W/2 + k - 1}$$

(4-18)

$$(b_{2,out})_{\ell s} = \sum_{j=1}^{H} \sum_{k=1}^{W} (f_2)_{jk}(b_{in})_{\ell - H/2 + j - 1, s - W/2 + k - 1}$$

Figure 4-34 shows the results of applying a series of convolutional filters to the same image. Figure 4-34a shows the original image with contrast enhancement. Figure 4-34b shows the same image after application of a 5 × 5 low pass filter and Figure 4-34c shows the same image after application of an 11 × 11 high pass filter. Figure 4-34d shows the same image after application of a Sobel edge detector.

Figure 4-35 shows the effect of filter size on desired frequency filter response. Figure 4-35(a) shows the high pass filter desired by the user, and Figures 4-35(b) and 4-35(c) show the frequency response of a 11 × 11 and 5 × 5 filter respectively. The frequency response of the 11 × 11 filter more closely matches the desired frequency response than the 5 × 5 filter.

High speed digital hardware is available for performing the operation in Equation 4-16. The same type of high-speed hardware is available for use with personal computers on special-purpose hardware boards designed to support image processing in a personal computer environment (see Chapter 9). This high-speed hardware makes it possible to perform convolutional filters within a few seconds or less on 512 × 512 imagery, depending on the size of the convolutional filter.

REFERENCES

1. Bernstein, R., "Digital Image Processing of Earth Observation Sensor Data," *IBM J Res & Dev* 20, 1, p. 40, (Jan. 1976).
2. Green, W. B., et al., "Removal of Instrument Signature from Mariner 9 Television Images of Mars," *Appl Opt* 14, 105 (Jan. 1975).
3. Wolf, M. R., "The Analysis and Removal of Geometric Distortion from Viking Lander Camera Images," *Proceedings of the American Society of Photogrammetry,* October 1975.
4. Keloway, G. P., *Map Projections,* London, Methuen and Company, 1946.
5. Castleman, K. R., *Digital Image Processing,* New York, Prentice-Hall, 1979.
6. Thompson, M. M., *Maps for America,* U.S. Geological Survey (U. S. Government Printing Office Stock Number 024-001-03145-1).
7. Colvocoresses, A. P., "Space Oblique Mercator," *Photogramm Engr* 40, 8, pp. 921–926, Aug. 1974.
8. Snyder, J. P., "The Space Oblique Mercator Projection," *Photogramm Engr & Remote Sensing* 44, 5, pp. 585–596, (May 1978).
9. Green, W. B., "Applications of Digital Image Processing Techniques to Problems of Data Registration and Correlation," *Proceedings of the National Computer Conference,* 1978, pp. 141–149.
10. Andrews, H., *Introduction to Mathematical Techniques in Pattern Recognition,* New York, Wiley Interscience, 1972.
11. Tou, J., and R. Gonzalez, *Pattern Recognition Principles,* New York, Addison-Wesley, 1975.
12. Blackwell, R. J., and D. H. P. Boland, "The Trophic Classification of Lakes Using ERTS Multispectral Scanner Data," *Proc Am Soc Photogramm,* March 1975.

13. Blackwell, R. J., and D. H. P. Boland, *Trophic Classification of Selected Colorado Lakes,* Jet Propulsion Laboratory Publication 78–100, January 1979.
14. Pratt, W. K., *Digital Image Processing,* New York, Wiley, 1978.
15. Gonzalez, R., and P. Wintz, *Digital Image Processing,* New York, Addison-Wesley, 1977.
16. J. Addington, Personal Communication.

5
Image Display

INTRODUCTION

A wide variety of devices are available that provide image display in various formats. Processed imagery can be viewed on a volatile display monitor that presents the digital data in video display format. Image data can be recorded on film, and photographic products can be produced from the original negative or positive transparency. Inexpensive hard-copy image recording devices are available that record image data directly from video input signals. This chapter describes the various types of image display equipment, including film recorders, hard-copy image recording devices, and volatile image display systems. It also describes nondigital methods that are used to store images for archival purposes, including microfiche, microfilm, and video disk systems for image storage, retrieval, and display. The chapter concludes with a discussion of the basic concepts involved in calibration of image output devices.

BLACK AND WHITE VOLATILE IMAGE DISPLAY SYSTEMS

The most common architecture for volatile image display systems involves the use of a digital storage medium (usually solid-state memory) from which the digital image data are read repetitively and converted to analog video format for display on a video monitor. The image data are transferred into the local memory from a host computer system, which can be a large mainframe system, a microprocessor controller, or another type of host computer. The image data are stored within the memory so that they can be accessed sequentially, line by line. Each line of image data is read out at the refresh rate of the monitor and converted to analog format for display. Video monitors typically refresh the full display screen every one-thirtieth of a second so that each image line will be read from digital storage and converted to analog format every one-thirtieth of a second. This concept is illustrated in Figure 5-1.

The host computer usually provides the overall control function for the display system and also handles the interface with the system user. The user communicates with the host computer, which interprets user requests and forwards detailed system-level commands to the display system.

The image display system usually operates under direct control of a *display controller*. The controller receives commands and image data from the host processor, routes image data into appropriate locations within the display memory, interprets commands issued by the host processor, and initiates actions on the basis of the information received from the host. The display controller can also transfer status information and other data back to the host computer.

The *image display memory* is configured to store image data for sequential access

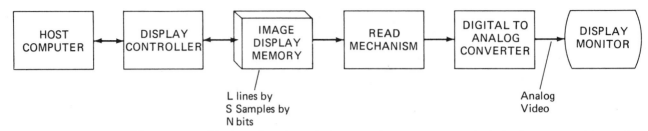

Figure 5-1. Black and white solid state refresh memory-based display system block diagram.

by the analog-to-digital conversion process. The display memory is limited in storage capacity and can hold a limited number of lines and samples of digital image data with a maximum number of bits per pixel. Typical configurations for black and white display devices include 256 lines by 256 samples by 8 bits, 512 lines by 512 samples by 8 bits, and 1,024 by 1,024 resolution by 8 bits. Many display systems are now marketed to provide a maximum storage capacity that can be configured under software control; the topic of display memory management is discussed later in this chapter.

Addition of Graphic Display Capability

The image data memory can be viewed as a stack of bit planes. A 512-line by 512-sample 8-bit display memory can be thought of as a stack of eight 1-bit planes, each 512 by 512 in size. Most available display systems provide an option enabling display of graphics information superimposed over the image data. Graphics display is usually achieved by adding an extra bit plane in which individual bits are turned off or on to form patterns for alphanumeric characters or graphical display. The graphics bit plane contains the same number of pixels as the image memory bit planes so that the graphics data are directly registered to the image data on a pixel-by-pixel basis. In black and white systems, the graphics plane bit is often incorporated as the most significant bit of each pixel intensity so tht pixels whose graphic bits that are turned on appear whiter than the whitest digital pixel intensity value. An 8-bit image display would then display a pixel value of 255 as the whitest pixel intensity, and a brighter white intensity would be reserved for pixels where the graphics bit is equal to 1.

The conversion of alphanumeric data into dot patterns within a bit plane is usually achieved with a hardware device called a *character generator,* and the conversion of vector data into the appropriate pattern of dots in a bit plane is performed by a *vector generator.* These devices are usually provided as part of an image display system and can be used under software control to create a desired graphics data overlay of image data on the volatile display.

Vector Generator. The operation of a vector generator is shown in Figure 5-2. A vector is usually specified to the display system in terms of the pixel coordinates of the desired end points of the vector. For example, a command may be issued to draw a vector from line 15, sample 12, to line 25, sample 15, on the display. The vector generator will determine which bits to turn on in the graphics plane to achieve the display of that vector.

One problem that occurs with raster display of vector data is the generation of a "sawtooth" effect for vectors that are not directly aligned either vertically or horizontally. Vectors that are drawn at angles will cause the vector generator algorithm to perform some type of round-off or nearest-neighbor interpolation in computing the pixel addresses of bits to be turned on in generating particular vectors. This will cause vectors to exhibit a jagged or sawtooth appearance when displayed. This problem is particularly noticeable when graphics data are displayed on image displays, since image displays usually have a total resolution of 1,024 square pixels or less.

Character Generator. Most character generators utilize a set of fixed patterns within read-only memory (ROM) to achieve alphanumeric display. The letter "a," for example, will be represented by a rectangular block of pixels within the ROM, and the appropriate pixel pattern for an "a" will be read from ROM and forwarded to the image display graphics bit plane when display of the character "a" is requested. A block size of 5 by 7 pixels for character representation in a raster display format is typical.

Character generators are often provided with a choice of type fonts. This is achieved by storing more than one set of character representations in ROM and accessing the appropriate set on the basis of software control or user command. It is also possible to store other characters in ROM, including non-Arabic text characters, scientific notation, and other special-purpose characters. Some display systems will provide random-access memory (RAM) rather than ROM, enabling the user to program his or her own character set within the display system and to change it as desired.

Software commands issued to display systems will usually provide the desired pixel coordinates of a particular letter, number, or symbol in terms of the location of one of the four corners of the block of pixels corresponding to the character. One example might be a command that specifies that the upper-left corner of the letter "a" must be placed at line 38, sample 104. The character generator will forward the appropriate pixel block from ROM to display memory, which will turn the appropriate bits on and off in the graphics bit plane to provide the character representation at the appropriate location. Figure 5-3 illustrates the basic operation of a character generator.

Character generators usually provide the capability of displaying characters horizontally on the display. Character generators that enable character display vertically or even at an angle on the display may also be available.

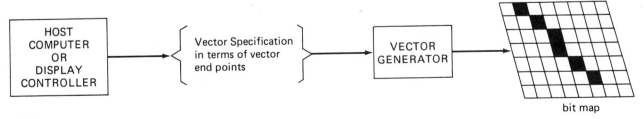

Figure 5-2. Operation of vector generator. Note sawtooth effect in the bit map vector display.

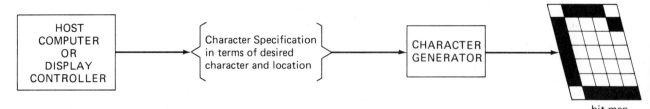

Figure 5-3. Operation of character generator. The bit map display contains a representation of the letter "C."

Use of Cursors in Display Systems

A *cursor* is a visible marker that can be positioned at a specified location on a volatile display either by software command or under the control of an interactive device operated by a user. The cursor is provided as a programmable 1-bit block of pixels representing a small matrix of dots (typically 5 by 5 pixels). The cursor dot pattern is centered at a specified location on the display under hardware or software control. The user can normally store the desired cursor pattern under software control. Typical shapes used for cursors within a 5 by 5 pixel pattern are shown in Figure 5–4. The display hardware also usually provides the capability of turning the cursor pattern on or off under either hardware or software control.

A cursor generator is used to produce the display of the selected cursor pattern. The cursor generator receives the desired position data from the host processor or the display controller and then forwards the pattern read from RAM to the graphics plane of the display device. In some implementations, the cursor generator will produce the cursor directly as an analog video signal, which is then clocked directly into the analog video stream.

Cursor Control by Interactive Hardware Devices.   A variety of devices are used to provide interactive user control of cursor position on a display system. Each of these devices operates in the same general manner. The user manipulates some physical device while viewing the display screen. There is a correspondence between the user's manipulation of a device and the location of the cursor as seen on the screen. As the user manipulates the device, the device generates a series of horizontal and vertical coordinates that can be read by the host computer or the display controller. These coordinates are then forwarded to the cursor controller through either software commands or hardware interconnections, and the cursor is positioned at the desired display location specified by the interactive device.

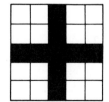 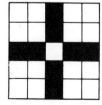 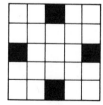  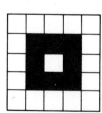

Figure 5-4.   Typical patterns used for a 5 × 5 cursor. Pixels shown here in black would appear bright white on the display, pixels shown here in white would display the image data pixel intensity at that location.

Several types of interactive devices are available as options on most commercially available image display systems. They include:

Mouse. A mouse is a device that rests on the working surface near the display. The bottom of the mouse device contains a ball that is moved as the mouse is moved around the working surface. The motion of the mouse provides two-dimensional coordinates to the display system. A mouse generally includes one or several depressable function keys that forward interrupts to the display system. These function keys are used in conjunction with the motion of the mouse to identify or select segments of the displayed image and/or to trigger functions or actions when the keys are depressed.

Trackball. A trackball is a round ball within a housing. A series of two-dimensional position coordinates is generated as the ball is rolled around in its housing.

Joystick. This device consists of a short lever that can be moved randomly by the user within some physical constraints. The two-dimensional position coordinates of the end of the lever are generated as the lever is moved.

Tablet. The user is provided with a flat pad and a pointer. The horizontal and vertical directions on the tablet correspond to the same directions of the display. The positions of the pointer within the pad area are read and provided to the host computer or display controller.

Light Pen. Light pens can be used in conjunction with clear overlays fixed to the video display or in direct contact with special-purpose display screens to provide two-dimensional coordinate input for display devices.

These interactive devices can be used for purposes other than cursor manipulation within image display systems. The use of interactive devices for control of image processing operations is described in detail in Chapter 6. Interactive devices can be used to control image processing functions, to select desired options from menus presented to the user, and to control interactive contrast manipulation and other image processing operations.

Black and White Display System Selection

Figure 5-5 shows the architecture for a fully configured black and white image display system that includes full graphics and cursor capability. The major system components include the solid-state image memory, the graphics overlay plane driven by a character and vector generator and through direct software commands from the host computer, and the interface with interactive hardware components.

Display systems are equipped with digital look-up tables that can be accessed directly by software within the host computer. The table performs contrast manipulation by modifying the digital pixel data on the basis of table-look up after the pixels are read from the display image memory and before they are input to the digital-to-analog conversion process. In this manner, contrast manipulations can be implemented without modifying the original image stored in display memory. This minimizes the data transfer time between host computer and display memory and also provides extremely rapid interactive image-manipulation capability. The look-

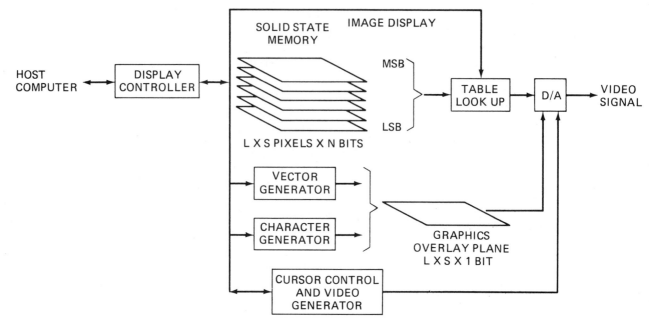

Figure 5-5.   Black and white volatile image display architecture.

up table contrast stretch is implemented on every readout of the display memory so that the results of a new stored table look-up are viewed on the display screen immediately after the table values are stored. In most display systems, the total time to store a new look-up table is less than 1 second.

The system designer must determine the nature of each of the components shown in Figure 5-5 when selecting a display system. The selection process usually involves a trade-off between available funds and system capability. Most systems are provided with a minimum set of image memory for a basic price. Additional memory for accommodating larger images or more bits per pixel is the most significant cost factor. Graphics capability and interactive user input devices also add to the cost of most systems, since these capabilities are offered as options to the basic system.

Display systems are now available with host microprocessors and local disk and/ or tape storage devices, providing local input-output capacity and limited image processing capability within a self-contained display system. These systems also incorporate limited image processing capability so that the entire system can be run in a "stand-alone" mode. A compact microprocessor-based system that provides self-contained input/output and processing capability is shown in Figure 5-6.

Display systems are also offered as computer peripherals. The display system, including controller, memory, and graphics and interactive device options is provided with an interface to a host minicomputer, mainframe, or microprocessor host system that provides overall control functions to the display device. The host processor handles user interface support and utilizes its own peripherals for image storage and input/output functions.

A fully configured black and white image display system is shown in Figure 5-7. This system has sufficient local memory for storage of two separate 512-square images and separate graphics planes for both images. The images shown on the two monitors include text information that has been overwritten, using the graphics

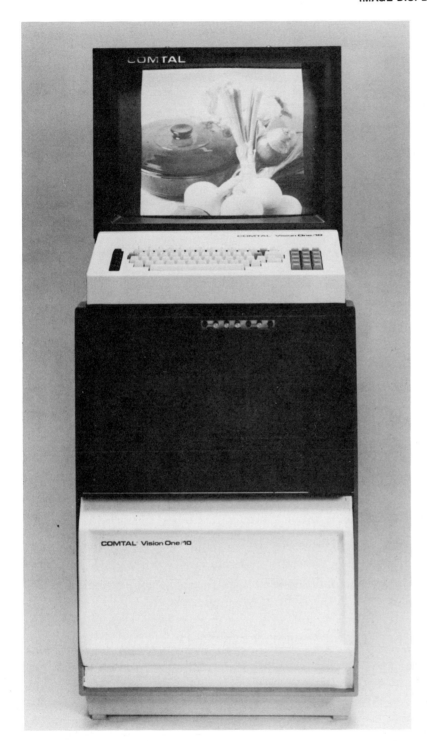

Figure 5-6.   A self-contained image display system with microprocessor controller and tape deck (COMTAL/3M).

Figure 5-7.   Image display system with interactive tablet. Character display is achieved using graphics overlay bit planes; note display of two separate images from the same solid state memory (COMTAL/3M).

planes. An interactive tablet is used to enter graphical information or to control the cursor; it is located at the right of the user keyboard.

COLOR VOLATILE IMAGE DISPLAY SYSTEMS

A schematic block diagram of a color image display system is shown in Figure 5-8. The first color volatile display systems provided separate blocks of solid-state memory for storage of red, green, and blue components of a color image. Three separate look-up tables were provided so that separate manipulation of the three component images was possible. Manipulation of the three look-up tables could be used to achieve a variety of false-color enhancements without modifying the basic image data stored within the display memory.

Color graphics overlay can be provided through use of three separate bit planes, one for each color of overlay (red, green, and blue). Each of the three separate graphics planes can be addressed separately by the host computer and display controller.

Color volatile image display systems provide a wide dynamic range of color for

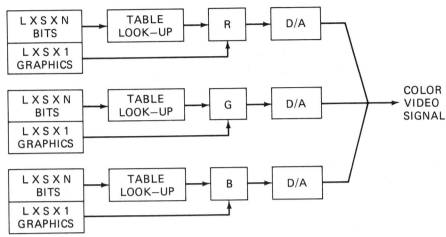

Figure 5-8. Color volatile display system architecture. *L* is number of lines, *S* is number of samples, and *N* is number of bits per pixel in the digital intensity.

display. The range of color inherent in three-color digital image data exceeds the range of color in standard broadcast television signals in the United States. Standard U.S. video is transmitted in NTSC format, which was created to transmit color video within the same communications bandwidth originally used for black and white television transmission in the 1950s. The range of hue and saturation data that can be transmitted was reduced in order to retain the limited communications bandwidth of black and white television signals. (See Chapter 4 for a description of the hue and saturation properties of color.) Image display systems generally utilize special color video monitors that accept separate red, green, and blue input analog video signals. The separate color format, called *RGB video,* is not compatible with broadcast video, and hardware converters are available that convert from RGB format to NTSC format for applications in which NTSC format video transmission of signals generated by image display equipment is desired. The conversion does introduce some degradation in the color content of the imagery.

Image Display Memory Management

Most commercially available image display systems now allow flexible and dynamic utilization of the image display memory. Figure 5-9 shows a schematic diagram of a block of solid-state memory that is 1,024 lines by 1,024 samples by 18 bits in size. The same block of memory can be configured in several ways for image storage, as shown by the dashed lines. The configurations shown in Figure 5-9 include the following:

1. A single 1,024-square three-color image
2. Four 512-square three-color images
3. Three 1,024-square or twelve 512-square black and white images
4. Sixteen 256-square three-color images or forty-eight 256-square black and white images

Roam and Zoom. Most displays will accommodate storage of images that are too large to be accommodated by the display monitor. As an example, a display system

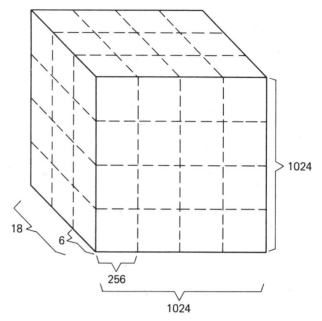

Figure 5-9.   Configuration of solid state memory of size 1024 × 1024 × 18 bits.

may be configured with the memory shown in Figure 5-9 and may have a display monitor that can display only color images that are 512 pixels square or less. A more common example might be large images (e.g., 4,000 pixels square) that cannot be accommodated by currently available color display monitors, which are generally limited to 1,024-square format or less. Many available systems are equipped with the capability to *roam* and *zoom* within the full image size contained in image memory when the display monitor cannot accommodate the full pixel resolution.

Figure 5-10 illustrates the concept of roam. The roam operation consists of extracting an image segment for display at full resolution on the display screen. As an example, Figure 5-10 illustrates the extraction of a 512-square color image segment from a larger image stored in image memory with resolution greater than 512 square.

The zoom function consists of enlarging a portion of the image in memory for display. As one example, consider a 1,024-square three-color image memory associated with a display monitor that can accommodate only 512 square images. The user may initially display the full image at one-quarter resolution on the 512-square display by selecting every other image pixel from every other line in the display memory. The user may then elect to zoom into a particular region within the image, and a selected image segment can then be displayed at full pixel resolution on the monitor. In some applications, zoom is used to perform segment magnification, using either pixel replication or intensity interpolation to generate the pixels created by the magnification. For example, a 256-square image segment can be displayed at 512-square resolution by replicating pixels or interpolating to generate the digital intensity of pixels created in the magnification.

Region-of-Interest.   Single bit planes are often provided within display systems that can be used as a ''mask'' to identify subsets of the displayed image that will be

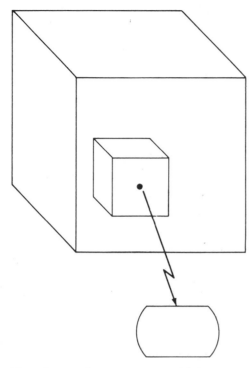

Figure 5-10.   Use of roam feature to extract image segment for display.

processed differently from the rest of the image. The subsets of the displayed imagery selected for specific processing are called "Regions of Interest (ROI)." One typical application in which ROI is utilized is selection of image segments that are displayed with a contrast enhancement different from the rest of the displayed image. It may be desirable, for example, to perform a severe contrast enhancement of an area of an image that represents a shadow in the scene in a case where the contrast enhancement of the total scene is acceptable. The ROI plane is used to identify the areas of the image that correspond to shadows, as opposed to other areas of the scene. Another application for the use of ROI might be magnification of a portion of the image located within a "window" identified through the ROI bit plane.

The basic concept of ROI is shown in Figure 5-11. An image is viewed on a display system and two regions have been selected for special processing. The regions are generally identified interactively by the user through the use of an interactive device (cursor or mouse). The single bit plane used for ROI identification contains zeroes everywhere except for the pixels corresponding to the two ROIs. The pixels in the ROI bit plane corresponding to the ROIs contain ones. This binary filter identifies the pixels in the ROI's which are processed using different look-up tables for different contrast enhancement, or are routed through alternative processing streams for other manipulation (e.g., enlargement or reduction). The pixels within the ROIs are then recombined into the video display stream for display. The final display contains both the original image and the specially processed ROIs.

Figure 5-12 shows the use of ROI processing in a color display. The color image represents a combination of SAR imagery acquired with the SIR-B shuttle radar imaging system and a topographic data set containing elevation data. For each pixel, the hue component of the color image contains the topographic data with higher

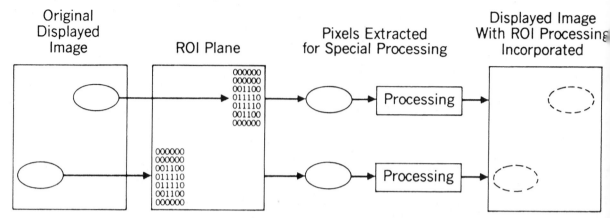

Figure 5-11. Region-of-interest concept.

pixel values corresponding to higher elevations, the saturation component has been set to mid-range (128) intensity, and the intensity component contains the SIR-B image. A ROI has been used to identify a segment of the image in which the display of the SIR-B data is suppressed, and within which the elevation data is contoured. Using an interactive device (joystick, mouse, trackball), the center of the ROI can be moved around the displayed image interactively, providing a "spotlight" effect into the image data.

Bit Plane Management.   Commercially available display systems incorporating microprocessor controllers provide user management of individual bit planes within the solid state memory. Commercially available systems now provide logical subsets of memory (generally 4 bits deep) that can be combined or utilized in a variety of ways under user control through software commands. The options available can include:

Image size. Multiple blocks of refresh memory can be combined to accommodate images larger than the display resolution, as shown in Figure 5-9.

Combined image and graphics display. If image memory is provided in logical units of less than 8 bits per pixel (usually 4 bits per pixel), image memory can be configured to accommodate both graphics data (generally 4 bits per pixel) and image data (8 bits per pixel or more) simultaneously.

Film looping. Software control of sequential display of multiple imagery stored in refresh memory is often provided, so that the equivalent of film looping can be achieved with digital image displays.

Look-up tables are generally provided that can be used to allocate specific bit planes to specific functions. Table look up can be used to provide graphics overlay on image data, to achieve separate table look up functions for image and graphics data stored concurrently in the same refresh memory, to control region of interest operation, and to control windowing operations on the display.

One commercially available display system incorporating many of these features is shown in Figure 5-13. This system incorporates control of up to 8 individual 4 bit deep memory segments, each with 1280 × 1024 resolution; a look-up table with 12 bits of input and 24 bits of output is provided, providing control of gray scale or color image or graphics output and control of other features as well (looping, region of interest, and overlays).

Figure 5.13.   An image display system featuring flexible control of refresh memory (Ramtek Corporation).

FILM RECORDING SYSTEMS

All devices that record digital imagery onto film operate with the same basic concept. A controlled-intensity light source is directed toward a particular pixel coordinate position in the focal plane, and the light source is focused onto a piece of film held in the focal plane of the recording device; the process is repeated for every pixel contained within the two-dimensional input image. The light-source intensity is modified at each pixel position in proportion to the digital intensity of that pixel.

The systems differ in the techniques used for generating the illumination and in the methods used for positioning the light source at the correct spatial location. They also differ in the size of film that can be accommodated, the size of the input digital image that can be accommodated, and the speed at which they record imagery onto film. Color film recorders utilize different technology to generate the color intensity for each pixel, and film recorders that can record only black and white imagery often represent a viable option to a system designer faced with a limited budget.

This section describes several types of systems that are designed to accept digital imagery as input and produce film output products. Other systems that produce direct hard-copy output with no photographic negative are described in the next section.

Flying Spot Cathode Ray Tube (CRT) Systems

The use of flying spot CRT systems for film scanning was described in Chapter 2. The same type of system can be used for recording. The main difference is that film scanning employs a single intensity spot directed to each addressable pixel location on the tube, whereas the spot intensity varies during recording. At each pixel position, the intensity is varied in proportion to the digital intensity of the individual pixel. The digital image is read by the system controller, and each pixel in turn is exposed by illuminating the appropriate spot on the CRT with an intensity proportional to the input digital intensity for that pixel. Color image recording usually is achieved by separately exposing three component images through different spectral filters (red, green, and blue). A film recorder system utilizing flying spot CRT technology is shown in Figure 5-14.

Currently available flying spot CRT recorders provide spot sizes ranging from 25 to 100 microns and accommodate input image sizes up to 4,096 square pixels. The larger spot sizes (above 25 microns) are produced by pixel replication so that a 100-micron spot size is obtained by replicating each input pixel four times and recording at the same fixed spot size (25 microns). For that reason, there is a trade-off between the input image size in pixels and the spot size for each pixel on the exposed negative. Normally, 4,096 square images can be recorded only at 25-micron spot size in this type of system.

These devices record imagery rapidly, with a typical recording time of approximately five minutes for a 1,024-square monocolor image with no pixel replication (assuming that the device controller can provide the digital pixel values at that rate).

Flying spot CRT film recorders have the same limitations on radiometric and geometric precision as flying spot CRT scanners. These considerations were discussed in Chapter 2. Systems are available that perform both scanning and recording. These systems are usually available with a choice of film holder and optics, accommodating a variety of film sizes ranging from 35-mm to 5-inch film.

Laser Film Recorders

Film recorders that utilize a laser as the active light source employ a single spectral line from the laser for black and white recording and utilize either filters or multiple spectral lines for color recording. The laser intensity is modulated in proportion to

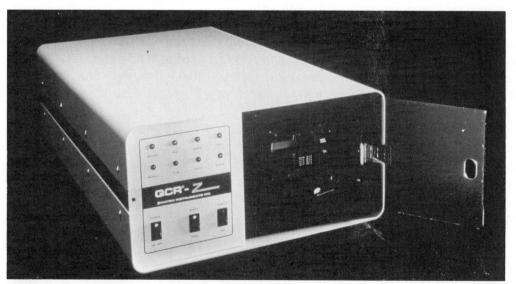

Figure 5-14.   Flying spot CRT-based film recording system (Matrix Instruments Incorporated).

the input digital intensity of each pixel and focused onto the film at the correct location.

The advantages of laser recording include high recording speed relative to other technologies and a high degree of geometric precision. The main disadvantages include high purchase cost and the maintenance support required to achieve consistent laser illumination and to retain the precision alignment necessary within the optical path of the recording system.

Light-Emitting Diode (LED) Recorders

LED recorders involve the use of a single LED light source positioned on a shaft in the center of a drum containing a piece of film. LED-based film scanners were described in Chapter 2, and film recorders using an LED as a light source operate in a similar manner. The LED intensity is modified in proportion to the digital intensity of each pixel; either the LED rotates within the drum, or the drum rotates about the fixed LED as the intensity fluctuates to generate a line of image data on the film. The LED is moved down the axis of rotation to generate additional lines of image data.

LED recorders provide spot sizes ranging from 25 to 100 microns. They can accommodate film sizes up to 8 by 10 inches, providing the capability of recording input images as large as several thousand pixels on a side. These recorders are slower than flying spot CRT or laser recorders, and they provide high geometric precision. They can be used for either black and white or color recording, and systems that can both scan and record film are available. A LED-based recording system was shown in Figure 2-24.

HARD-COPY OUTPUT DEVICES

Several relatively low-cost devices are available that generate hard copy of imagery that is displayed in video form on display monitors. These devices provide image products that are generally of lower quality than products generated from original negatives produced on film recording systems. They are popular because of their low cost and because a user can obtain a direct copy of an image that he or she is viewing on a volatile display without experiencing the delay involved in film recording, photo processing, and printing.

Figure 5-15 shows a schematic of one type of device used for direct hard copy of black and white imagery. This type of device involves image exposure onto dry silver copy paper, with heat treatment as the development mechanism. The input to this type of device is a standard black and white analog video signal. These devices are connected directly to black and white display monitors driven by digital image display devices. The user pushes a button to obtain a hard copy of the image on the screen in front of him. Typical exposure and development time for these devices is approximately 8 seconds. With proper maintenance, these devices usually provide black and white products with from 16 to 32 gray shade rendition.

These devices operate by moving a segment of the video image data to an exposure station as the paper moves. The full image is recorded by changing the segment at the display position as the paper is moved. One system of this type utilizes a linear fiber-optics array to transfer a segment or window of the input video signal to the exposure position.

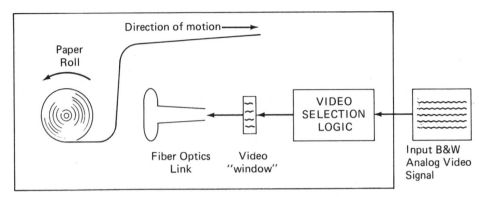

Figure 5-15. Schematic of video-driven black and white hard copy image recorder.

A second type of hard-copy recording device also utilizes video signals as input but incorporates small, high quality color CRTs to transfer the image onto film. These devices accept either black and white or color image input and utilize RGB video as input for color product generation. The video signal is used to drive an image onto a compact CRT contained within the unit; the image is focused onto instant film located in the focal plane of the device. Figure 5-16 shows one of these systems.

These devices may be limited in resolution to the image size inherent in standard video format (typically 512 samples by 512 lines) and provide limited gray shade rendition in black and white. For color recording, these devices are not limited by the inherent color limitations of the NTSC format described earlier, because color hard-copy systems usually accept RGB-format video signals. These devices are much less expensive than film recorders and thus provide an inexpensive means of obtaining rapid black and white or color hard copy almost immediately. They are particularly useful in an interactive image processing environment. These devices also provide an inexpensive method of obtaining "quick look" hard copy in situations where higher-quality photographic products may be produced later with a higher-quality film recording system.

The distinction between film recorders and instant hard-copy devices is diminishing with the appearance of the CRT-based hard-copy devices. This is because many of the rapid hard-copy devices now come equipped with film holders that enable image transfer directly from RGB video to 35-mm film or even 8 by 10-inch positive transparency film. The instant color hard-copy recorders remain limited to the quality and image size imposed by the limitations of analog video but do provide an extremely low-cost approach to obtaining medium-quality image products in a rapid manner.

NONDIGITAL IMAGE STORAGE DEVICES

The cost of digital storage continues to decrease rapidly. Despite this trend, analog storage is still cheaper than digital storage, and many image processing systems incorporate analog media for archival storage of large image data bases. This means that imagery originally generated in digital format is converted to analog format (such as video format on video disk or film products) for archival storage. The analog storage devices generally include a computer interface so that the analog

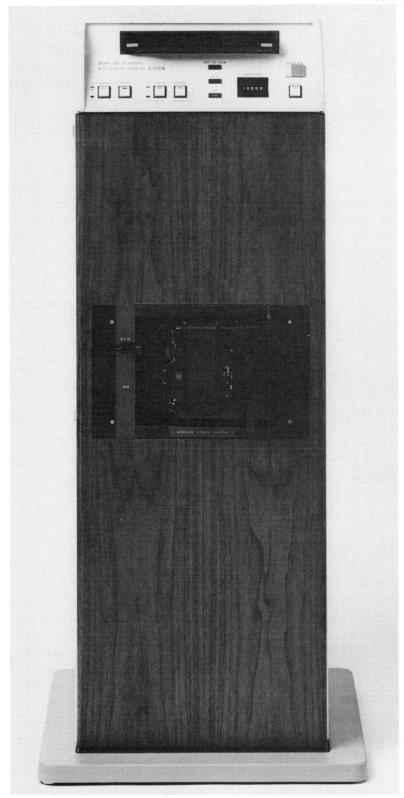

Figure 5-16. Quick-look hard copy color camera system (Dunn Instruments).

image data base can be queried, using computerized data base management techniques operating on a set of image-associated identifiers. Image retrieval from analog storage usually implies computer-controlled access to the analog medium.

The advantage of archival storage on analog media is that analog storage enables retention of a large image data base in a compact manner on relatively inexpensive media. This provides rapid user interrogation and browsing capability. The disadvantages of analog archival storage include the following: (1) The conversion from digital format to analog degrades the quality of the image data. (2) Additional digital processing cannot be performed directly on the archived imagery; the analog imagery must be reconverted to digital format for further processing, and the reconverted digital version will not have the quality of the original digital image that existed before conversion for archival storage. The ideal situation involves utilization of analog storage for browsing and data base interrogation, coupled with the availability of the original digital versions of the images selected for further processing by the user after browsing through the data in analog format. The digital archive can be kept in inexpensive off-line storage, and individual images can be recalled for on-line use, based on user requests.

This section provides a brief description of several types of sytsems that have been used to maintain archival image data bases on analog media. There are no "standard" devices available in this area yet, and systems are generally developed by system designers who adapt analog devices intended for other uses.

Microfilm and Microfiche Devices

Microfilm devices record large numbers of images onto small film strips (typically 16- or 35-mm film sizes). Each image is indexed by its relative position on the film roll, and computer-compatible image-associated data can be entered into an indexed data base to aid retrieval.

Microfiche devices record a set of images onto a fixed-size card. Typically, microfiche systems will record approximately 60 or 98 images on a card that is approximately 3 by 5 inches in size.

Microfilm and microfiche systems are popular in office and commercial environments, since film is an inexpensive and compact way to store documents; each page of a document is photographed, and the image of the page is merged onto a roll of microfilm or onto a particular position on a microfiche card. Commercially available devices provide access to individual images based on user interrogation of computerized indexes within a few seconds of a user request. The retrieval is performed by positioning the proper image within an optical device that magnifies the image and displays the enlarged image to the user. Computer-driven microfilm and microfiche systems that format computer output directly onto film are also available.

The vast majority of microfilm and microfiche systems are designed for photographic storage of document material. As such, they are not designed to provide the gray shade or color image rendition required for digital image storage and retrieval. Document material is normally photographed on high-contrast film, and the photographic result is equivalent to a 1-bit digital image. For this reason, special photographic procedures must be established to generate a digital image data base on mirofilm or microfiche media. Once the image data base is created on this media, commercially available equipment can be used to store, interrogate, and retrieve the image data.

Figure 5-17 shows a system adapted for use at the Jet Propulsion Laboratory's Regional Planetary Imaging Facility, based on a concept originally developed at the California Institute of Technology. The viewers shown in the figure are commercially available computer-controlled microfiche card readers. Image data bases were generated on microfiche film cards and stored within these readers. The image catalogs containing a variety of image descriptors (see Chapter 7) were interrogated by users, and images satisfying user search criteria were displayed as shown. The microfiche storage mechanism provided a compact and efficient method of browsing through an image data base of several thousand images and provided a rapid mechanisms for viewing selected imagery that did not require expensive on-line digital storage of the full image data base. For this purpose, the quality degradation that occurred when converting from digital format to microfiche imagery was acceptable.

Figure 5-17. Archival image data base query and retrieval system utilizing computer-controlled microfiche viewers. User queries are entered via the terminals, and appropriate imagery is displayed under computer control (Jet Propulsion Laboratory Regional Planetary Image Facility).

It should be noted that microfilm and microfiche recording systems that provide limited gray shade or color rendition of image data are beginning to appear on the market. Some of these devices are even computer-driven. It will probably be possible in the future to develop microfilm- or microfiche-based systems for archival image storage that rely completely on commercially available components.

DIGITAL IMAGE STORAGE DEVICES

Optical Disk Technology

There are currently three basic types of optical disk technology commercially available that are relevant to the storage, retrieval, and display of large volumes of digital image data: videodisk, compact disk-read only memory (CD-ROM), and optical digital disk.[1]

Video Disk. High-density videodisks based on optical technology emerged originally as an alternative to videotape. These disks feature a recording "track" similar to that of phonograph records. Video image data are converted frame by frame into digital representation and recorded onto the recording track. The track is permanently etched wherever a "1" bit appears in the digital data. The playback is performed by optical means, where ones or zeros are determined by the reflective return signal of a small laser light source that scans the recorded track. The digital image is converted to analog video format as the track is read, and the analog signal is played back on a video monitor. All data is recorded within the video (and audio) format of broadcast video (NTSC format).

Videodisks are ideal in a situation involving many copies of the same source material. A expensive master disk is produced, and relatively inexpensive copies can be replicated for economical distribution to multiple sites. This technology provides storage capacity of approximately 50,000 images per side.

Video disk technology offers an alternative to microfilm or microfiche as a storage medium for large data bases in applications where access is required at a large number of sites. The master disk can be generated from either video or film source data. The advantages over film storage include (1) Video disks are physically more rigid than film and far less likely to be damaged or to cause mechanical problems in the retrieval system. (2) Video disk storage is significantly more compact than microfilm or microfiche storage. (3) The video disk playback mechanism is widely available on commercially available consumer-oriented equipment. The main limitation for the storage of image data is the limitation to NTSC video formats, both in terms of spatial and radiometric resolution.

CD-ROM. Compact audio disks have emerged as a commercially viable alternative to analog recordings. These disks are used to store digitized audio signals, and audio playback is achieved through the use of compact disk (CD) players designed to convert the digitized signal back into analog audio signals. CDs are 4 3/4 inches in diameter, and provide sufficient digital storage for 75 minutes of stereo audio playback. The storage and readback of digital data from these disks is achieved in a manner similar to the videodisks described above.

The CD media can be used to store any type of digital information, not just digitized audio signals. The computer industry is now capitalizing on that fact, and producing peripheral equipment designed to read digital data stored on CDs. CDs designed to be used for digital computer data storage applications are generally referred to as compact disk-read only memory (CD-ROM).

The advantage of CD-ROM over video disk is the generality of data storage that can be achieved using the CD technology. CD-ROM can be used for generalized storage of digital data, and is not limited to NTSC-compatible video data storage. It is similar to video disk in that it is cost effective in applications in which wide distribution of a data base to a large number of separate users is required. CD-ROM can be used to store text information, image data of varying formats, and other digital data. Standards governing data format are emerging, and storage capacities of 600 megabytes per disk is the current standard. This corresponds to over 500 images (1024 square, 8 bits per image) of capacity on a small compact disk.

Optical Digital Disk. Commercially viable optical disk storage media for high-capacity high-density storage of digital data are now emerging. These disks provide approximately 1 gigabyte (1×10^9 bytes) of storage per side on a 12-inch disk. Other formats in the process of development include both a 5 1/4-inch and 14-inch format.

This medium is designed for the digital computer peripheral mass storage marketplace. At the current time, this technology is write once-read many (WORM) technology. Digital data can be stored onto the optical disk, and then read at any time, but the data cannot be erased from the medium. These disks are not replicated from a master disk. Instead, each disk is used directly as a computer peripheral, with data entered onto the disk as dictated by the applications requirements and objectives. Copies of optical digital disks are made in a manner similar to duplicating digital magnetic tapes. The technology is most relevant to applications involving large volumes of archival storage of digital data over long periods of time.

The technology by which digital data is stored on optical digital disks varies with the manufacturer. Most techniques rely on changes of reflectivity within a material deposited on a stable substrate, located below transparent protective material. The data is recorded and read using small lasers in the read/write heads of the drives.

Use of Optical Disk Technology for Distributed Image Data Base Applications. The use of inexpensive optical disk storage media makes possible the distribution of a full image data base to a large number of users located at a variety of remote locations. The remote users can access a central computer facility that maintains the image catalog for user query and interrogation, and the central computer can issue retrieval commands to the optical disk storage device located at the user's facility. This concept is illustrated in Figure 5-18. The user generates a query, the central computer generates display commands that control the device at the user facility, and the remote user views the imagery that meets the search criteria.

DISPLAY SYSTEM CALIBRATION

It is necessary to strive for consistency in image display so that the same digital data values are consistently perceived as the same displayed intensity. It is necessary to establish a relationship between digital intensity values and output intensity for every display device and to maintain that relationship as consistently as possible over long periods of time. These relationships are referred to as *calibration curves,* and maintenance of consistent calibration curves for every display device is the only

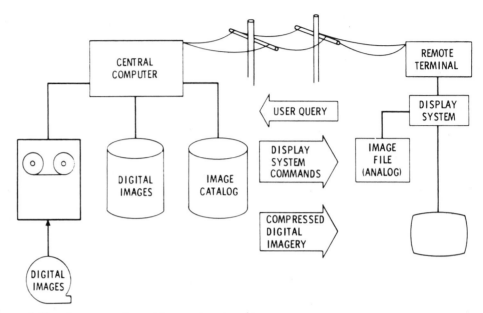

Figure 5-18. Interrogation of image data base by a remote user with resident analog display system.

way to guarantee that the same image will appear the same to a user when displayed at two different times or on two different display devices.

The calibration curve for black and white film recording is usually defined in terms of the relationship of digital intensity to density on the original negative after film exposure and film processing. The most common relationships established for black and white display on film are logarithmic or linear (i.e., the relationship between density on the original negative and input digital intensity values is either logarithmic or linear). A typical linear relationship is shown in Figure 5-19.

The particular relationship for black and white film recording is determined by the combined effect of the film recorder, the choice of film, and the photo processing. The desired calibration curve is usually difficult to attain by adjusting these three components, and a contrast manipulation look-up table is normally used within the film recording device to manipulate input gray shades into the desired relationship. Gray wedges are used to determine the relationship between digital intensity and film density. Most image processing systems also annotate images with gray steps so that the actual relationship between digital intensity and gray shade on an image product can be determined subjectively on each photographic product. This topic is addressed in detail in Chapter 7.

The density on the original negative is not the only parameter that can be used to calibrate black and white film recording and photo-processing systems. Other parameters that can be used to maintain photo-product calibration standards include density values measured on second-generation negatives, reflectance values derived from a first-generation print made from the original negative, and density or transmittance values measured from positive transparencies.

It is normally necessary to develop special calibration targets and to record and process them periodically to determine whether the film recording process is within the calibration specification for the particular facility. If deviation from the calibration standard is observed, it may be necessary to adjust the film recorder or the

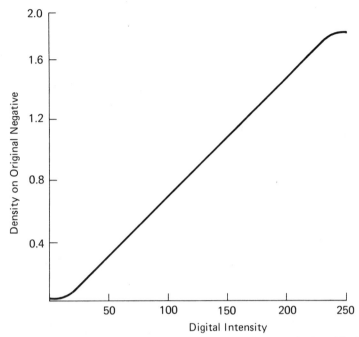

Figure 5-19.   Typical film recording calibration curve. A linear relationship between density on original negative and digital intensity is maintained, except for regions near black and white where the film saturates as shown.

photo-processing procedures or to modify the look-up table within the film recorder in order to reestablish system calibration.

Calibration of color film recording is more complex. Color calibration usually is based on calibration targets generated with known hue and saturation steps (see Chapter 4), and the relationships between film density, transmittances, or print reflectances and digital values of hue and saturation are used to specify and control the calibration.

Similar calibration procedures must be developed for hard-copy image recording devices and for volatile display systems and their associated monitors. Most image processing systems will include more than one display device. When that is the case, an overall system calibration standard must be established and maintained. A system that includes a volatile display and a hard-copy output device must ensure that the user will receive a hard-copy version of the displayed image that matches the image he or she views on the volatile display. Volatile display devices and image recording devices must be calibrated and maintained so that consistent image rendition is achieved independent of the display medium that is used.

REFERENCE

1. McQueen, J. and R. W. Boss, *Videodisk and Optical Digital Disk Technologies and their Applications in Libraries, 1986 Update.* Chicago, American Library Association, 1986.

6
Image Processing Software Design Concepts

INTRODUCTION

This chapter deals with the details of designing a software system for digital image processing. The philosophy outlined in this chapter is based on the concept of separating the various required functions into a set of discrete software modules that fall within several broad categories, including the following:

Individual image processing modules. These modules perform the mathematical operations on digital images. They incorporate the various algorithms described in Chapters 3 and 4 as well as others not described in this text. Typical functions provided by image processing modules (IPMs) include contrast manipulation, filtering, and geometric transformation. These modules operate within a particular computer system and are supported by capabilities provided by the operating system resident on the computer. They may also be supported by other capabilities provided by software developed specifically to support image processing operations. The types of support software that may be available can be divided into the categories listed below.

General-purpose subroutines. A set of subroutines may be available that support a variety of operations required by most image processing modules. These support functions may include input/output (optimized for image data transfer), transfer of user requests to individual IPMs, and display packages that provide an interface between a processing module and a hardware display (volatile display, film recorder, etc.). These subroutines are used by individual processing modules as required, and development of a generalized set of subroutines can minimize the effort required to develop image processing applications software.

Image processing executive. A set of image processing modules can operate directly under control of the computer operating system provided by the manufacturer of the computer hardware. The user must then understand the operating system and must learn the operating system job-control language in order to perform image processing. Many users wishing to perform image processing and image analysis may not be familiar with the particular operating system or may not have had experience in computer processing of any sort. It is often desirable to create an executive program that supports user interaction with an image processing system. The executive can be written in a "user-friendly" manner; the communication with the user can be at a high level, enabling the user to describe functionally the image processing operations that are to be performed. The executive then translates the user requirements into a set of commands and data allocation job-control statements that are forwarded to the computer operating system for execution. The user is thus not required to learn the often complex details of operating system control functions and job-control language, and the executive translates the user's simple requests into the required operating system syntax.

Image data base management system (DBMS). This system provides the mechanism for cataloging, storing, retrieving, and annotating the set of images currently resident on a particular system. Ideally, the DBMS will be used (a) to control storage of digital image data on peripheral storage devices (disk and tape), (b) to maintain a catalog of all images currently available within a particular facility, (c) enter new images into the catalog as they are acquired, (d) catalog multiple versions of the same image as they are created by processing and enhancement of the initial version of the image, and (e) catalog and index all hard-copy photographic products produced by the image processing system. The DBMS should also retain image-related information for every image; this information may include data relating to the acquisition of the original image (e.g., sensor identification, filter position, shutter speed, film scanner device identification, etc.) and other data relating to an individual image (e.g., longitude and latitude coordinates, solar elevation angle, patient name for an X-ray or tomographic image, etc.). The DBMS provides the capability to annotate images produced on hard copy or on volatile display, based on user requests.

Computer operating system. The hardware manufacturer (or other source) provides a software operating system that includes the basic job control functions and data file management functions for the particular system. The manufacturer (or other source) also provides a set of compilers and assemblers for a variety of languages (e.g., FORTRAN, C, PASCAL, Assembly Language, etc.). The image processing system developed on a particular computer will be implemented and operated within constraints established by that operating system and the selection of a particular set of programming languages. The image processing system may take advantage of capabilities and languages provided by the operating system, or many of the capabilities may be revised or replaced by alternative capabilities that are optimized for image processing if they constrain performance or flexibility in image processing applications.

The various categories of software interact with each other in a variety of complex ways to achieve image processing. Figure 6-1 attempts to show the various interfaces that may exist within an image processing system that is performing processing on the basis of user requirements. Each element of the system can utilize capabilities provided by other elements as processing is performed. In the most successful software systems, the user is not aware of the complex interactions that occur between the various software components in response to processing requests. In the ideal system, the user simply provides a functional request (e.g., "Perform a linear stretch from 20 to 50 on the red image and display the result on monitor B") and then views the desired result that appears rapidly on the specified monitor. The user is unaware of the complex series of operations set into motion by rather simple and straightforward processing requests.

Figure 6-2 indicates the variety of operations initiated by a simple request to stretch an image. The computer operating system, the image processing executive, the DBMS, and the IPM that performs contrast enhancement all assume control of the processing at various stages and then interact with one another to perform the

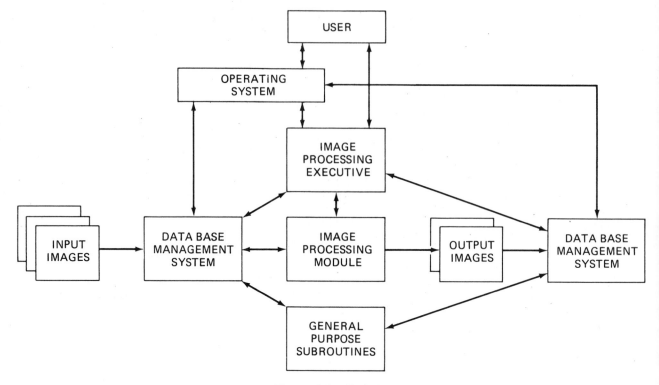

Figure 6-1. Software system interfaces.

operations initiated by the user's request. Interface files are generated to pass information between the various categories of software in the system. Figure 6-2 illustrates the need for creation of simple user interfaces with image processing systems. If users had to control every step of the actual flow of processing shown in Figure 6-2, communicating with the computer operating system and the various software components within the system at a detailed level, they would quickly become frustrated with the system and abandon their efforts.

This chapter describes design considerations for image processing modules, outlines the detailed design of digital formats used to store image data on tape or disk, and outlines design considerations for IPMs that are utilized interactively in conjunction with direct user input and volatile display systems. A full image processing software system is described at the end of this chapter. Chapter 7 deals with design considerations for image data base management systems and with the details of image annotation for image display of hard-copy image products.

The design concepts outlined in these two chapters are generally applicable to systems developed for medium- to large-scale mainframe computers and for minicomputers. Many of these concepts may also be applicable to systems implemented on microprocessors. Not all of the design guidelines presented here apply to microprocessor-based systems. Software development for microprocessor-based systems should accommodate the constraints and limitations imposed by that environment. Microprocessors are well suited for specific image processing applications and are widely used for a limited set of image processing applications. The material presented here is directed primarily toward the system designer who is concerned with implementation of a system that will provide a variety of flexible capabilities in a minicomputer or medium- to large-scale mainframe computing environment. The

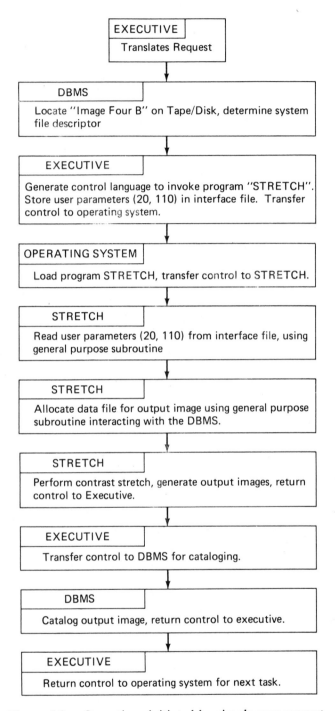

Figure 6-2.   Operations initiated by simple user request.

subject of image processing in a personal computer environment is addressed in Chapter 9.

DIGITAL FORMATS FOR IMAGE STORAGE

The detailed image processing operations performed within a general-purpose image processing system are performed by a set of IPMs. Each module is designed to perform a single function or a set of functions with options determined by the user. The IPMs can be used as building blocks to create a series of desired image processing operations for a specific application. The concept of modularity is illustrated in Figure 6-3. The programs called "program 1" and "program 2" perform the image manipulation operations desired by the user. It is generally desirable to design IPMs that can process images from a variety of sources, images with a variable number of spectral components, and images of varying size. One of the easiest ways to achieve this design goal is through definition of a general format used to store digital images on tape or disk. All programs within a particular image processing system are then designed to read images in that standard format and to produce processed imagery in the same generalized standard format.

An image processing system design based on a generalized common digital image format can accommodate a variety of image types and sizes. This concept is illustrated in Figure 6-3. Digital imagery is produced by a variety of sources or sensors, as discussed in Chapter 2. The software system can accommodate imagery produced by different systems by including a set of IPMs that are used to convert digital imagery from the format in which it is provided by a sensor or scanner into the generalized format used throughout the software system. These conversion modules, called *logging programs,* are the first programs to be run in any processing sequence. In Figure 6-3, two choices are shown at the start of the processing sequence. If the image is delivered on magnetic tape in some particular format, the logging program converts the data from the original format to the standard system format. If the image source is a film scanner or video digitizer connected directly to the computer system, the logging program will read the digitized data and output a sampled image in the standard system format.

The definition of a standard image format also provides generality in the selection of output medium for the processed image. The software system can include a series of format-conversion modules that read an image in standard system format and convert it into appropriate format for display or hard-copy recording. This is also illustrated in Figure 6-3.

Once a standard format is established, a set of system-level subroutines is written, to be used by all the IPMs. These subroutines perform the operations associated with reading and writing standard format images, and they provide important pa-

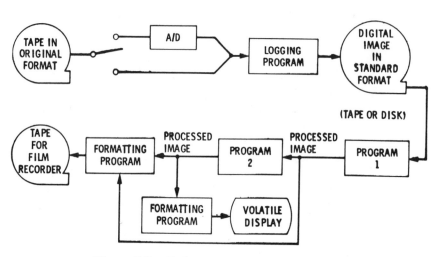

Figure 6-3.   Software system modularity.

rameters (e.g., image size and number of spectral channels) to the applications programs.

One recommended design of a standard image format is shown in Figure 6-4. Each digital image is stored as a single file on tape (or a single disk data set containing multiple records on disk). The first record of the file is a "header record" containing a variety of information, including the size of the image, the number of spectral channels, the number of bytes per pixel, etc. This record will be discussed in detail later in this section. The digital pixel data follow the header record and are stored line by line, with one (logical) record per line of image data. For efficiency, the digital pixel data are often "blocked," minimizing the number of end-of-record gaps within a tape file and maximizing the use of each track on a disk storage device. Blocking factors are discussed at the end of this section.

Contents of Header Record

The header record is designed to provide a consistent means of storing image-associated data required by applications processing modules. There are several classes of data that can be stored in a header record. The possible classes of header data are described below; they are listed here as examples of data classes that can be established by the software system designer. The image format descriptor class is usually found in most digital image formats.

Image Format Descriptor.   Includes information regarding the size of the image, the number of spectral channels, and the format in which the pixel data are stored. Parameters that should be included in this descriptor include the following:

Image size: number of lines and samples.
Number of spectral channels.
Pixel code: includes the number of bytes per pixel and an indicator of the data

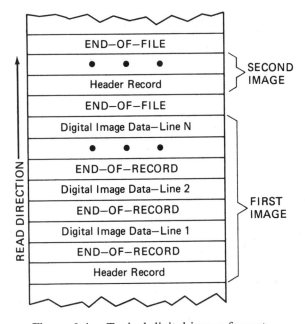

Figure 6-4.   Typical digital image format.

format in which the pixel data are stored. The possible formats include (1) unsigned binary integer, (2) single precision floating point, (3) double precision floating point, (4) complex data, etc.

Tape or disk blocking factor: the number of logical records contained within each physical record.

Image-Associated Data. This section of the header record is normally in the same format for specific sets of images. As an example, all LANDSAT TM images processed within a particular system would have the same format for the image-associated data section of the header record, but images acquired from a film scanner and processed on the same software system may have a different format for the image-associated data. The type of information that can be stored as image-associated data within a header record can include the following:

Identification of the data source (e.g., LANDSAT 5, film scanner B, etc.)

Longitude/latitude/solar elevation angle/camera viewing angle (for remotely sensed imagery)

Information extracted from telemetry returned with remotely sensed imagery (camera temperature, filter position, shutter speed, ground receiving station identification, day of mission, spacecraft time, etc.)

Processing History. It may be desirable to add information describing the processing performed on each image to the header record as the processing occurs so that the final output version of the processed image has a history of the processing appended to it. The information can include the following:

Names of programs used to process the image, in the sequence in which they were executed

Identification of the version of each program used

Parameters used by each processing module

Image Histogram. It may be desirable to store the image histogram as part of the header record. This enables IPMs to perform image manipulation operations based on histogram analysis directly, without computing the histogram. It also provides histogram data for image display and output formatting programs that may need access to the data for display and annotation purposes.

User-Supplied Annotation. The user may wish to append descriptive information to a digital image, either when the image is entered into the system via the logging program or at some stage of the processing. This type of information can be incorporated in the header record.

The physical header record can consist of a set of logical records; it should be designed to accommodate a variable number of records for each class of data. One design of a header record format is shown in Figure 6-5. The header record can be of fixed length (e.g., 1,800 bytes) and can be divided into logical subdivisions (e.g., 72 bytes). There can be more than one header record preceding the digital pixel data, depending on the volume of data associated with a particular image. Each 72-byte logical record contains a descriptor indicating which of the several classes of data is contained in the logical record. These are shown in byte position 72 of each

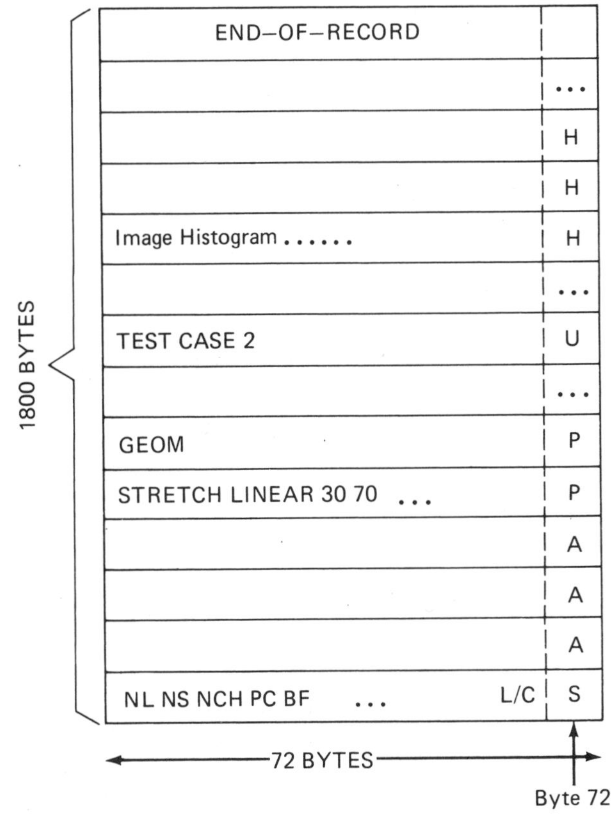

END—OF—RECORD	
	...
	H
	H
Image Histogram	H
	...
TEST CASE 2	U
	...
GEOM	P
STRETCH LINEAR 30 70 ...	P
	A
	A
	A
NL NS NCH PC BF ... L/C	S

1800 BYTES

72 BYTES

Byte 72

Figure 6-5. Typical design of image header record.

logical record in Figure 6-5. The descriptors shown in Figure 6-5 correspond to the following classes of data:

S	Image format descriptor (mandatory in this sample format)
A	Image-associated data (may or may not be present)
P	Processing history (may or may not be present)
U	User-supplied annotation (may or may not be present)
H	Image histogram (may or may not be present)

The first logical subrecord shown in Figure 6-5 contains the image format descriptor data; it also contains an indicator in byte 71 that indicates whether additional header records follow this first record. If byte 71 contains an ''L,'' this is the last header record; if byte 71 contains a ''C,'' the next record in the file is another header record. This convention can be followed for all subsequent header records, with an ''L'' in byte 71 indicating the last header record.

Figure 6-5 contains additional examples of typical contents of each of the data types described in this section. The header record is usually written in ASCII or EBCDIC characters, although specific fields (e.g., the image histogram) may contain binary data. Use of ASCII or EBCDIC allows output formatting routines to easily extract the information contained in the header records for annotation of output imagery.

The header record is usually generated by the logging program that converts digital image data into the standard system format. Figure 6-6 illustrates the functional operation of the logging program. Note that the logging program often requires access to a variety of data sources in addition to the digital image data. This is particularly true when the image-related data are stored in data files that are separate from the image data file provided as input to the system.

Tape and Disk Blocking Factors

Digital image pixel intensity data can be stored on magnetic tape line by line, with each physical record corresponding to a single digitized line of pixel intensity data. When this format is selected, every digitized line of image data is followed by an end-of-record (EOR) gap that is typically 0.75 inches long. An 8-bit image that is 512 pixels square and is recorded as a single spectral component would occupy 1.07 inches of 9-track tape for every line if it is recorded at a density of 1600 bits per inch (bpi):

$$(512 \text{ bytes/record}) \times (1 \text{ inch}/1600 \text{ bytes}) + .75'' \text{ EOR gap} = 1.07''$$

The total length of tape required to store this image is

$$512 \text{ lines} \times 1.07 \text{ inches/line} = 548 \text{ inches (approximately 46 feet).}$$

A large amount of tape can be saved by *blocking* digital image data on tape. When data are blocked on tape, each physical record on the tape is divided into a set of *n* logical records. Figure 6-7 illustrates one method of blocking a 512 by 512 image onto tape. Each physical record contains 2,048 bytes, enough to accommodate four lines of image data. Each physical record thus contains four logical records, and a *blocking factor* of 4:1 has been achieved. The blocking factor is entered into the system header record so that each applications program can determine the

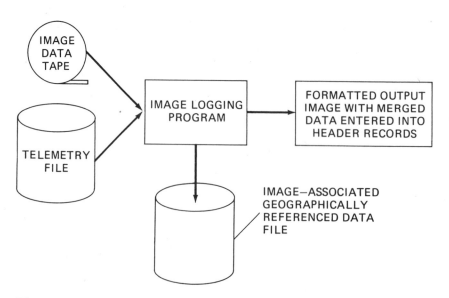

Figure 6-6. Functional operation of image logging program.

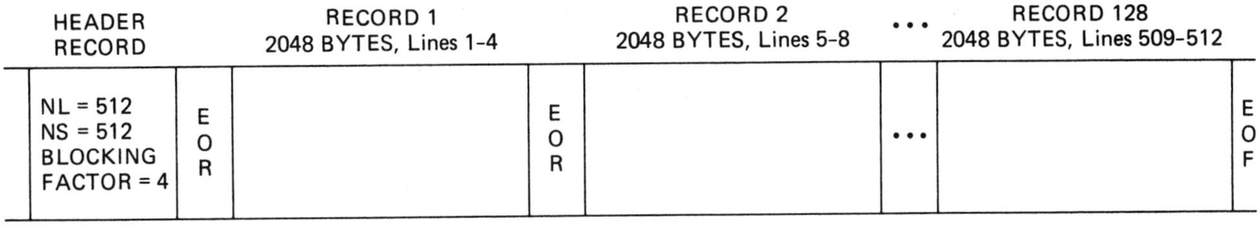

HEADER RECORD		RECORD 1 2048 BYTES, Lines 1–4		RECORD 2 2048 BYTES, Lines 5–8	...	RECORD 128 2048 BYTES, Lines 509–512	
NL = 512 NS = 512 BLOCKING FACTOR = 4	E O R		E O R		...		E O F

Figure 6-7. Illustration of blocked tape format.

physical and logical location of an individual line of image data within the tape records.

The 4:1 blocking factor illustrated in Figure 6-7 will result in a significant saving of space when this image is stored on 9-track 1600 bpi tape. Each logical record will require 2.03 inches of tape:

$$(512 \text{ bytes/logical record}) \times (4 \text{ logical records/1 physical record}) \times$$
$$(1 \text{ inch/1600 bytes}) + .75'' \text{ EOR gap} = 2.03''$$

The total image will require $(512/4) \times 2.03'' = 260$ inches (approximately 22 feet). The 4:1 blocking factor saves approximately 24 feet of tape relative to the unblocked format.

Tape blocking also saves program execution time, since the number of records read from (or written to) tape is reduced. The only drawback to tape blocking is that the size of the memory buffers within computer memory must be increased to acommodate the larger record sizes that result from tape blocking. Particular care should be taken when operating with virtual storage computer operating systems. Generation of large storage buffers within a virtual storage structure can increase the input/output overhead associated with a particular image transfer operation, since the virtual system may in fact generate a large amount of swapping between real memory locations and the peripheral disk storage that is used to accommodate the overflow from main storage.

Optimal utilization of disk storage devices for image storage can also result in significant increases in efficiency. Disks usually store data within tracks of fixed size (typically on the order of 7,200 bytes). The image processing software system should allocate disk storage on the basis of an optimal assignment of image lines to physical tracks on the disk. As many image lines as possible should be stored on each physical track. As an example, if a track size is 7,200 bytes and an image is 512 × 512 8-bit pixels, then 14 lines of pixel data can be stored on each physical track. Many image processing algorithms operate sequentially, line by line, through the image. If image data are optimally stored on disk storage devices, a single head movement to address a particular physical track will provide a block of lines to the IPM with a single disk access.

The ideal image processing system design will allocate the functions of optimizing storage on disk or tape to a set of general-purpose subroutines or to the DBMS component of the system. This frees the applications programmer from the need to design and optimize details of image storage and provides him or her with a general-purpose capability that can be incorporated into many different applications processing modules.

IMAGE PROCESSING PROGRAM MODULE DESIGN CONCEPTS

Basic Module Structure and System-Level Subroutines

This section discusses the design considerations associated with development of individual image processing modules. An IPM is a program designed to perform a particular operation on one or more input images. IPMs should be written as parameter-driven routines and should incorporate a variety of options that can be selected by the user to provide maximum flexibility. Centralization of image processing functions into a minimum number of highly flexible IPMs minimizes the effort associated with learning to operate an image processing system and maintaining the software resident on the system.

Figure 6-8 contains a top-level flowchart of an IPM written to perform contrast enhancement. The double boxes indicate operations that are performed in general-purpose system-level subroutines; these subroutines provide basic input/output operations capability and can be used by many IPMs. Use of standard system-level subroutines for operations required by many IPMs provides standardization of common functions throughout a set of applications programs resident on a particular image processing system.

A useful set of system level subroutines might include the following:

TLABEL: Reads headers (see previous section) and returns a set of data items extracted from the image header record to the calling program. These parameters can include the image size, data format of the pixel data in the image, image-associated data, histogram data, user-supplied data, and processing history data.

OPEN: Ensures that tape or disk storage devices are available for input/output of image data. May also read header record of images used as input and transfer header data to the calling program. May also write header record onto tape or disk as the first step in generating the output image resulting from processing to be performed by the IPM issuing the subroutine call.

READ, WRITE: Read or write full image or specified image segment to or from auxiliary storage devices (tape or disk). These routines handle the detailed translation from image coordinates into physical location of image data within tape or disk files. They handle the details of the translation on the basis of the blocking factors associated with the packing of logical records into physical records, as described in the last section.

GETPAR: Transfers parameters controlling the processing from the image processing executive or operating system job control stream to the individual IPM.

HIST: Computes the histogram of a full image or specified image segment.

LABEL: Generates header record for an image created by the calling IPM.

CONVERT: Provides conversion between binary, EBCDIC, and ASCII formats.

NCONVERT: Converts numerical pixel data from one format to another (byte, halfword integer, floating point, etc.

DISPLAY: Provides interface with hardware display systems. Transfers image data, graphics data, cursor control data, and other data between main computer memory and image display device.

The applications programmer is able to concentrate on the design details of the image processing algoriths if a general-purpose set of system level subroutines is

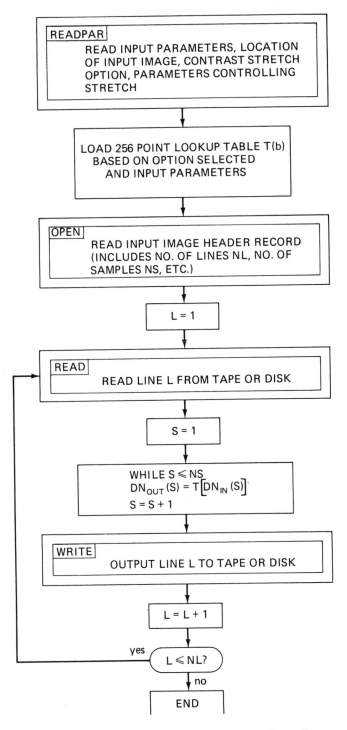

READPAR
READ INPUT PARAMETERS, LOCATION
OF INPUT IMAGE, CONTRAST STRETCH
OPTION, PARAMETERS CONTROLLING
STRETCH

LOAD 256 POINT LOOKUP TABLE T(b)
BASED ON OPTION SELECTED
AND INPUT PARAMETERS

OPEN
READ INPUT IMAGE HEADER RECORD
(INCLUDES NO. OF LINES NL, NO. OF
SAMPLES NS, ETC.)

L = 1

READ
READ LINE L FROM TAPE OR DISK

S = 1

WHILE S ≤ NS
$DN_{OUT}(S) = T[DN_{IN}(S)]$
S = S + 1

WRITE
OUTPUT LINE L TO TAPE OR DISK

L = L + 1

yes   L ≤ NL?

no

END

Figure 6-8.   Contrast-enhancement program flow diagram.

available. In the example shown in Figure 6-8, the applications programmer uses
subroutine calls to achieve input, output, and parameter transfer from user to the
IPM. The main effort involved in generating the IPM for contrast enhancement is
centered on design and coding of the image processing operations that are to be
performed, not on designing and coding the detailed system level interfaces required

to support the input/output functions. The general-purpose set of subroutines thus minimizes the time required to develop applications software.

Options and Parameters

The system designer should try to isolate operations common to a large number of applications within a single general-purpose IPM. As an example, contrast enhancement is achieved by loading a look-up table that provides the transformation of input intensity levels into a different set of output intensity levels (see Chapter 3). Other functions that are also achieved through a table look-up, such as contouring and bit-clipping, should also be implemented as options within the IPM that performs contrast enhancement. Even within the contrast-enhancement algorithm, a variety of options are available (e.g., linear, "ramp CDF," etc.), and each of these should be available by specifying an option to a general-purpose contrast-enhancement IPM rather than by invoking different IPMs to perform different types of enhancement.

Table 6-1 shows one version of the options that might be available within the contrast-enhancement module that is flowcharted in Figure 6-8. Figure 6-9 shows the logic required within the module if the available options are those listed in Table 6-1. Figure 6-9 thus represents an expanded view of the functions that are performed within the second box of the top-level flow diagram in Figure 6-8. The user invokes the preferred option by specifying a keyword that indicates the option desired. The user also may be required to enter additional parameters controlling the processing, depending on the option that is selected. The program operates with a "default" mode; if the user enters no keyword, the program assumes that a linear stretch from 100 to 200 is desired and performs that operation. The default mode is normally used to enable the most frequently requested program option to be invoked as a default. If no keywords specifying a particular option are supplied by the user, the program is written to perform the most commonly utilized function based on the designer's experience and judgment.

Figure 6-9 illustrates the fact that option selection affects only the actual numerical values stored in the look-up table. The other operations of the program perform independently of the entries actually stored within the table. In this manner, a variety of operations, each of which can be implemented by a table look-up, have been provided by a single IPM operating on the basis of user-provided option selection. This design is superior to an alternate design concept in which individual programs with different names might be used to perform each individual operation. Development of an option-drive flexible module also enables incorporation of additional

TABLE 6-1 CONTRAST-ENHANCEMENT PROGRAM OPTIONS

PARAMETER OR KEYWORD	FUNCTION	DEFAULT
LINEAR,MIN,MAX	Perform linear stretch between MIN and MAX	LINEAR,100,200
EXPONENTIAL,A,B	Perform exponential stretch, $b_{out} = A \exp (B\ b_{in})$	LINEAR stretch is performed
CLIP,n	Clip n most significant bits	LINEAR stretch is performed

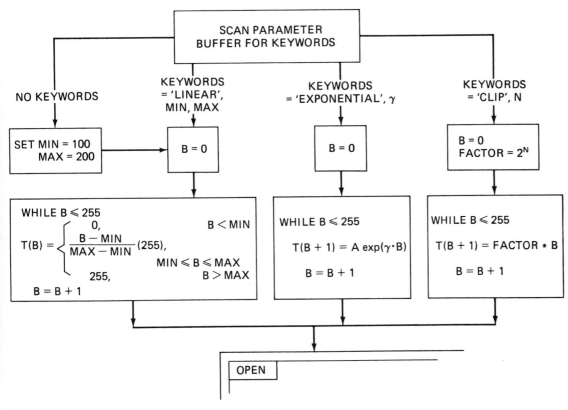

Figure 6-9. Detail of table generation based on selection of contrast-enhancement option.

options easily, without the need of developing an entire new program simply to add an additional enhancement technique to the system.

A more complex example of the options available within a general-purpose IPM is shown in Table 6-2. The parameters and options listed in Table 6-2 are some of the options available on the ASTRTCH2 program within the Jet Propulsion Laboratory's VICAR image processing system. ASTRTCH2 performs contrast enhancement on the basis of analysis of the image histogram, as described in Chapter 3. A

TABLE 6-2 ASTRTCH2 Program Parameters

PARAMETER	FUNCTION	DEFAULT
EXCLUDE,b_1,b_2	Excludes digital intensities between b_1 and b_2 from histogram computation	$b_1 = 0$, $b_2 = 0$
LPERCENT,p_{low}, HPERCENT,p_{high}	Define percent of histogram to be saturated in performing linear stretch	$p_{low} = p_{high} = 3\%$
SMOOTH	Perform ramp CDF stretch	Automatic linear stretch
COMP	Complement output image	No complement
AREA,ℓ_1,ℓ_2,s_1,s_2	Compute histogram from rectangle of pixels between lines ℓ_1 and ℓ_2 and samples s_1 and s_2	Use full image
SPEED,NSPD	Use only every NSPDth pixel in performing histogram computation	NSPD = 1

variety of options are available, and default values are provided for the parameters associated with each individual option selected.

Input/Output Buffering

Image processing operations fall into two general classes, based on the ratio of the time required for the mathematical computations to the time required to perform the input/output operations associated with the particular algortihm. Operations that require a substantial amount of processing time (and thus require a significant amount of resources from the central processing unit, or CPU) are called *CPU-bound*. The speed at which a CPU-bound task can be completed is constrained by the speed at which the required mathematical operations can be performed. An operation whose speed is limited by the rate at which image data can be transferred between peripheral storage devices and the CPU is called an input/output bound, or *I/O-bound,* operation.

Contrast enhancement normally is an I/O-bound operation. The arithmetic operations required to perform a contrast enhancement are usually achieved by table look-up procedures, and these can be performed extremely quickly for each pixel. The computation is usually completed for a block of pixel data well before the system can access and deliver the next block of pixel data to the processor or transfer the processed data out to a peripheral storage device to make room in memory for the next block to be processed. The processor must wait to perform the contrast enhancement on the next block of pixel data until (1) the system has transferred out the last block of processed data and/or (2) the system has transferred the first elements of the next block of data into main memory for processing. The speed at which the data transfers are achieved determines the speed at which the total image processing operation will occur.

Fourier transformation is an example of a CPU-bound operation. If a one-dimensional transform is to be computed for a single line of image data, it is likely that the required data transfers between peripheral storage and memory will occur faster than the actual computations associated with the transformation. The system's I/O devices will be ready to accept or transfer data to or from peripheral storage before the CPU has completed the mathematical operations on the data. The speed of processing in this case will thus be determined by the speed of CPU rather than by the speed of the data transfer operations.

The total time required to perform an image processing operation is determined by the *throughput speed.* For most image processing applications, the throughput speed will be approximately the same as either the input/output data transfer time associated with the particular operation (I/O-bound operations) or the CPU time for CPU-bound operations. This section describes a double buffering technique that is useful in minimizing the throughput time for I/O-bound jobs. The technique is useful in situations where storage space in main memory is available.

Double buffering is a technique that achieves a "look ahead" capability when transferring image data from peripheral storage to main memory. Two storage buffers are established in memory, each large enough to accommodate a full line of image data (or a full logical record if the image data are blocked). Two things occur when an applications program issues a "read next line" request: (1) A flag is reset to indicate which of the two buffers is currently filled with data ready for computation. (2) A physical read operation is initiated from the disk or tape unit containing the input image, transferring the next sequential line (or logical record) of pixel data from peripheral unit into the alternate buffer in memory. The image processing operation utilizes the data that are available within the main memory buffer from the previous physical read, and the transfer of the next sequential block of image data from peripheral storage is overlapped with the image processing operation in progress. The image processing operations thus occur at maximum speed, without waiting for data transfer to occur; meanwhile, the next image line is transferred into the alternate memory buffer, where it will be available when the applications program issues the next "read next line" request.

Figure 6-10 presents a time line for the double buffering mechanism. The FLAG variable is used to indicate the next memory buffer to be used for processing operations. It alternates in value between 1 and 2, changing value each time a physical transfer of data from peripheral device to memory is completed. The two buffers are denoted as BUFFER(1,j) and BUFFER(2,j), where the index j is used to denote pixel sample position along each line, and BUFFER(1,j) or BUFFER(2,j) is determined by the value of FLAG each time the program issues a "read" request.

INTERACTIVE PROGRAM MODULE DESIGN CONSIDERATIONS

An interactive IPM is designed to be directly controlled by a user through commands and auxiliary input entered through a keyboard, terminal, or other interactive device during execution. An interactive module also provides direct and immediate output results for display on a volatile display device. Many IPM's are designed to be run in a batch mode, with no user intervention possible during program execution. Noninteractive modules can be executed as part of a batch job stream or can be initiated by a user at a terminal, but no user intervention is possible during execution, and immediate visual display of processed results is normally not available. This section deals with design considerations for interactive modules that are specifically intended to be highly responsive and user-driven and also intended to provide immediate visual display of the results of the interaction between user and computer system.

This section begins with a summary of the various types of input devices used to control processing in an interactive environment. The general structure and operation of interactive IPMs is outlined, and the various techniques that can be used to

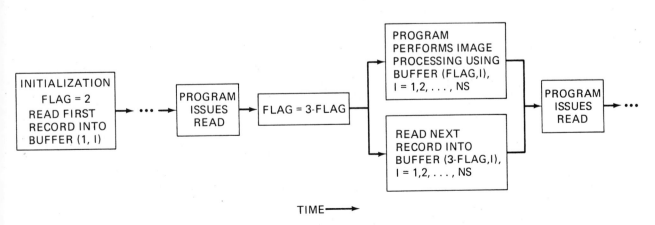

Figure 6-10. Double buffering for image input.

control processing with a trackball or joystick unit are outlined. The use of menus to control processing is described at the end of this section.

Input Devices

Keyboard/Cathode Ray Tube (CRT).   These devices are standard computer-compatible terminal devices used to control processing from a user location. The user enters commands and parameters, using a typewriterlike keyboard, and the computer can display alphanumeric data on the CRT. Terminals used for the control of image processing need not differ from terminals used for general-purpose communication with computer systems in a wide variety of applications. However, there are terminal features that can prove useful in image processing, including the following:

Special-Purpose Function Keys. Most terminals include an extra set of keys that supplement the standard typewriterlike keyboard. Each key of the special set forwards a unique character to the computer when the key is struck. Most special-purpose keys can generate more than one input character, through the use of "shift" or "numeric" keys that can be depressed at the same time a function key is depressed. Special-purpose function keys can be used to control program options and choices during image processing program execution. For example, selection of a single function key could dictate the selection of a particular enhancement option in a given program module. The use of function key to avoid the need for entering a series of text commands to an IPM provides an efficient and "user-friendly" interface.

Graphics. Many terminals can display both alphanumeric and graphics data on the same CRT. This can be extremely useful in image processing. One of the most common uses of graphics display during image processing is image histogram display. A graphics display can be used to show an image histogram and to indicate the modified histogram that will result after a contrast manipulation. Graphics terminals can also be used to display digital filters that are applied to image data, to show the intensity distribution along line segments within an image, and display the multispectral histograms derived from the components of a multispectral image. Many image display systems also include graphics planes, as described in Chapter 5. The use of graphics terminals can supplement the graphics display capability provided with image display systems, and it also enables display of image data without overwriting image data with graphics information.

Color. Alphanumeric terminals and graphics terminals with color display capability are now readily available from commercial sources. Color can be used to discriminate between the types of data displayed on a CRT. It can also be used effectively in user communication. Display of information in particular colors helps in "prompting" the user for required input and alerting the user to specific situations arising during program execution; it is also used for a variety of other purposes. Color is especially useful in displaying graphics data associated with multispectral imagery, since a particular color can be used to display data associated with one particular multispectral component.

Mice, Trackballs, and Joysticks.   These devices are normally used to position a cursor, or special visual indicator, on a display screen. Most image display devices provide the capability of displaying a particular marker at any pixel location within the display format. The size and shape of the marker are usually determined by the user or programmer. These markers are called *cursors,* and a variety of options for cursor size and shape are possible, as described in Chapter 5.

The basic concept of mouse/trackball/joystick unit operation was described in Chapter 5. Basically, the mouse/trackball/joystick provides a pair of (*x,y*) coordinates that are read by the computer system through an interface with the display system. The coordinates generated by these units can also be used to control processing in an interactive environment. Several examples of the use of cursor coordinates for control of image processing are included in this chapter, in a special section dealing with that topic.

General Structure and Operation of Interactive Modules

The central processing component of an interactive IPM is shown within the dashed box in Figure 6-11. There are usually three main elements within the module. One element interprets user input provided by one or more of the available variety of user input devices described above. The second element performs the actual image processing and manipulation. The third element controls display of processed imagery and other output; it includes the instructions used to send information in

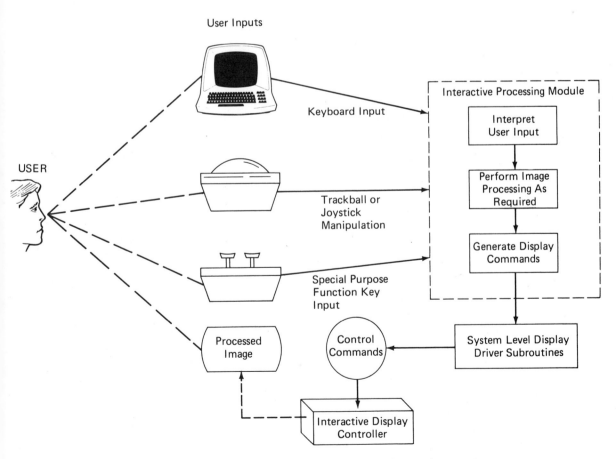

Figure 6-11.   Interactive processing module functional overview.

alphanumeric or graphical form to a variety of output devices and the terminals and displays at the user location.

The interactive IPM utilizes a set of general-purpose system-level subroutines during execution. These subroutines are designed to service the interfaces with the user input devices (terminals, graphics displays, etc.) and the output display devices (digital image displays, graphics overlays, etc.).

Interactive modules are designed to achieve minimum response time between input of a user request and display of the processing results on a volatile display. The interactive module and the supporting system-level subroutines should make maximum use of capabilities provided within the hardware components interfaced to the computer system. As one example, use of the table look-up feature in digital display hardware to implement a contrast manipulation can result in a total elapsed time of less than 1 second between the time a user requests a particular contrast stretch and the appearance of the enhanced image on a volatile display. Use of other local display capabilities can result in similar rapid response to user input requests.

Interactive IPMs should also make maximum use of capabilities provided within the input devices. The input of user commands, options, and parameters should be designed to require a minimum of typing on the part of the user. In addition, the command structure used for interactive processing should be simple, straightforward, and well suited to an environment characterized by users who may be unfamiliar with computer technology. The use of function keys, trackball or joystick units, and menu structures to control image processing should be maximized in order to minimize the effort required of an untrained user to learn to use the system.

Use of Manually Controlled Devices

Figure 6-12 indicates one use of a trackball unit to control image processing in an interactive environment. The analyst utilizes both a computer terminal and a trackball unit to control image processing in an interactive environment. The application shown in Figure 6-12 relates to water quality. LANDSAT imagery is used to determine the quality of water in a variety of lakes and to compare water quality determined from LANDSAT multispectral data with quality determined by direct chemical measurements. The cursor controlled by the trackball unit was initially used to indicate the approximate center of a lake within the LANDSAT scene. The cursor was also used to define a rectangle enclosing the lake; the rectangle was extracted from the LANDSAT scene, magnified, and displayed over the original scene on the image display. A binary mask was then generated, with white denoting pixels thought to be water and black denoting nonwater pixels, based on multispectral analysis. The cursor was then used to mark all water pixels extraneous to the lake of interest, and they are deleted from the binary mask.

This example illustrates several uses of a manually controlled device (MCD) such as a mouse, trackball, or joystick, within a single applications program. The specific utilization of the trackball at each point in time is determined from commands entered from the keyboard. MCDs can be employed in a variety of ways to control image processing operations. Some of the ways in which these devices can be used are listed below.

Contrast Manipulation. The (x,y) coordinate pairs read from an MCD position can be interpreted as the end points of a linear contrast stretch. As the MCD is

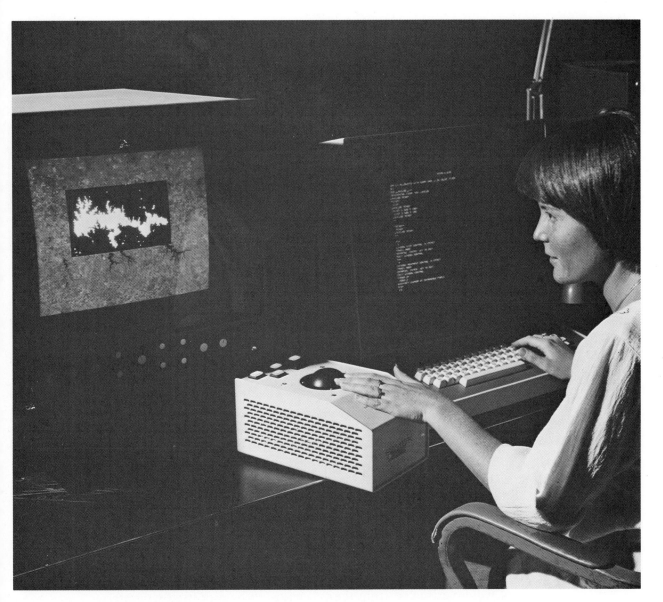

Figure 6-12.   Use of trackball to control interactive image processing (Jet Propulsion Laboratory).

moved, the degree of contrast enhancement changes, and use of the table look-up feature within the display hardware provides the capability of performing an "instant" stretch. The displayed image changes appearance as the MCD is manipulated. The coordinate pairs can also be used to control other types of contrast manipulation. The coordinates can control the centroid and width of a Gaussian stretch, the slope and offset of a linear stretch, or the upper and lower percentages of saturation in an automated linear enhancement based on the image histogram.

Plotting.   The MCD can be used to trace a line or curve through the image in conjunction with the cursor, and the digital intensity of the pixels lying on the traced profile can be plotted on a graphics display or on the graphics plane of an image display device. Figure 6-13 shows a plot of pixel intensities along a line segment selected with an MCD.

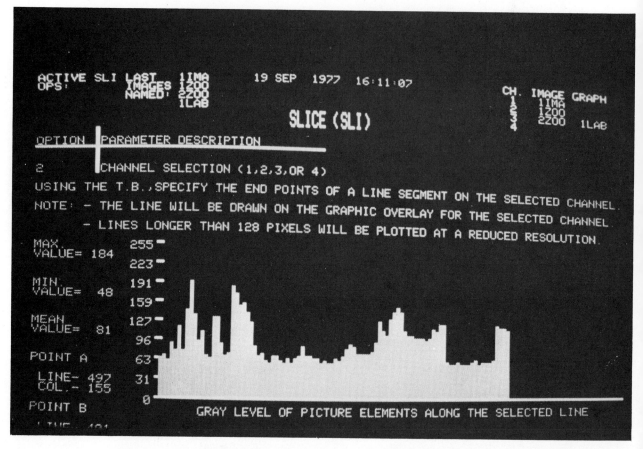

Figure 6-13. Plot of pixel intensity along a line segment drawn through an image, using a trackball/cursor unit (Unisys Defense Systems).

Shape Outlining. The motion of a cursor driven by an MCD can define a segment of an image for a variety of purposes. It may be desirable to determine the average digital intensity within the segment or the brightness distribution (histogram) within the segment. The segment may contain a particular feature of interest (e.g., a lake) that will be extracted from the full image to be processed separately.

Parameter Control. An MCD may be used in conjunction with the hardware cursor to define parameters for image processing. This can be achieved in a variety of ways. The cursor can be used to define the shape of a digital filter to be applied to an image. It can define the transfer function for a contrast manipulation. It can be used to indicate points within a graphical display of the image histogram that determine the input parameters for a contrast manipulation operation.

False-Color Manipulation. A cursor can be used to control the false-color display of digital intensity information. As one example, suppose a set of color transformations is stored within a display device look-up table, as shown in Figure 6-14. In this example, it is assumed that the adjacent colors stored in the look-up table are designed so that immediate neighbors in the table represent visually high-contrast color differences (e.g., red is stored next to yellow, purple next to gold, etc.). The example in Figure 6-14 assumes 8-bit input pixel digital intensities, and 255 different

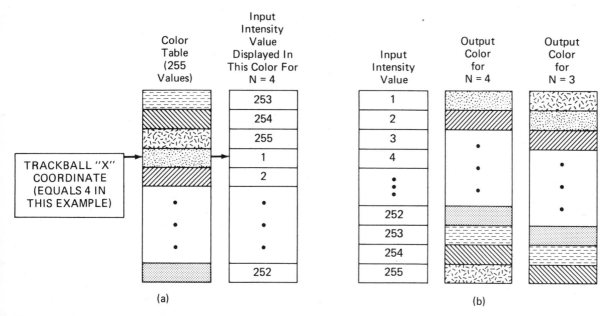

Figure 6-14.   Control of color look-up table using trackball. (*a*) Example showing relationship between prestored colors in table and input digital intensity values for a trackball coordinate equal to 4. (*b*) Relationship between input digital intensity values and colors assigned to those intensity values for different trackball coordinate values. Note significant variation in color assignment resulting from a change of only one step in trackball position.

colors are stored in the look-up table. If digital intensities from zero to 255 are transferred through the look-up table, the 255 colors will be transferred in sequence to the display device. An MCD can be used to modify the starting location of intensities transferred through the look-up table. One of the two coordinates read from the MCD can be used to change the starting location within the look-up table. If the coordinate is denoted as C, the lowest intensity value (zero) will be assigned the Cth color, the next intensity value (1) will be assigned the (C + 1)th color, etc. The motion of the MCD can be used to "roll" through the color look-up table. If a sequence of high-contrast color transitions is stored in the table, a small change in x-y coordinate will produce a very large visual change in the appearance of the false-color image on the display device. The MCD can be maneuvered until the region of interest is displayed in a desired false-color enhancement on the display screen.

Stereo Analysis.   MCDs can be utilized effectively in conjunction with hardware cursor capability in performing stereophotogrammetry. A stereo image pair can be displayed on a hardware device so that it can be viewed in stereo or three dimensions. The MCD can be used in conjunction with applications software to position a stereo cursor in three-dimensional space so that it appears in the proper location within the three-dimensional image. The software actually drives two cursors, one within each component of the stereo pair.

The MCD can be used to trace elevation profiles, as shown in the Viking Lander stereo pair in Figure 6-15. The graphics plane of a hardware display device is used to superimpose the stereo image of elevation profiles drawn along the surface of Mars, using a trackball-controlled cursor operated by a photogrammetrist viewing the scene in three dimensions. Each of the nearly vertical traces corresponds to a difference in azimuth bearing of 1° for the Viking Lander surface sampler arm

Figure 6-15.   Viking Lander 1 stereo pair acquired in July 1976. The vertical lines superimposed on the image lie approximately 4 inches apart on the surface and were generated from a trackball/cursor unit under control of a photogrammetrist viewing the scene on a stereo display (NASA/Jet Propulsion Laboratory)

located between the stereo camera pairs (see Figure 2-7). Figure 6-16 shows a series of isoelevation contours drawn with a trackball-controlled cursor and the graphics plane of a hardware display device.

Feature Correlation.   MCDs can be used with a cursor to mark common features within two views of the same area of an object. This is useful when one is performing image differencing, where two views of the same area are available that correspond to two different time periods. In general, the geometric references of the two images differ, and an MCD-controlled cursor can be used to mark or identify the same point within both images. Location of a series of common points within a pair of images can then be used to perform a geometric transformation of one of the images so that it is geometrically aligned with the second member of the pair. It is

Figure 6-16.   Viking Lander 1 stereo pair with isoelevation contours superimposed. The graphics data are overlaid so that they can be viewed in stereo on a stereo display system (Jet Propulsion Laboratory).

then possible to perform image differencing. The same type of procedure can also be used to compute elevation of isolated features within a stereo pair. The same feature is marked with a cursor that is controlled by an MCD, and a computation of the elevation of the feature can be performed if the reference geometry for both component images is known.

Menu-Driven Interactive Image Processing Systems

One technique that provides a simple user interface that can be learned with a minimum of training is the *menu*. At every point in the processing at which the user needs to make a decision, a "menu" is presented that includes a list of the options or choices available at that point. The user selects one of the options, usually by positioning a cursor next to the selection or by indicating the desired option through use of a special function key or numeric key on a computer terminal. Processing then proceeds, based on the option selected, and the user may be prompted for additional input (e.g., numerical values for parameters required by a particular algorithm).

A *tree-driven menu structure* is shown in Figure 6-17. A tree-drive system presents a series of menus to the user. The first menu may outline a series of general options that are available. Once one of the general options is selected, another menu appears, providing another set of choices relating only to the general option that has been selected initially. Figure 6-17 indicates some typical details that might be presented within menus associated with contrast manipulation. The first level of menu allows the user to select from a series of image processing functions (contrast manipulation, digital filtering, geometric transformation, etc.). A series of second-order menus is then available, and the second-order menu for contrast manipulation may present a choice of linear, Gaussian, or automated linear enhancement. If automated linear enhancement is selected, a third level menu may present a further selection of options (ramp CDF, saturation of upper and lower ends of the image histo-

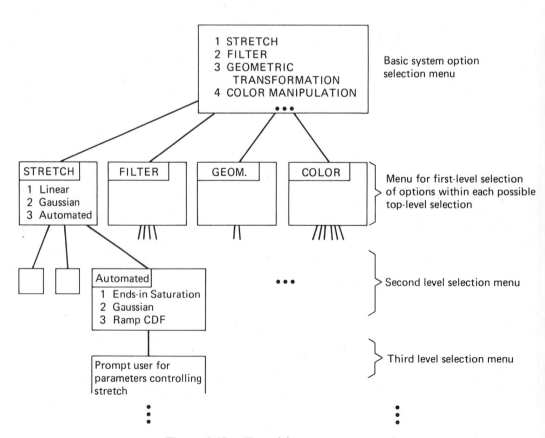

Figure 6-17.   Tree drive menu structure.

gram, etc.) and may also prompt the user directly for parameters required by the algorithm selected.

The use of menus allows an inexperienced user to perform sophisticated image processing quickly and easily. The system provides continuous support, guiding the user through the options available within the system and prompting him or her for input parameters as they are required. There is no need for the user to learn complicated syntax or the grammar of an image processing executive language in order to process images. The main disadvantage of a menu-driven system is the need for development of the software that supports the menu selection system. This can be minimized by generating a set of system-level subroutines that support the menu display and user communication functions; these subroutines can be utilized by the applications programmer.

Figures 6-18 and 6-19 show two menus displayed by an image processing system operated under user control through the use of a tree-driven menu structure. The first menu, in Figure 6-18, describes the 13 top-level options available to the user and prompts for a single numeric input to indicate function selection. If option 1, "Image Input/Output," is selected, the menu shown in Figure 6-19 indicates the available options within the particular module. The user is again prompted for a selection of one of the available options. User selection of option 6, "Generate Synthetic Image," is illustrated in Figure 6-19. The user will next be prompted to provide the additional information required to generate a synthetic image (e.g., size of the image to be generated, distribution of digital intensity desired, etc.).

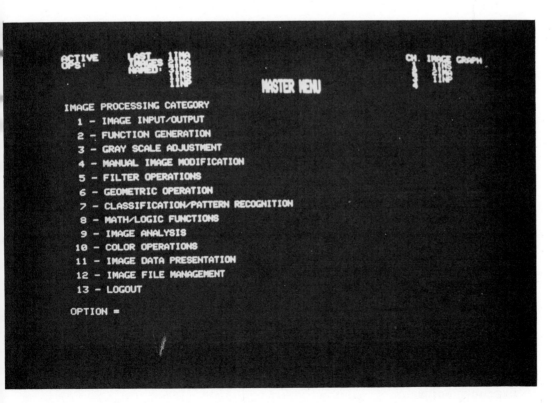

Figure 6-18. Top-level menu, presenting basic system processing options to an interactive user (Unisys Defense Systems).

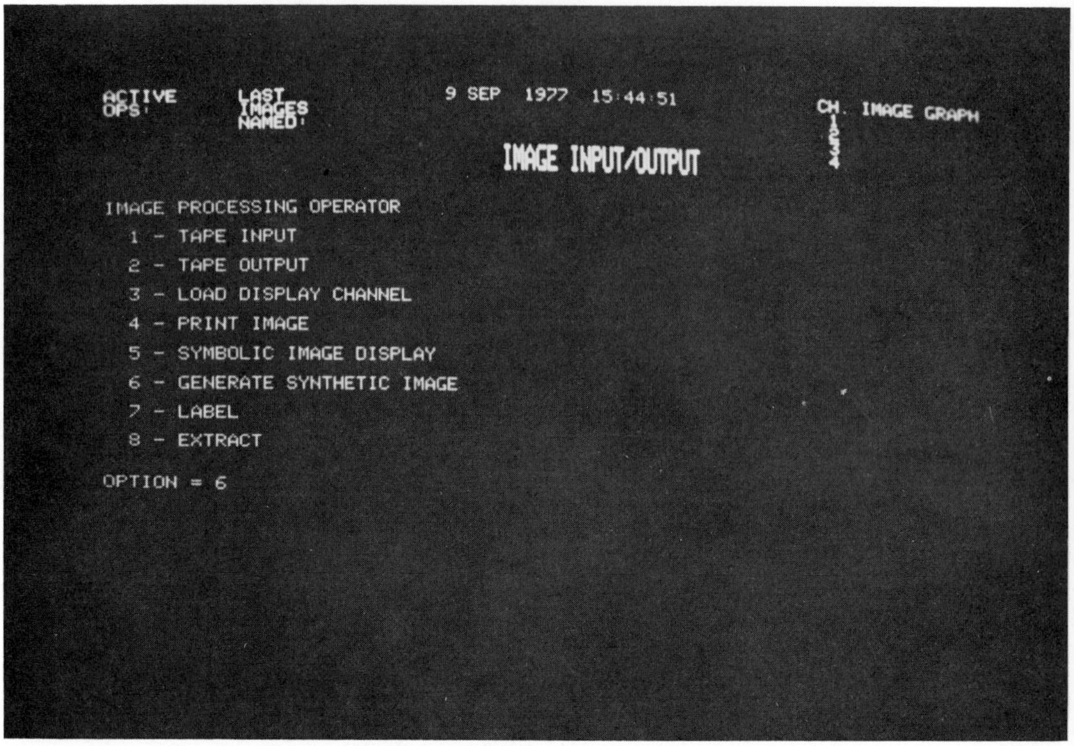

Figure 6-19.   Second-level menu, corresponding to option 1 in Figure 6–18 (Unisys Defense Systems).

IMAGE PROCESSING SOFTWARE SYSTEM OVERVIEW

This section summarizes the types of image processing program modules that may be resident within an image processing system. Not all image processing systems will require all the software described here, and there are additional capabilities not described here that may be part of some individual systems. The intent is to group image processing software within broad general categories and to provide a complete summary of the types of software that may exist within image processing systems. The system designer can use the software categories and modules described here as a checklist during design of a particular image processing system, adding and deleting capabilities and regrouping the modules as required to meet a specific set of applications requirements.

Figure 6-20 contains a summary overview of a general-purpose image processing software system. The software has been grouped within four broad categories: executive software, preprocessing modules, processing modules, and output modules. In addition, a set of utility modules is listed; these modules are generally required in any system and are useful for image analysis and in development and check-out of more complex image processing modules. The set of system-level subroutines discussed earlier in this chapter is not shown explicitly in Figure 6-20, but those subroutines are utilized extensively within the modules shown in Figure 6-20.

Executive Software

The *executive software* controls the execution of image processing jobs and handles the data storage and management functions during task execution. It may consist

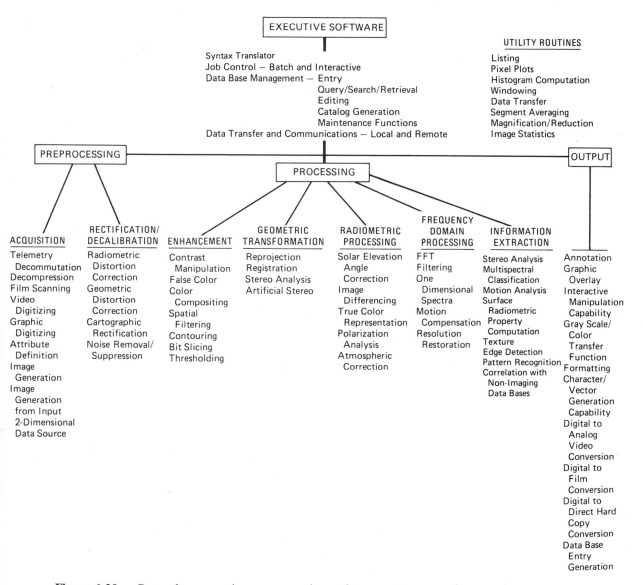

Figure 6-20. General-purpose image processing software system overview.

of the computer operating system, as provided by the hardware vendor, or it may include a set of software designed specifically to interface directly with an image processing user that supplements the functions provided by the computer operating system.

Preprocessing

Two categories of preprocessing software are indicated in Figure 6-20. *Acquisition software* modules convert image data from their original input form into the standard digital image format used throughout the system. *Rectification* or *decalibration* software applies a set of operations to imagery derived from particular sources designed to transform the image data into a standard reference format, remove sensor-induced distortions, and remove noise and other artifacts from the image data. Both classes of preprocessing software are designed to prepare digital image data for processing by the more general modules included under the "processing" category.

Acquisition software modules generate digital imagery in the standard image format from data that can be provided in a variety of input formats. The input imagery can be digital, or it can be provided as film transparency or video data, or it can even be input as a set of coordinate values by a coordinate digitizer. Imagery in digital format can be provided within a more general telemetry stream, and software may be required to extract and format the digital image data embedded within a general telemetry format. Telemetry decommutation and decompression are included in the acquisition category.

It may be necessary to accommodate image data acquired by a remote sensing system that is provided on digital tape in a format that differs from the standard digital format in use within the particular software system. The "logging programs" described earlier in this chapter fall into the preprocessing category.

Preprocessing can also include software modules designed to create image data from data sources that are not originally digital in nature. It is possible, for example, to digitize contour maps and to generate "elevation images," in which digital intensity values that are proportional to elevation are assigned to each pixel. These images are generated by digitizing isoelevation contours from a map and then generating the pixel intensity values by spatial interpolation performed between the digitized contours.

The rectification and decalibration modules may be applied to every image derived from a particular source (film scanner, digital camera system, etc.). These operations may include removal of system-induced distortions, including radiometric and/or geometric distortion introduced by the imaging system, scanner, or digitizer. It may be necessary to perform digital filtering for noise suppression or removal or to apply special algorithms to reduce random noise or telemetry system-induced bit errors.

Some applications may require that all images be transformed to a common geographic or geometric reference frame before further processing can occur. These functions are all included in the preprocessing phase shown in Figure 6-20.

Processing

The processing modules shown in Figure 6-20 include several broad classes of software that perform the processing and manipulation of digital imagery. Many of these techniques are described in Chapters 3 and 4 and in the references cited in those chapters. Ideally, these modules will be able to accommodate image data from a variety of sources. In many cases, however, it is not possible to develop general-purpose modules that can accommodate a diverse range of image sources.

Enhancement modules constitute the set of functions described in Chapter 3. They include the basic capabilities of contrast manipulation, color and false-color processing, enhancement filtering, contouring, and thresholding. These modules usually are written as general-purpose modules capable of accepting any type of image presented in the common system digital image format. They may be highly interactive or batch-oriented, depending on the exact nature of the applications requirements.

Geometric transformation modules provide the capability of transforming imagery into a variety of spatial formats. The most commonly used modules perform cartographic projection, and general-purpose geometric transformation modules can be used to perform digital registration and to produce transformed imagery representing modified view perspectives. Special-purpose modules for analysis of stero image pairs can be developed, including modules designed to perform stereophotogrammetry. Stereo can also be used as an enhancement tool, and modules can be developed that generate an artificial pair of stereo images from a single input image, where the third dimension is proportional to some quantity of interest within the image (e.g., local intensity variation).

Radiometric processing modules are usually designed to assist in scientific analysis of digital image data. Programs can be written to remove the shading introduced into planetary images by variation in incident solar elevation angle across the field of view of the camera system. Radiometric modules include programs written to perform quantitative measurement of differences in intensity between two images recorded of the same area as well as programs that analyze and manipulate surface color properties, using multispectral image components. Remotely sensed imagery can be used to derive polarization properties of a surface or atmospheric polarization or transmission properties. Intensity correction of remotely sensed imagery for radiometric variation introduced by a planetary atmosphere is possible by using software designed for that purpose.

Frequency domain processing describes the set of software used to manipulate digital imagery by filtering, using digital filters designed for a particular purpose. The Fourier transform of a digital image can be computed in either one or two dimensions, and analysis of the resulting frequency spectra can be useful in scene analysis. Digital filters can be applied either in the spatial domain (using convolutional filters) or in the frequency domain (applying the desired frequency filter directly to the Fourier transform of the digital image). Filtering in the spatial domain is preferable, since convolutional filtering avoids the need to perform the Fourier transform twice (once to obtain the frequency representation of the digital image, and again to perform the inverse transform after the digital filter has been applied). Correction for loss of resolution (owing to digital sampling, system optics, or atmospheric effects) can be achieved by application of the appropriate frequency filter. It is also possible to remove the effects of blurring caused by motion by applying the appropriate digital filter. The use of special-purpose hardware to aid in digital filtering has become common, and array processors are now in widespread use within the image processing community. For many minicomputer-based image processing systems, special-purpose hardware for digital filtering is a necessity if there is a significant amount of filtering to be performed in the particular application.

Information extraction is a broad category, and many of the topics within that category have not been dealt with in this text. The modules in this category are designed to extract particular information from one or more digital images. Examples of information extraction include determination of the elevation profile of a surface from a pair of stereoscopic images, determination of surface materials from a set of multispectral images, and measurement of the degree of roughness of an arterial wall from an x-ray image. The modules listed in this category are all designed to assist a human interpreter in performing image analysis, and in some cases they replicate the functions performed by a human analyst. Information regarding cloud motion can be derived from a series of time-sequential digital images, using software that correlates the imagery to determine the relative motion of identifiable features within the time sequence. One or more images can be used to determine the radiometric properties of a surface if the viewing geometry and illumination geometry are known. Surface texture can be determined by using a variety of algorithms that measure local variance within a digital image. A variety of techniques can be used to detect and follow edges within an image, and the degree of roughness of an edge can be computed quantitatively. Pattern recognition is fully developed technology in its own right[1] and deals with techniques for identification of shapes, objects, and features within digital imagery, using automated techniques. Image data can be correlated with data contained in nonimaging data bases and can be combined with auxiliary data in quantitative computations; as one example, land use derived from a multispectral image of an urban area can be combined with population data contained in an auxiliary data base to develop an estimate of air pollution for regions located within that urban area.

Each of the information-extraction techniques described here provides quantitative data based on input digital imagery. The data derived from the imagery can include parameters such as the following: the number of cornfields located within the image area, the surface elevation of each pixel in the image area, the number of veins located within the X-ray that has been digitized, the number of rocks located in the path of a moving robot equipped with television cameras, and angular reflectance of the surface material located at each pixel location within the image. This listing is intended to indicate the types of information that can be derived from digital imagery, and each system designer will eventually develop one or more modules that perform information extraction for specific applications.

Output Modules

Output modules include several types of software. There is a basic set of modules within every image processing system that converts an image stored in standard system format to the appropriate digital format for display or film recording so that the results of computer processing can be viewed by an analyst. There is usually one module for each type of output device, and each module can contain a variety of options corresponding to the capabilities of the particular hardware components used for image output and display.

A set of modules or system-level subroutines should also be available for annotation and labeling of the output imagery. This topic is discussed in detail in Chapter 7, but the basic functions include addition of tic marks, gray scales, and annotation around the borders of the image data. Other routines may be available that merge or superimpose graphics data with digital image data.

Software modules are also required in order to enter new versions of images into the system catalog and to enter descriptive data regarding enhanced imagery into the system catalog. This topic is also discussed in Chapter 7.

Summary

This section has provided an overview of a large general-purpose image processing software system containing a variety of software in several categories. The complete image processing software system will contain modules for user communication, preprocessing, processing, and output of image data as well as a variety of other software capabilities including general-purpose subroutines that provide basic capabilities required by a variety of applications modules. The intent of this section has been to describe the large variety of software necessary to perform efficient digital image processing.

Image processing systems can range from a minimal system to a highly complex system. A minimal system utilizes the computer operating system capabilities for the user interface, processes image data acquired from a single source, possesses a limited number of applications processing modules, and provides output to a single display or recording device. A complex system provides the capability of accommodating a variety of image sources, includes hundreds of applications modules, and provides output to a variety of output display devices, with control driven by an image processing executive capable of supporting multiple simultaneous image processing users. The basic design rules of system modularity, standard digital image format, incorporation of parameter-driven options within applications modules, and extensive use of general-purpose system-level subroutines should govern both types of system. When these basic rules are followed, it is easy to expand or modify the software system to accommodate more image data sources, more applications, additional output devices, and a more sophisticated user interface.

REFERENCE

1. Andrews, H., *Introduction to Mathematical Techniques in Pattern Recognition,* New York, Wiley-Interscience, 1972.

7
Image Data Base Management

INTRODUCTION

Most image processing facilities quickly discover that there is a need to keep track of a large number of digital images that are available in a variety of formats. There is a need to enter new images into the image processing system, to record the location of newly acquired images, and to retrieve input images by means of search criteria that utilize a variety of information associated with each image. A single input image may be processed several times on a particular system, and a series of processed image products can be produced from the same input image. There is a need to identify the processing that has produced each version of the image, and there may be a need to determine the processing that has produced a particular hard-copy image product. It may also be necessary to keep track of the processed versions on digital storage (tape or disk) for future access.

Image products can be produced that involve multiple input images; a mosaic of several images is a simple example of this type of processing. It may be necessary to keep track of the particular images used to produce the amalgamated product or of the specific versions of particular images used to produce the result.

Most facilities require a mechanism for locating image data on computer-compatible storage devices (tape and disk). In addition, facilities producing hard-copy photo products require a means for annotating the hard copy with identification of the image data used to produce the product, the processing that was performed, and other auxiliary image-associated data. A unique descriptor is often required to distinguish hard-copy products generated by an image processing system.

Every image processing system will produce an expanding data base of digital imagery. The data base must be maintained and kept current, with the imagery of lowest utilization transferred off-line to archival storage. As the data base expands in size, it is necessary to develop efficient tools to interrogate the image data base in a variety of ways. The image data base will contain a variety of image-associated data in addition to the basic digital pixel data. The image-associated data enable query and interrogation of the image data base. It should be possible to interrogate the data base to locate on tape, disk, or film hard copy a set of images satisfying a particular search criterion. Typical data base queries can be structured in the following ways:

"What are the disk data set names of the files containing the LANDSAT MSS images taken in 1979 of the Orlando, Florida, region in the IR-1 filter on days when the cloud cover was less than 30 percent?"

"What processing was performed to produce the image on film roll number 4719, file number 14, and what sensor was used to acquire the original image?"

"What are the film production identification numbers of all Viking Lander 1 images taken with the High Resolution 4 Diode after 4 P.M. local Mars time after the hundredth day of the mission that have been radiometrically corrected, high pass filtered, and contrast-enhanced?"

"List the data set names for all images that have not been accessed for the last 4 weeks."

These queries are typical of those which may arise in facilities in which the data base size is more than a few hundred images. A data base management system is required in order to keep track of large numbers of digital and hard-copy image products and to maintain the data base itself (as illustrated by the last query in the examples given above).

This chapter describes the use of image descriptors in an image data base management system and the design of image catalogs utilized as part of an image data base management system. The annotation of hard-copy products is discussed, and recommendations are made regarding the information used to annotate and uniquely identify hard-copy image products.

IMAGE DESCRIPTORS

A variety of information can be associated with every version of a digital image that is available within the image data base maintained on a particular system. An image that is entered into a particular system will initially have a variety of descriptors associated with it. The descriptors can include the identification of the image source (digital remote sensing system, video digitizer, film scanner, etc.), information about the conditions under which the image was acquired, and a variety of additional information of various types. The image may be processed once or several times, and additional information relative to the processing performed to generate each version of the image can be accumulated as processed image products are created. Processed versions of the original image may be retained within the system image data base in digital form, and hard-copy products of the original and/or processed forms of the images may also be produced.

This section describes several types of information that may be associated with digital imagery. The concept of a unique image identifier is described, and examples of information associated with digital imagery and processing history information are presented. The next section describes the use of this information within image catalogs used for query and retrieval of image data and for unique identification of hard-copy image products.

Unique Image Identifier

Each digital image that is entered into an image processing system should be assigned a unique identifier when it is initially acquired. The unique descriptor that distinguishes one acquired image from any other image acquired by the same device or any other device will be called the *unique image descriptor* (UID). One useful unique descriptor combines the date and time of image acquisition with some identification code that indicates the sensor, device, or system acquiring the image.

One example of a UID might be the following descriptor associated with an image originally scanned by a film scanner:

SA.880302.101322

This UID would refer to the image scanned on a film scanner denoted as Scanner A within a particular facility on March 2, 1988, at time 10:13:22. A second example of a UID that might be assigned by a film scanning system might be the following:

SA.0327.C

This type of identifier might be assigned by a scanner system containing a cycling counter; the particular example might indicate the 327th image scanned on the third cycle of the image counter (the letter "C" is used to denote the third cycle of the image counter). This type of identifier involves fewer characters per UID than the use of date and time but is limited in the number of images that can be assigned unique identifiers and may be subject to inadvertent recycling of the image counter as a result of hardware problems or power interruptions. The date and time identifier has the advantage of guaranteed uniqueness of each UID but requires more characters and is more cumbersome to use when entering computer commands or identifying images verbally.

An example of the use of cycling frame counter in assignment of UIDs is the following UID utilized on the Viking Lander Mars mission:

12A153/26

This identifier described an image acquired with Lander spacecraft number 1, camera 2; the letter "A" denoted the frame counter cycle, the number 153 denoted the image number within cycle A, and the number 26 indicated the day of the mission on which the image was acquired. The mission day was included to retain UID uniqueness if the spacecraft were to acquire more than 26 times 999 images (in which case the cycle indicator would have reset from "Z" to "A") and to guard against ambiguity if the cycle counter inadvertently reset.

Image-Associated Data

A variety of information can be associated with each image processed or stored in an image processing system. The information includes sensor identification of the source of the image, the spectral band represented by the image, shutter speed or exposure level of the image, information relative to the viewing geometry, a description of the image contents, etc. The various types of image-associated data were described in Chapter 6, when the concept of a general format image header record for stored imagery was introduced.

The variety of information available about images can vary significantly. The image-associated data can be used when searching an image data base for the subset of images satisfying some search criteria. It should also be added to the image data as annotation on hard-copy image products. Figure 7-1 shows an enhanced version of an astronomical image. This color product was produced as a composite, using three separate astronomical plates that were acquired at different times. The image-associated data are displayed within the annotation block below the image area in Figure 7-1 and include the following items:

NGC1097: Identification of the galaxy that was imaged

DEC 5 1975: Date on which the three source images were acquired

EXP 80 M: Exposure time

13A0 FILT UG5 PLATE 1414: Identification of the filter used during exposure and the plate number of the first exposed plate

RA 2 45 24 DEC -30 23(1975): Right acension and declination of the galactic cluster

4 METER CERRO TOLOLO: Identifies observatory at which plate was exposed and the telescope used

PDS SCAN 50 MIC SPOT 48 MIC SPACING: Describes the particular film scanner used and the spot size and spot spacing used in scanning the plates

Information regarding the processing performed to generate the image shown in Figure 7-1 is found below this information. Next, the source images for the color composite are identified as follows:

103A0 is the blue component

127 is the green component

098 is the red component

The remaining information in the annotation in Figure 7-1 will be discussed in later sections of this chapter.

Figure 7-2 shows a color composite LANDSAT MSS image developed from enhanced versions of three of the four spectral components returned by the LANDSAT multispectral scanner. The descriptors in the information block contain a variety of information derived from several sources, including the following:

1426-12070: UID for the LANDSAT MSS image. 1426 denotes the 426th image acquired by LANDSAT-1; 12070 represents the time of image acquisition.

Spectral components: The color composite was obtained by merging bands 5, 6, and 7 from the LANDSAT MSS. The spectral band numbers are displayed offset by one position in the image header and appear color-coded in the composite so that the viewer can determine the color assignment for each component spectral band.

11Sep73: Date of image acquisition

VATNAJOKULL, ICELAND: A cultural identifier determined by using a software table look-up in a table indexed by longitude and latitude.

N64-12/W017-20: Longitude and latitude of the image.

HDG200: Spacecraft heading.

SUN EL 25 AZ 164: Solar incident angle in azimuth and elevation coordinates relative to the center of the image.

PC121 SCALE 79.83M/PXL: The PC121 code is a processing code that identifies the image processing performed by the logging program used to convert from LANDSAT tape format into the standard system format (see Chapter 6). The particular code identifies the type of geometric rectification, radiometric, correction, cartographic registration, and other processing performed on the original LANDSAT MSS image to produce the version entered into the system image data base. The SCALE parameter, indicating the number of meters per picture element, is also computed by the logging program, which scaled the original image into a particular geometric reference frame.

*SAR – *STRETCH, etc.: This is an abbreviated processing history for the image shown in Figure 7-2, and it indicates the programs that have been used to process the image and produce the hard-copy product.

05-22-76 171840 JPL/IPL: These identifiers are the date and time at which the component images were written to tape for film recorder playback and the facility at which the film recording was performed. The color composite shown in Figure 7-2 was made by superimposing three separate exposed negatives in a photo lab; the three unique negative identifiers are thus superimposed and printed in three different colors on this product.

Processing History

The two examples in the last section were included to indicate the variety of information that is associated with every digital image input into an image processing system. The amount of information associated with processed versions of a single input image can also be extensive. Several processed versions of a single input image can be produced by an image processing system over the course of time, and it is important to keep track of the processing performed in generating each version.

In most applications, it is difficult to utilize digital imagery without knowing a variety of information pertaining to the image. It is difficult, for example, to utilize a remotely sensed image without additional information regarding the location of the image within some geographic reference system, the time of day and season under which the image was acquired, the sensor acquiring the image, and other information. A digital version of an X-ray or tomograph is useless if the name of the patient and the time and circumstances under which the image was acquired are not known.

In a similar manner, it is often difficult to utilize a processed or enhanced image product without knowing the details of the processing involved in generating that product. It is necessary to understand which algorithms have been applied to the image, the geometric reference of the output product, the parameters used in enhancing the image for display, and other important parameters in order to perform image analysis on enhanced or processed imagery. It is thus important to develop a file containing the history of processing that has led to each processed version of digital image produced on a particular system.

Figure 7-3 contains a Viking Lander image with extensive annotation, including a variety of information associated with the original image and additional information regarding the particular processing performed to yield the product shown in the figure. Note first the three geometric scales around the image itself. The three scales have been added by a program designed for that purpose. The inner scale indicates the line and sample coordinates within the image. The particular image shown in Figure 7-3 is actually the third segment of a much wider image acquired by the Lander camera, and the second pixed scale indicates the pixel coordinates of the image segment within the full camera pixel coordinate system. Notice also that the Lander camera acquired images by scanning from bottom to top of the field of view so that the vertical pixel scales run in opposite directions. The third geometric scale around the segment indicates image coordinates in camera azimuth and eleva-

Figure 7-3. Viking Lander image of Mars. The annotation block includes image associated data and parameters added by several programs used to process the image, and the histogram (Jet Propulsion Laboratory).

tion viewing coordinates; these coordinates are actually used in commanding the camera for image acquisition, and so it was necessary to provide a mechanism for translating between camera pixel coordinates, image segment pixel coordinates, and camera azimuth/elevation coordinates when viewing an image product.

The annotation below the image segment contains a variety of image-associated data of the type discussed previously in this chapter. The data contained in this section have been derived from a variety of sources. Many of the data are returned as part of the image telemetry (e.g., camera identification, spacecraft identifier, etc.). Other data were returned in engineering telemetry streams (e.g., temperatures) or derived from ground-based software (e.g., solar azimuth and elevation at the time of image acquisition). All the data had to be merged into a single data file corresponding to this particular image. Missing data are flagged by inclusion of asterisks.

This image has been time-tagged in a variety of ways. The time at which image acquisition began on Mars is included in Mars time as Local Lander Day and Time (LLD/T) and in Greenwich Mean Time as EVENT D/GMT (missing in this particular example). The time at which the telemetry transmission of this image was received on earth is also included as Earth Received Day and Time (ERD/T). The ERD/T annotation is desirable because multiple transmission of the same image from spacecraft storage to earth was possible and was frequently performed to overcome transmission difficulties. Annotation with ERD/T served as an unambiguous unique identifier for each transmitted version of the same image.

The actual ground processing history for the image product shown in Figure 7-3 begins with information derived from the logging program (see Chapter 6). The logging program determined the number of missing lines in the full camera image, the number of gaps within which lines in the full camera image were missing, and the percentage of missing lines. Although the percentage missing was quite high for the full image, which is the value included in the annotation in Figure 7-3, the percentage was low for the segment shown in the figure.

The source tape and file of the original image are included in the product annotation, and the output tape and file number (missing here) can also be added to an annotation block so that the processed image can be located on tape at a later date.

The remaining annotation describes the particular geometric reference to which the image segment has been projected. The geometric rectification in this case included removal of camera-system geometric distortion and projection to a standard cartographic projection in Viking Lander coordinates. The detailed parameters describing the projection and reference location of this segment within the georeference coordinate system are thus included in the annotation block. This information is generated by the applications program that performs the rectification.

The histogram, mean digital intensity, and standard deviation are also included as annotation. All the information that has been added as annotation is required if the image segment is to be scientifically useful. In order to make intelligent use of the hard-copy image product, the end user must be able to establish the processing that has been performed, the parameters used in the processing, and the image manipulation and enhancement that has been performed. It is especially useful if the available processing history information can be provided to some extent directly on hard-copy image products. It is often useful to present one level of available information within the product annotation and to retain a more detailed level of information in a computer-accessible data file, enabling users to obtain all available information relating to the particular product.

Unique Processing Identifier

A single source image may be processed in a variety of ways to produce many different products in a variety of hard-copy forms. Each of the processed images will be associated with the UID of the source image, and it becomes necessary to add an additional identifier so that multiple versions of the same source image can be identified unambiguously.

The easiest way to differentiate between multiple versions of the same source image is to assign a unique product identifier (UPID) to each version at the time that it is recorded onto film or otherwise rendered into hard-copy photo-product form. The UPID should be included in the annotation on hard-copy products.

Each UPID should provide the mechanism for determining the sequence that has been performed to yield the particular photo product. The other annotation may also indicate the types of processing that have been performed and other information about the photo product, as we have seen previously. The UPID should serve as an index into a more complete computerized file containing the names of the programs used to process the image in the order they were executed, the parameters used in the various algorithms, and other detailed data regarding the processing that was performed.

The date and time of film recording or hard-copy generation is a useful UPID. A typical UPID for an enhanced photo product might be of the form

$$YR/MO/DAY/hhmmss$$

where YR, MO, and DAY indicate the date of recording the image onto film, and hhmmss indicates the time (in hours, minutes, and seconds) at which recording occurred. Computerized image catalogs, which are described in the next section, can be used to determine the processing that has produced a particular photo product annotated with a UPID.

Figure 7-3 includes a UPID found on the bottom of the annotation block. The UPID in Figure 7-3 is of the type just described, and the image shown was recorded at 7 minutes after midnight on July 27, 1976. The UPID annotation block also includes an identification of the facility at which the image was produced as well as the initials of the individual responsible for the processing ("JB2") and the descriptor identifying the film roll number on which the original negative is located ("L1142AX").

In this case, the UPID can be used to interrogate a computerized file to determine details of processing not shown on the annotation block. In addition, photographic products can be obtained by specifying the film roll number and the UPID of the desired image product to the archival data storage facility where the original negatives are archived.

IMAGE CATALOGS

Image catalogs are computer-compatible files of auxiliary data associated with the images stored within an image data base. The following examples represent typical operational requirements that can be met by creating and maintaining active image catalogs:

1. The need to locate particular images or a class of images on digital storage (magnetic tape or disk)

2. The need to locate hard-copy image products on film, microfiche, videodisk, or other media
3. The need to interrogate large image files to locate images satisfying search criteria
4. The need to determine the processing steps and algorithm parameters used in generating a particular hard-copy image product.

Image catalogs containing the image-associated data and processing history information associated with particular UIDs and UPIDs are used to meet these requirements. These catalogs can be used to unambiguously relate particular source images (or processed versions) with the variety of information associated with them. This section discusses techniques used to create image catalogs, the structure of image catalogs, and the use of image catalogs in storage and retrieval of photographic products.

Use of Header Records as a Source of Catalog Entries

The use of header records within standard digital image formats used to store image data was described in Chapter 6. The header records are used to store the various types of image-associated data. The use of header records guarantees that the various types of ancillary data will remain associated with the image as processing is performed. Additional information is added into the header records as each new version of the image is created so that the processing history information is available within the image header records. Every version of every image thus includes an up-to-date set of information within the header record that can be used to trace the image from its origin through to the most recent algorithm that has been applied to generate the current version.

The information within the image header records can serve as the source of data for formatting software that adds annotation and borders to image data before film recording. The annotation blocks shown in Figures 7-1 through 7-3 were derived from the header records of the versions of the imagery portrayed in those figures.

A separate computer-compatible image catalog can be generated by extracting the header data from each version of each image produced on a particular system and transferring it into a specially formatted data file that serves as the system's image catalog.

Image Catalog Structure

Figure 7-4 illustrates one representative structure for an image catalog. In this example, the information derived from image header records has been divided into five categories (note that the five categories correspond to categories flagged with particular alphanumeric characters within the image header record structure described in Chapter 6). Image catalogs should be structured to minimize the search time associated with the most commonly performed catalog searches or queries. Figure 7-4 indicates one important design concept. The catalog has been divided into subfiles, allowing searches of available subsets without requiring a search of the entire file for many queries. This structure is made possible through the use of *pointers*. Each entry in the subfiles includes pointers to the other subfiles, as shown by the arrows in Figure 7-4.

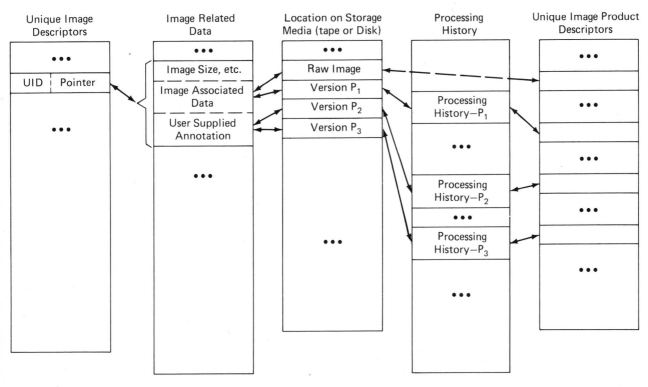

Figure 7-4. Structure of sub-files in an image catalog.

The shortest subfile shown in Figure 7-4 is the subfile containing the UIDs. A search for particular UIDs would require only a search of the shortest table or subfile in the catalog. Each UID entry would also include pointers to the other subfiles denoting the positions at which additional information relating to the particular UID can be found. A simple search for the disk data set name assigned to a particular UID would involve a search of the short UID subfile, location of the desired UID and extraction of the corresponding disk data set name from the "Location on Storage Media" subfile. Access to the disk data set name would be determined by a pointer in the UID file that indicates the location of the disk data set name within the "Location" subfile.

Pointers are used in both directions when image catalogs are structured as shown in Figure 7-4. The "location" file thus contains pointers indicating the location of the UID corresponding to each entry in the "location" file.

More complex searches of image catalogs can involve several subfiles or all the subfiles, depending on the complexity of the user queries. It is important to monitor the use of image catalogs and to develop a mechanism for determining the most frequent types of user queries. Optimal structuring of the image catalog into appropriate subfiles can enable rapid interrogation of large image data bases; conversely, nonoptimal catalog structuring can result in long search times for queries that the user considers straightforward and routine. Note that the subfiles themselves can be ordered and structured in an optimal manner, again reflecting the most frequent use of the image catalog.

The type of catalog structure shown in Figure 7-4 can accommodate the diverse types of user queries listed as examples at the beginning of this chapter. Many commercially available data base management system software packages can be adapted for use in creating, structuring, and maintaining image catalogs. In some facilities, user needs may be met with a less complex catalog structure that can accommodate a small number of query types. Regardless of the number of images in the image data base and the complexity of the image-associated information, each processing facility will ultimately have to develop the ability to keep track of the images processed on the system and the image products produced by the system.

Generation of Image Catalogs

Figure 7-5 illustrates the various stages of image processing that can produce entries into an image catalog. The first entry can occur when a particular image is read into the system, using the "logging program" described in Chapter 6. The logging program determines the UID, and the UID and the location on tape or disk of the digital image are transferred to the catalog file, after the image has been converted into the standard digital image format established for the particular image processing system. A variety of image-associated information may also be stored into the header records associated with the logged image at that time.

The original source image may undergo a variety of image processing operations that generate one or more processed versions of the original image. Each time a new version is created, the processing history is entered into the header record of the processed image.

A formatting program normally is used to prepare the data file used as input to a film recorder or other device used to generate hard-copy products. The formatting program reads an image in standard digital image format and produces a version compatible with the film recorder or other hard-copy device. The formatting program adds annotation, borders, and other information to the image that later appears on the film products. In addition, the formatting program can be used to assign the UPID for the hard-copy product and can enter the UPID into the image catalog file, as shown.

The image catalog can also be used to store the location of processed versions of

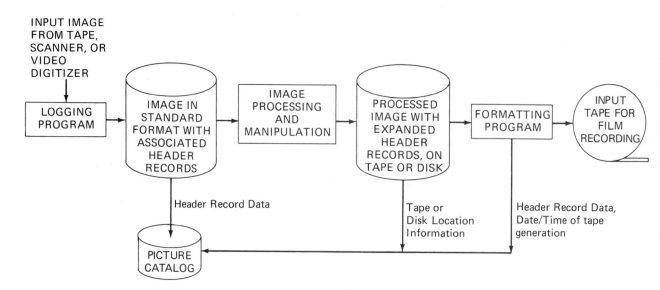

Figure 7-5.   Creation of Image Catalog entries.

images that are not produced in hard-copy form. The system software should allow for entry of location data (location of processed image versions on magnetic or other storage) in versions for which a hard-copy product is not produced. This operation is also shown in Figure 7-5.

Storage and Retrieval of Photographic Products

It may become advisable to store or archive all negatives produced within a particular facility in a central file. The reasons for central storage include environmental protection of original negatives, a need for central archival storage of all products produced on a particular study, contract or experiment, or a lack of adequate distributed environmentally appropriate film-product storage facilities.

A computer-compatible film hard-copy index is required to catalog a central film archive of any substantial size. The central archive will usually access original negatives by a "film roll number" or other device that indicates the image content of archival rolls or sets of exposed and developed film negatives. The original negatives will be retained in a central archive, and other photo products (duplicate negatives, positive transparencies, and prints) will be distributed to users.

Correspondence should be maintained between the system used to store film products in an archival storage facility and the UID and UPID information contained in the image catalog so that the processing that generated a particular photographic product and the image used in that product can be determined. If the film archive facility uses a particular filing scheme (e.g., film roll number and frame number on the roll), that information should be entered in the image catalog. Alternatively, a smaller computer data base can be used to maintain a record of the correspondence between UID, UPID, and location within the archival film storage facility.

Users will tend to place two types of orders for additional hard copy products:

1. Orders will be placed for additional photo products by specifying the photo archive index (e.g., roll and frame number).
2. Orders will be based on image catalog interrogation, with desired image products specified by UID and/or UPID.

The image catalog, possibly used in conjunction with a smaller file correlating UID, UPID, and photo products, can be utilized to accommodate both types of request.

TECHNIQUES USED FOR HARD-COPY IMAGE ANNOTATION

A hard-copy image product, or an image displayed on a volatile display, is generated as an array of pixels that are forwarded to the display device. The most basic method of displaying an image consists of forwarding the pixel data corresponding to the digital image to the display device. When imagery is displayed in that manner, the display does not include a variety of additional information that may be required for image analysis or for specification of further processing. The display of image data in hard-copy or volatile formats usually requires the addition of "extra" pixels around the borders of the actual digital image data. The "extra" pixels are used to display alphanumeric information, graphics, tic marks, gray scales, and other information that may be useful. Annotation is added by translating alphanumeric characters into blocks of pixels, and image-associated information is converted from alphanumeric format into patterns of pixel dots representing the alphanumeric characters. The annotation information usually consists of the image-associated data described in this chapter.

The image products used in several figures in this chapter serve as examples of annotated hard-copy image products. The image shown in Figure 7-3, for example, represents a product generated by adding several hundred "extra" pixels to a digital image that was originally 512 pixels square. The gray step wedges are written to the film recorder as blocks of pixels of fixed digital intensities, with each gray step represented as 20 × 20 block of pixels. Other pixel patterns of all-white pixels are used to generate the tic marks, alphanumeric annotation, and histogram data shown in Figure 2-3. The full image transmitted to the film recorder to generate the product shown in Figure 7-3 is approximately 800 × 1024 pixels; several thousand pixels were required to incorporate the gray wedges, pixel scales, annotation, and histogram display added around the borders of the original 512-pixel-square image.

This section describes the techniques used to add gray wedges, tic marks, histograms, and annotation to image products. The majority of the material is relevant to hard-copy photographic products that are generated from film recorders or other hard-copy devices. Some of the information presented here may also be relevant to volatile display of image data (e.g., it may be useful to display numbered pixel scales around the edge of a digital image shown on a volatile display).

Gray Step Wedges

Gray step wedges are often displayed as part of hard-copy image products. They may also be useful when they are added to imagery displayed on a video monitor. They are constructed from blocks of pixels containing uniform digital intensity values. If intensity data are represented by using 8 bits, then blocks of pixels with intensities separated by 16 digital intensity levels could be used to construct a step wedge containing 16 steps. Figure 7-3 includes one example of a gray step wedge constructed in this manner.

The step wedge is written in both increasing and decreasing intensity order in Figure 7-3, and wedges are added at both the top and bottom of the image data. This is often done to determine the degree of radiometric uniformity of the recording or display device. Image display devices often exhibit spatially nonuniform radiometric properties, and the effect can be observed by comparing gray step wedges placed in different positions within the recording or display format. The example in Figure 7-3 consists of four separate step wedges, two placed above the image data and two placed below. Note that the whitest steps in the step wedges saturate at different points in the digital intensity range when the wedges at the top of the figure are compared with the wedges at the bottom. This indicates that spatially dependent radiometric distortion has occurred in generating the photographic product used as the source of Figure 7-3. This example illustrates one use for step wedges. A rapid qualitative evaluation of the radiometric fidelity of an image product can be made through inspection of the gray step wedges displayed along the image data.

Gray step wedges also enable a user to relate digital intensity values to the gray shades present in the image product or image display. The gray wedges correspond to a series of known digital intensity values, and the gray shades visible on a displayed image can be related to the numerical data through use of the gray step wedge.

Gray step wedges are also incorporated for quantitative control of the film recorder/photo-processing systems or volatile display device. The reflectance of individual steps can be read from hard-copy prints, or the transmitance of the individual steps can be read from a film transparency, and a calibration specification can be established by a particular facility that relates desired reflectance or transmitance to the digital intensity values. Contrast-manipulation table look-ups can be employed to manipulate the digital intensity data before film or volatile display in order to retain the desired relationship between film product or display characteristics and digital intensity levels in the computer, as discussed in Chapter 5.

Pixel Scales

It is often necessary to determine the line and sample coordinates of particular features within an image. The addition of pixel scales around the border of displayed imagery provides a mechanism for reasonably precise visual location of the coordinates of selected features. Pixel scales can be seen on the image border in Figures 7-1 and 7-2.

Pixel scales consist of patterns of pixels that are generated outside the image area on image products. Several types of tic marks are in common use, and several examples are shown in Figure 7-6. Scales can be generated as patterns of white pixels on a black background or vice versa. The most commonly used technique involves highlighting of individual lines or samples at discrete intervals within the image. The first example in Figure 7-6 shows a pixel scale in which every fifth pixel is highlighted by adding a "tic mark" at the image border every five pixels. In addition, every twenty-fifth pixel is highlighted by lengthening the tic mark, and even longer tic mark is used to highlight every hundredth pixel. Examples of other pixel scales are also included in Figure 7-6, including one in which integers are used to aid in distinguishing every group of 100 pixels.

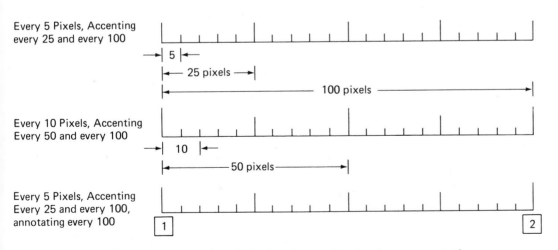

Figure 7-6.   Three examples of pixel scales used as hard copy annotation.

Geometric Reference Scales

In many applications, it is necessary to determine the spatial location or orientation of an image within some reference coordinate or to understand the camera's viewing geometry. As an example, images transformed to a particular cartographic projection are often displayed with longitude and latitude coordinates superimposed or incorporated within the annotation block. Thus, annotation of image products with geometric reference information is often important.

Figure 7-7 is an image of the Martian surface acquired by the Viking Lander spacecraft. There are three geometric reference scales visible on the left and top borders of the image. The innermost border can be used to determine the line and sample coordinates of pixels within the image. The middle scale contains the pixel coordinates as scanned by the Lander camera system, referenced to a camera system-centered pixel coordinate system. The Lander facsimile cameras acquired images by scanning sequential vertical lines from the bottom to the top of the camera's field of view. In camera coordinates, the pixel at line and sample coordinate location (1,1) lies at the lower-left corner of the displayed image; the middle pixel scale is used to reference pixel coordinates in that camera-referenced coordinate system.

The outer scale corresponds to a camera-centered coordinate system that was used to command the camera for image acquisition and for cartographic representation of the Martian surface surrounding the spacecraft. Particular locations in the camera field of view could be addressed in terms of azimuth and elevation angles relative to a particular reference point within the Lander camera system. The Lander camera was capable of imaging almost a full 360° horizontally and 80° vertically. The vertical (or elevation) angles were represented within a range of from −20° to +60°, with 0° representing an elevation straight out from the reference point within the camera. Horizontal (or azimuth) angles were actually represented in two different coordinate systems, one centered about a reference point within the camera and a second centered about a reference point on the Lander spacecraft. The horizontal scale in Figure 7-7 includes annotation in both azimuth coordinate systems.

The outer pixels scales were used to position individual images relative to other images when forming mosaics. In addition, image acquisition was controlled by entering the starting and ending azimuth and elevation angles for each image into the command sequence transmitted to the Lander spacecraft. The angular coordinate system was heavily utilized for mission planning and during mission operations, and it was therefore advisable to annotate individual images with reference marks denoting the angular coordinates of the pixels within the image.

This example was included to illustrate the variety of geometric reference annotation that may be required for specific applications on image products.

Image Histogram

The image histogram, representing the distribution of intensity within the digital image, is often included as part of the image annotation. It can be displayed as part of the annotation on hard-copy image products and can be displayed as an optional graphics overlay with images displayed on a volatile display system. The histogram serves as an important tool in image analysis and can also be used as an indicator of the processing that has been performed to yield a particular image product.

Figure 7-7. Viking Lander Mars image, with three geometric coordinate scales added around image border (Jet Propulsion Laboratory).

An image histogram for a black and white image is shown in the annotation area in Figure 7-3. For multispectral imagery, the histogram of each component image would be displayed.

The graphical representation of an image histogram is a plot of the percentage of image pixels at each digital intensity value. The input data for the histogram consist of a table of numbers containing the number of pixels at each intensity level. The first step in generating a graphical display of the histogram is to convert the distribution to a percentage distribution by dividing the table entries by the number of pixels within the image. The second step involves allocation of the number of pixels to be used in the annotation area for presentation of the histogram. If, for example, 100 pixels is allocated for histogram display in the vertical direction (see Figure 7-3 for one example), the percentage data are scaled so that 100 pixels corresponds to the maximum percentage within the histogram.

In practice, it often turns out that a large percentage of the pixels within an image occur at one or a few brightness levels. This can be caused by a variety of factors. One example would be the presence of a black border around an image, which would cause a large percentage of the image pixels to be at zero intensity. When this is the case, the histogram would exhibit a single vertical "spike" at one intensity level (or a few spikes at a few intensity levels), and the remaining detail in the histogram would be supressed because of the scaling factors that is computed on the basis of the maximum percentage found in the histogram data. Table 7-1 contains a portion of an image histogram illustrating this phenomenon. Forty percent of the pixels have intensity values of 119, whereas the next highest percentage at any intensity level is 10 percent. Figure 7-8 shows a plot of the histogram data contained in Table 7-1 for a case in which 100 pixels is allocated in the display for histogram data. Scaling to the maximum percentage would yield a graphical display such that 1 percent in the image histogram would correspond to 2.5 pixels vertically in the graphical display, as shown in Figure 7-8.

The problem with Figure 7-8 is that the detailed intensity distribution is difficult

TABLE 7-1. CALCULATION OF IMAGE HISTOGRAM SCALING FACTOR

IMAGE HISTOGRAM		BAR LENGTH IN PIXELS	
DIGITAL INTENSITY	PERCENTAGE	@ 2.5 PIXELS/PCT.	@ 10 PIXELS/PCT.
0	0.1	0	1
. . .	. . .	. . .	. . .
115	1.	3	10
116	2.	5	20
117	7.	17	70
118	8.	22	80
119	40.	100	100*
120	10.	37	100
121	4.	10	40
122	2.	5	20
123	1.	3	10
. . .	. . .	. . .	. . .

* denotes supressed spike

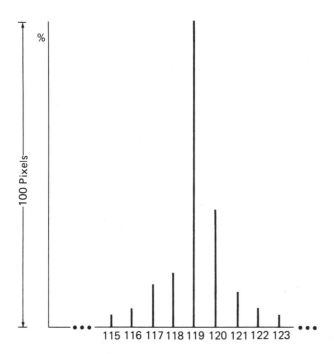

Figure 7-8. Graphical histogram display using maximum percentage to determine scaling factor.

to interpret. The total available space allocated for vertical display is actually fully utilized only in plotting one of the histogram values; the remaining histogram values are plotted utilizing less than 40 percent of the available display space.

For these reasons, it is often advisable to incorporate a more sophisticated scaling algorithm into routines for graphical display of histogram data. One technique incorporates rejection of the first n maxima in the histogram before determining the scaling factor. Table 7-1 and Figure 7-9 illustrate the effect of excluding the first maximum from the scaling computation. If the first maximum is excluded, the scaling of the graphical display is determined by using the next highest percentage found in the histogram table. In the case shown in Table 7-1, the next highest percentage is 10 percent at a digital intensity of 120. If that value is used to compute the scaling factor, a value of 10 pixels per percentage results, and the resultant histogram display is shown in Figure 7-9. A dot is placed over the spike, or spikes, that are eliminated from the scaling factor computation in order to indicate that the value as plotted is in fact lower than the actual value for that particular digital intensity. With the new scaling factor, the value of 10 percent is plotted as a vector of length 100 pixels, versus a length of 37 pixels when the original scaling factor was applied. This technique enables improved display of the intensity variation and efficient utilization of the physical space allocated for histogram display.

Unique Product Identifier

The unique product identifier (UPID) is used to distinguish between individual photographic products. The UPID can be included as part of the annotation block on hard-copy image products. It unambiguously identifies the particular version of the image that is displayed, and it can be used as an index to access more detailed

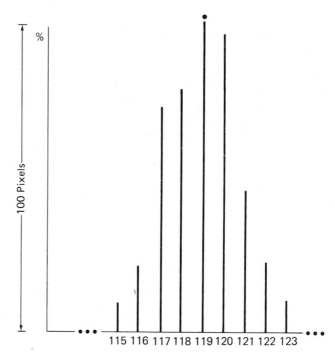

Figure 7-9.   Graphical histogram display using supression of first maximum prior to calculation of scaling factor.

computerized information relative to the processing performed to produce that version.

The use of the UPID in an image annotation block can be seen in Figure 7-3. The UPID is identified as the "IPL PIC ID" contained within the data block at the bottom of the figure. The date and time annotation discussed earlier in this chapter has been used as the UPID in this case.

8
Binary Image Processing

INTRODUCTION

In recent years, systems and supporting peripheral devices have emerged designed to capture, enhance, store, retrieve, and display digitized document material. These systems treat scanned document material as binary images, representing pixels in the scanned imagery with a single bit of intensity (pixels are either "on" or "off," corresponding to black or white in the original document material).

The technology involved in scanning, processing, and displaying binary imagery is a subset of more general image processing technology. The techniques used to capture images of documents, convert intensities to binary representation, and display bit-mapped imagery has been available for several years. The recent growth in the number of digital document processing systems has been motivated by the emergence of optical disk storage devices. Optical disks make it possible to store large volumes of binary imagery at relatively low cost, in systems requiring minimal floor space, power, and air conditioning. Currently, twelve-inch optical disk media can store approximately one gigabyte of data on each side. A single 8 1/2 by 11 inch page scanned at 200 pixels per inch resolution will require 500 kilobytes of storage after conversion to 1 bit per pixel intensity representation. Standard data compression techniques described later in this chapter result in a typical compression factor of 10:1, so that a typical page of document material requires 50 kilobytes. An optical disk can thus store 20,000 pages of document information per side. A 50 disk jukebox can store 2 million pages of document information. The development of high-density optical disk storage equipment, coupled with development of relatively low-cost high-resolution bit mapped displays, microprocessors, and high-speed communications links, has made possible the evolution of digital document storage systems.

This chapter reviews the configuration of typical digital document storage and retrieval systems, and the functions generally performed with those systems. Document scanning of the various sources of document material (paper, microfilm, and microfiche media) is described, and the image processing operations performed to reduce the scanned imagery to one bit/pixel representation are reviewed. Compression techniques used on binary imagery are described. The use of halftoning to represent continuous tone (gray-shaded) imagery with binary imagery is described. The chapter also includes a summary of the special purpose equipment used to scan and display document imagery.

OVERVIEW OF DOCUMENT PROCESSING SYSTEMS

System Overview

A typical document processing system is shown in Figure 8-1. These systems typically include some or all of the following components:

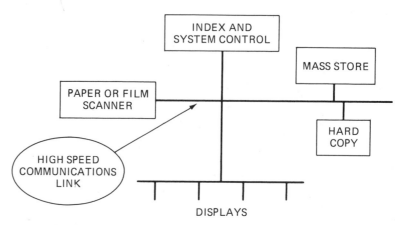

Figure 8-1. Typical document image processing system.

Image scanners. Specialized scanners for converting document material into binary image representation are commercially available. These units are designed to scan paper, microfilm, and microfiche media. Special scanners for scanning large format drawings, such as engineering drawings, are commercially available. The scanners generally scan document imagery at 6 or 8 bits per pixel and convert the scanned imagery into compressed binary imagery. Various image enhancement techniques are utilized to process input imagery to yield a bimodal histogram intensity distribution to facilitate the conversion into one bit per pixel intensity representation.

High-speed communications interface. Even compressed binary imagery represents a significant volume of digital data. If a general rule of 50 kilobytes per 8 1/2 by 11 inch page is used, it will take over five seconds to transfer a scanned document page across a standard 9600 baud RS232 communications link in a point-to-point connection. Most systems involve multiple users, a communications path with multiple nodes (scanners, workstations, storage devices, etc.), and overlapping access to large image data bases. The transfer rates required to support an acceptable system response generally dictate that a high-speed distributed communications pathway exist within a digital document processing system. In many applications, even standard high-speed network connections such as Ethernet* may not be adequate to support the total communications requirements. High-speed local area networks are generally designed for optimal transfer of text data blocks, and are not necessarily optimal for the transfer of large volumes of image data at high speed.

Mass storage. Most document image processing systems now incorporate optical disk storage devices as the archival mass storage component. Magnetic disk is also utilized for transient storage of document material at various points within the system where buffer storage is required.

Displays. Display of digitized document material requires the use of high resolution bit mapped display equipment. In general, compressed image data is transferred across the high-speed communications path to the workstations for display; high-speed decompression at the display equipment is required.

Hard copy output device. A high-resolution printer is required to produce hard

---

*A registered trademark of Xerox Corporation

copy output of document imagery. These units generally tend to be laser printers in today's systems.

Index and system control. Document image processing systems require the same image data base management and control functions as the other image processing systems described earlier in this text.

Functional Overview

Figure 8-2 represents the functional flow of document information within a typical system. Document material is scanned using special-purpose scanning equipment and converted to binary representation. Most systems provide the functionality for quality review of scanned imagery prior to committing the scanned imagery to long term archival storage. Scanners incorporate image-processing operations to create binary imagery from scanned information, and it may be necessary to rescan the source material with different processing options to yield an acceptable binary image representation of the source material. The quality control operation provides the capability of identifying images requiring rescan.

Once the scanned imagery passes the quality control operation, it is generally transferred to long-term archival storage media (typically an optical disk). At this point, it is indexed, using techniques similar to those described earlier in this text for image data base management. The degree of indexing and the number of levels of index data required generally vary with the specific application.

The archival image data base is available for query and retrieval by users. Users enter search parameters controlling their query, and image data (either entire documents or sections or pages of specific documents, depending on the degree of complexity of the image index file) are retrieved and displayed on high-resolution bit-mapped display equipment. Users can obtain hard copy renditions of the displayed imagery as desired, using high-resolution laser printers designed for the production of bit-mapped binary image hard copy.

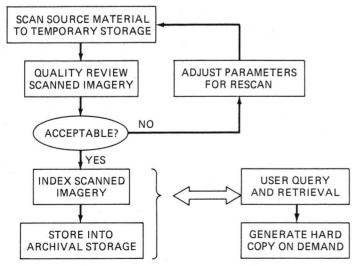

Figure 8-2. Functional view of a typical document image processing system.

IMAGE ACQUISITION

Scanners

The scanners used for the acquisition of document material generally utilize CCD sensors. Image data is initially captured at 6 or 8 bits per pixel. Image processing is applied to reduce the intensity to 1 bit per pixel. The image processing most generally applied includes convolutional filtering and adaptive thresholding.

Convolutional filtering is generally applied to enhance high spatial frequencies. Most commercial scanners utilize 3×3 or 5×5 convolutional windows and apply some sort of high pass filter to the scanned imagery. High pass filtering is used to enhance spatial detail corresponding to text and line drawings, or to perform edge detection. Some scanners may incorporate adaptive filters, where the gain of the filter is varied depending on the spatial intensity variation within local areas across the image.

Adaptive threshholding is another means of isolating text and line drawings from the page background in a scanned image. A contrast enhancement is performed within a moving local window (generally a 3×3 or 5×5 window), where the contrast enhancement is designed to yield a bimodal histogram. The "valley" of the bimodal histogram is used to separate black and white intensities, and becomes the decision point used to generate the binary pixel intensity value (1 or 0).

Figure 8-3.   Paper scanner. The operator feeds single sheets of document material which are converted to a binary image format (TDC).

Data media containing document material can consist of paper (8 1/2 by 11 inches or larger), microfilm (16mm or 35mm), or microfiche of various standard formats. Engineering drawings can also be stored on "aperture cards," which are computer cards designed to incorporate a small photographic inset image of an engineering drawing and punched alphanumeric index data on the remainder of the card.

A commercial paper scanner is shown in Figure 8-3, and a cutaway diagram of the paper transport is shown in Figure 8-4. This scanner can capture single- or double-sided documents on various sizes of paper ranging up to 11 by 17 inches. The scanner incorporates adaptive thresholding and high frequency enhancement processing, as well as compression, and can process material at a rate of under two seconds per page, scanning both sides of the page.

Scanning Resolution

The application requirements generally dictate the scanning resolution required for capturing document material in digital image format. The standard measure used to quantify document scanning resolution is the number of pixels per inch repre- In digital document systems, this measure is referred

and office material, scanning resolutions of from 150 quate for resolution of the original document material. ocuments with detailed line drawings, chemical or math- type (4 point type for example), higher resolution scan- nned document material thus requires a significant he same storage and communications problems present n this text designed to handle black and white or color er pixel). Table 8-1 shows the number of bits required page scanned at various resolutions.

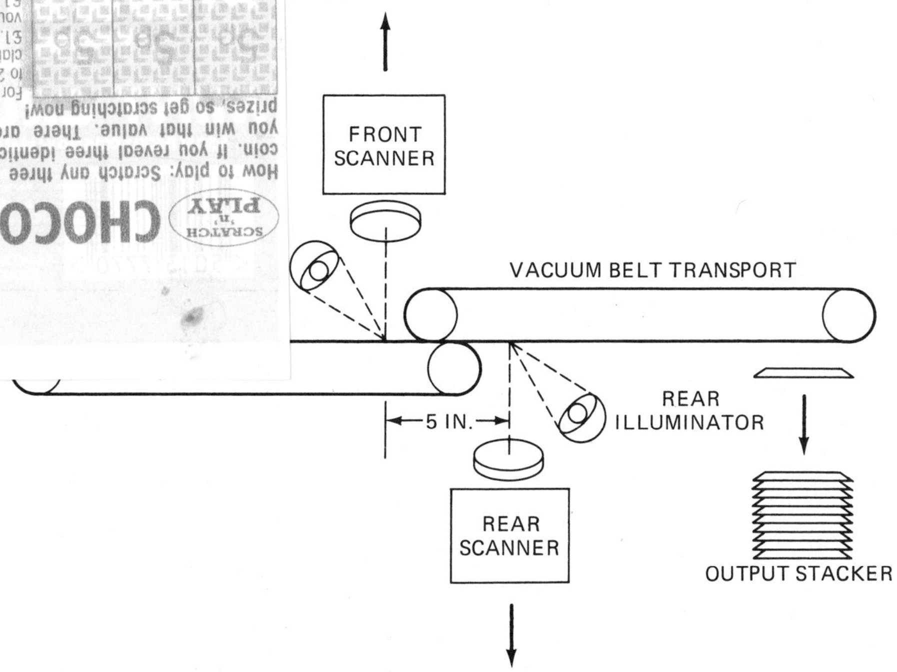

Figure 8-4. Detail of the paper transport and imaging systems for the scanner shown in Figure 8-3 (TDC).

TABLE 8-1.   IMAGE SIZE IN PIXELS FOR AN 8½ × 11 INCH PAGE

DOTS/INCH	PIXELS	NUMBER OF BITS
50	425 × 550	2.34×10^5
100	850 × 1100	9.35×10^5
150	1275 × 1650	2.10×10^6
200	1700 × 2200	3.74×10^6
300	2550 × 3300	8.42×10^6
400	3400 × 4400	1.50×10^7

Figures 8-5 and 8-6 show the same document material scanned at resolutions of 150 and 300 dpi. The 150 dpi scan resolution is adequate to resolve only the largest type fonts. 300 dpi is adequate for most material on the test target; 300 dpi scanning is generally adequate for resolution of 4 point type.

IMAGE COMPRESSION

The volumes of data produced in scanning, storing, and transferring document imagery make it mandatory to compress the image data efficiently in order to make economic digital document handling systems feasible. Data compression significantly reduces the cost of storage devices and communications paths within digital document handling systems.

Data compression standards originally developed for facsimile transmission equipment are currently used for document storage and retrieval systems. The compression standards were developed by the International Telegraph and Telephone Consultative Committee (CCITT), and are referred to as CCITT Group 3 or CCITT Group 4 compression.

CCITT compression is based on the statistical nature of scanned binary document imagery. Scanned document material usually consists of large amounts of white space, with local clusters of black pixels representing text or line drawings. If a typical scan line within a digital image is examined, it is generally (a) either all white or (b) is represented by long strings of white pixels interrupted by short strings of black pixels. Because of the statistical nature of the scanned material, it is possible to use *run length encoding* to achieve image compression. Run length encoding involves replacement of the scanned pixel values with code words representing the run lengths of black and white pixels along a scan line. The code words are designed to require less bits than the bit strings they represent.

An examination of digitized document imagery also reveals that there is a high degree of correlation between adjacent scan lines. Statistics indicate that transition from black to white or from white to black that occur on a scan line are likely to occur on the next adjacent scan line within a few pixel positions of the transition on the first line. It is possible to utilize two-dimensional coding schemes to encode only the transitions between black and white, and to use code word assignment that allocate the fewest numbers of bits to the most likely pattern of bit transition between adjacent lines. CCITT Group 3 compression utilizes a combination of one dimensional run length encoding and two-dimensional coding based on bit reversal between adjacent lines. CCITT Group 4 compression utilizes only the two-dimensional coding based on bit reversals.

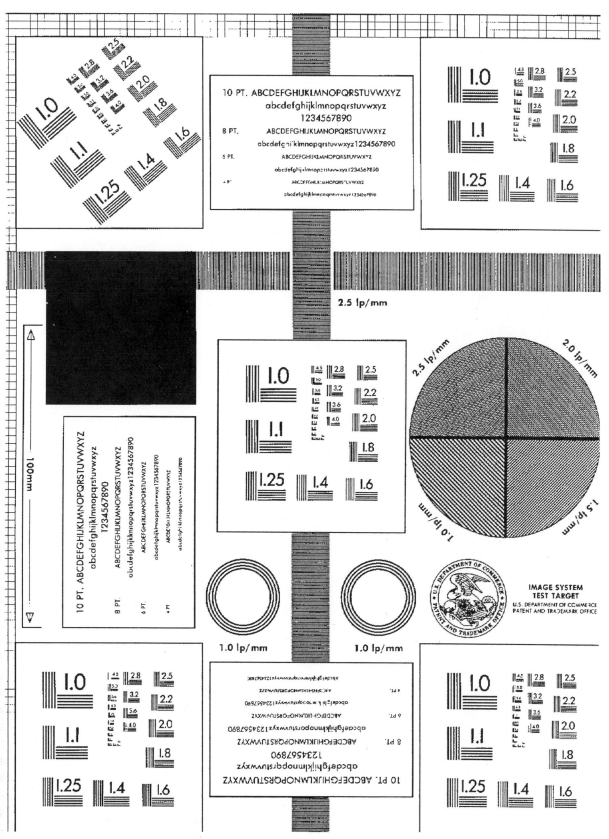

Figure 8-5.   Digital image representation of a test target scanned at 150 dots per inch (target courtesy of U.S. Patent and Trademark Office).

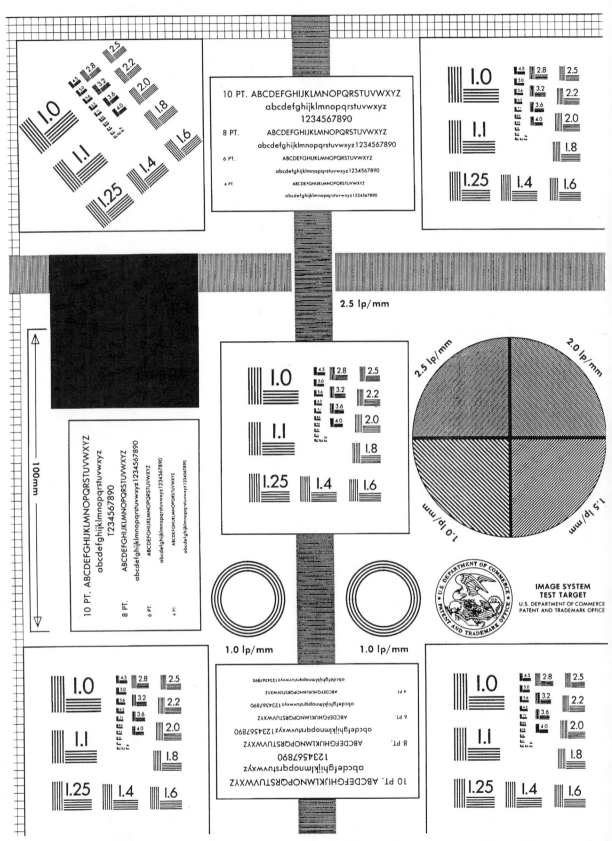

Figure 8-6. Digital image representation of the same test target as Figure 8-5, scanned at 300 dots per inch (target courtesy of U.S. Patent and Trademark Office).

CCITT Group 3 Compression

If a sufficient number of document examples are analyzed, it is possible to determine the statistics of black and white run lengths within a typical standard set of documents. The CCITT has established nine standard pages are representative of a large class of documents[1], and determined the black and white run lengths within that set of imagery. White and black run lengths can be ordered by the frequency of occurrence. A set of code words can be developed to represent the run lengths, with the number of bits in the code word being the lowest for the most commonly occurring run length, and highest for the least frequently occurring run length.

Huffman Encoding is used to encode the pixel run lengths in the CCITT Group 4 standard. Huffman codes are variable length code words that produce optimal encoding with minimum redundancy. The use of Huffman encoding guarantees that the compressed imagery will be produced with the lowest possible number of bits per image for the statistical set of images selected to derive the run length codes.

Figure 8-7 illustrates the tree structure associated with Huffman encoding for a simple example considering only six statistically occurring white pixel run lengths within a scanned image. If the six run lengths are designated R_1 through R_6, assume the following arbitrarily assigned distribution for the probability associated with each white run length within the image in this example:

$$P(R_1) = .35$$
$$P(R_2) = .25$$
$$P(R_3) = .20$$
$$P(R_4) = .10$$
$$P(R_5) = .07$$
$$P(R_6) = .03$$

where $P(R_n)$ is the probability of occurrence of a bit string of length R_n. Figure 8-7 shows the tree structure that assigns unique code words to each run length, with

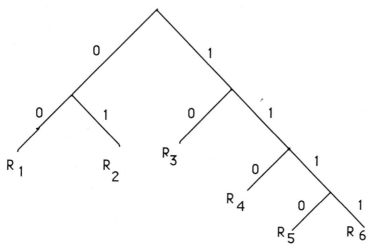

Figure 8-7.   Huffman coding tree structure example.

the most probable run lengths assigned the shortest code words. The code words assigned to represent white pixel run lengths for this example would be:

$$R_1 \ 00$$
$$R_2 \ 01$$
$$R_3 \ 10$$
$$R_4 \ 110$$
$$R_5 \ 1110$$
$$R_6 \ 1111$$

This type of tree-structured encoding yields a set of unique codes that can be decoded sequentially as the encoded bit stream is transmitted serially. The most frequently occurring run lengths will be represented by the shortest code words, and will be decoded more rapidly than less frequently occurring run lengths that are represented by longer code words.

The CCITT Group 3 compression algorithm utilizes Huffman code words to represent "make up codes" and "terminating codes" in encoding single lines. "Make up codes," incorporating code words of 9 bits or less, are used to represent run lengths in multiples of 64 pixels. "Terminating codes" are used to represent run lengths of less than 64 pixels.

Figure 8-8 shows the "make up codes" used to represent multiples of 64 black or white pixel run lengths. A white run length of 64 pixels is represented by the 5-bit code word 11011, a black run length of 128 pixels is represented by a 12-bit code word 000011001000, etc. Figure 8-9 shows the "terminating codes," used to represent pixel run lengths of less than 64 pixels. Black and white run lengths are encoded differently because the statistics of white run lengths differ significantly from the statistics of black run lengths in scanned imagery.

A run length of 137 white pixels would be encoded using two code words:

make up code for a white run length of 128 pixels; 10010
terminating code for a white run length of 9 pixels: 10100

The compressed bit sequence would be 1001010100. The total number of bits encoded to represent this run length is thus 10 bits, and a compression factor of 13.7:1 is achieved in this example (137/10).

The actual degree of compression achieved in practice on document material is highly dependent on the image content. Figure 8-9 shows that short run lengths can be encoded with code words of more bits than the actual run length itself (e.g., a run length of 2 white pixels is represented as a 4-bit code word). If images are extremely "busy," with a significant amount of high frequency variation, it is possible to obtain "negative compression" using this algorithm. In addition to the image content, it is possible for improper or noisy scanning of the original document material to cause this effect, due to the introduction of "salt and pepper" noise into the scanned imagery.

This discussion has considered only one-dimensional run length encoding up to this point (each scanned line of pixels is encoded independently). The CCITT Group 3 standard is actually a modified Relative Element Address Designated (READ) code that combines one-dimensional run length encoding with a two-dimensional coding scheme. The two-dimensional encoding scheme is based on the fact that

White run lengths	Code word	Black run lengths	Code word
64	11011	64	0000001111
128	10010	128	000011001000
192	010111	192	000011001001
256	0110111	256	000001011011
320	00110110	320	000000110011
384	00110111	384	000000110100
448	01100100	448	000000110101
512	01100101	512	0000001101100
576	01101000	576	0000001101101
640	01100111	640	0000001001010
704	011001100	704	0000001001011
768	011001101	768	0000001001100
832	011010010	832	0000001001101
896	011010011	896	0000001110010
960	011010100	960	0000001110011
1024	011010101	1024	0000001110100
1088	011010110	1088	0000001110101
1152	011010111	1152	0000001110110
1216	011011000	1216	0000001110111
1280	011011001	1280	0000001010010
1344	011011010	1344	0000001010011
1408	011011011	1408	0000001010100
1472	010011000	1472	0000001010101
1536	010011001	1536	0000001011010
1600	010011010	1600	0000001011011
1664	011000	1664	0000001100100
1728	010011011	1728	0000001100101
EOL	000000000001	EOL	000000000001

Note — It is recognized that machines exist which accommodate larger paper widths whilst maintaining the standard horizontal resolution. This option has been provided for by the addition of the Make-up code set defined as follows:

Run length (black and white)	Make-up codes
1792	00000001000
1856	00000001100
1920	00000001101
1984	000000010010
2048	000000010011
2112	000000010100
2176	000000010101
2240	000000010110
2304	000000010111
2368	000000011100
2432	000000011101
2496	000000011110
2560	000000011111

Figure 8-8.   Make-up codes used CCITT Group 3 compression standard.

White run length	Code word	Black run length	Code word
0	00110101	0	0000110111
1	000111	1	010
2	0111	2	11
3	1000	3	10
4	1011	4	011
5	1100	5	0011
6	1110	6	0010
7	1111	7	00011
8	10011	8	000101
9	10100	9	000100
10	00111	10	0000100
11	01000	11	0000101
12	001000	12	0000111
13	000011	13	00000100
14	110100	14	00000111
15	110101	15	000011000
16	101010	16	0000010111
17	101011	17	0000011000
18	0100111	18	0000001000
19	0001100	19	00001100111
20	0001000	20	00001101000
21	0010111	21	00001101100
22	0000011	22	000001101111
23	0000100	23	00000101000
24	0101000	24	00000010111
25	0101011	25	00000011000
26	0010011	26	000011001010
27	0100100	27	000011001011
28	0011000	28	000011001100
29	00000010	29	000011001101
30	00000011	30	000001101000
31	00011010	31	000001101001
32	00011011	32	000001101010
33	00010010	33	000001101011
34	00010011	34	000011010010
35	00010100	35	000011010011
36	00010101	36	000011010100
37	00010110	37	000011010101
38	00010111	38	000011010110
39	00101000	39	000011010111
40	00101001	40	000001101100
41	00101010	41	000001101101
42	00101011	42	000011011010
43	00101100	43	000011011011
44	00101101	44	000001010100
45	00000100	45	000001010101
46	00000101	46	000001010110
47	00001010	47	000001010111
48	00001011	48	000001100100
49	01010010	49	000001100101
50	01010011	50	000001010010
51	01010100	51	000001010011
52	01010101	52	000000100100
53	00100100	53	000000110111
54	00100101	54	000000111000
55	01011000	55	000000100111
56	01011001	56	000000101000
57	01011010	57	000001011000
58	01011011	58	000001011001
59	01001010	59	000000101011
60	01001011	60	000000101100
61	00110010	61	000001011010
62	00110011	62	000001100110
63	00110100	63	000001100111

Figure 8-9.   Terminating codes used in CCITT Group 3 compression standard.

image data is highly redundant across adjacent scan lines. Statistically, if a black-white transition occurs on a given scan line, the odds are that the same transition will occur within plus or minus 3 pixels in the next scan line as well. The modified READ encoding utilizes two adjacent scan lines in developing optimal Huffman code words for image compression.

The CCITT Group 3 compression standard incorporates a "K factor." The first line of every group of K lines is encoded using one-dimensional encoding, as described earlier. Between every Kth line, the two-dimensional encoding scheme is used. The K factor guards against loss of line synchronization. In digital image processing systems, K=infinity is often used.

CCITT Group 4 Compression

The CCITT Group 4 compression standard utilizes only the two-dimensional encoding scheme based on pixel intensity transitions occurring in adjacent lines. There is no "K factor" available in the Group 4 encoding standard.

A complete description of the one- and two-dimensional CCITT standards for compression is contained in reference 2. Reference 3 contains a description of both CCITT algorithms and other encoding schemes that can be used to compress binary imagery.

The CCITT compression standards may not provide the optimal compression for specific types of imagery, but the fact that a standard has been defined and accepted has resulted in widespread use of this technique. Hardware components are now commercially available that incorporate the compression/decompression algorithms for both CCITT Group 3 and Group 4 compression standards.

BINARY IMAGE DISPLAY

Binary image display systems operate in the same manner as the digital image display systems described earlier. Images are stored in one or more pages of bit-mapped image-refresh display memory. The fact that document imagery requires only one bit per pixel for display significantly reduces the amount of refresh memory required for digital document displays, and the cost of document display workstations is generally lower than more general image display systems.

The following features are desirable in a digital document display workstation:

Hardware image compression/decompression. Binary document imagery is generally stored in a compressed format. Transfer of stored imagery to the display equipment in compressed format is desirable to reduce the communications bandwidth required between storage and display, and to reduce system network data traffic. Commercial hardware for the decompression of imagery based on the CCITT compression standards is now available, and can be incorporated into display equipment to provide high-speed decompression at the workstation. Compression may be required if image manipulation is performed at the workstation, to enable compressed image data to be transferred from the workstation back to archival or temporary storage.

Image Manipulation. Capability for roam, zoom, intensity reversal, and rotation supported by hardware is desirable.

Image Storage. It may be usedul to provide adequate bit-mapped storage to accommodate several pages of document material at the workstation. This provides high-speed next page/last page display capability without the delay introduced by communications transfer of stored imagery across the communications interface.

Interface capability. Display equipment incorporating standard communications interfaces is more easily integrated within a total system than equipment with specialized interfaces. Display equipment supporting commercial bus and communications interfaces is now available.

Figure 8-10 shows a block diagram for a commercially available document image display workstation. This device can be equipped for image compression/decompression, image processing functions, and multiple pages of display memory. In addition, interfaces to optical disk equipment, scanners, and other input/output equipment are supported via standard interfaces. Figure 8-11 shows a picture of this equipment in use.

Display Resolution

There is a relationship between the resolution at which images are scanned and the resolution of the image display device used in a specific system. Since most images will be scanned at 200 dpi or greater resolution, it is generally not possible to display a full scanned page (typically 8 1/2 by 11 inches) on a display that supports less than 1700 by 2200 pixels. Even with this resolution display, 8 1/2 by 11 inch material scanned at greater than 200 dots per inch cannot be displayed in full page mode on the display screen. Generally, subsampling is used to reduce the number of pixels in the scanned image to the number of pixels that can be accommodated by the image display. Another option is storage of the full resolution image in the display bit-

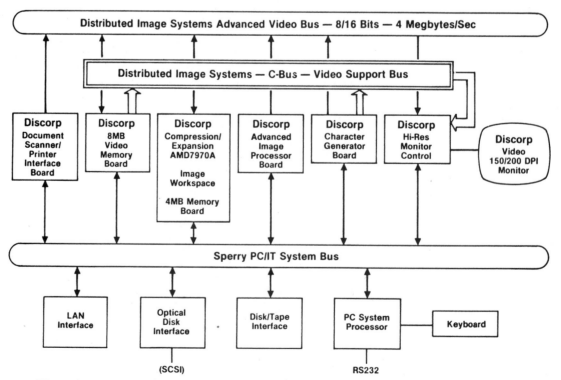

Figure 8-10. Block diagram of a commercially available high-resolution binary image processing and display workstation (Distributed Image Systems Corporation).

Figure 8-11. Image and user interface display on the high-resolution workstation shown in Figure 8-10. The screen resolution is adequate to display an 8 1/2 by 11 inch image at 150 dots per inch and user interface menus adjacent to the image.

mapped memory, and the display of segments of the scanned images at full resolution on the screen.

Figure 8-12 shows an example of the various ways in which a 1700 by 2200 pixel display can be utilized to display a variety of scanned image formats. A display of an 8 1/2 by 11 inch image at 150 dpi will require only 1275 by 1650 pixels, leaving room for user interface menus on the side of the displayed image in vertical ("portrait") mode. If the same page is displayed in horizontal ("landscape") mode, there is room available for menu display on the bottom of the screen. The same display can also accommodate full resolution of an 8 1/2 by 11 inch image scanned at 200 dpi, as shown in the figure.

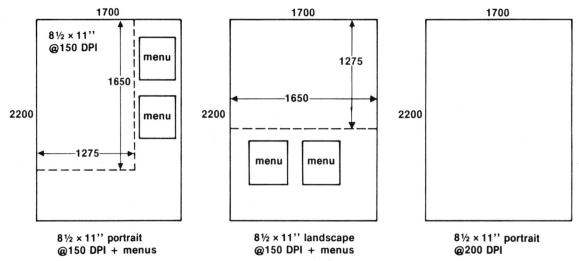

Figure 8-12. Three methods of utilizing a 1700 × 2200 pixel resolution display format.

HALFTONING

Digital halftoning is a technique that can be used to display gray-shaded imagery using patterns of ones and zeroes. This technique allows storage and display of gray-shaded imagery within digital document image processing systems that accommodate only binary imagery.

The basic process in image halftoning is depicted in Figure 8-13. The gray-shaded image is divided into segments. These segments can be rectangular or can be other defined shapes. The average pixel value is computed in each segment. The average gray shade in the image segment defines the binary pattern to be output for that segment in the output binary image. Low gray shades will be represented by a large number of black pixels in the output segment, intermediate gray shades will produce output binary image segments with the number of white and black pixels more

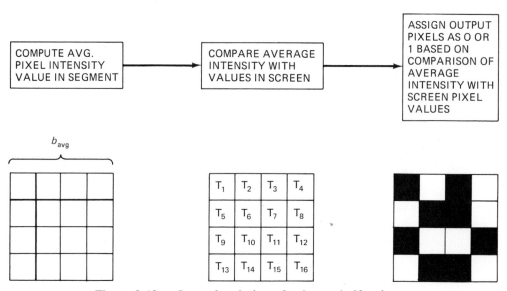

Figure 8-13. General technique for image halftoning.

nearly equal, and high gray levels will be depicted in the output image by a large number of white pixels in the output binary image segment.

The halftoning process is performed as depicted in Figure 8–13. The average intensity, b_{avg}, of the segment is computed. The halftone screen consists of a matrix of the same size as the image segment. Each position in the halftone screen contains a threshold intensity, T_i. b_{avg} is compared to each intensity value at each position in the halftone screen in turn. A white pixel is output at all positions at which b_{avg} exceeds the threshold intensity value T_i, and a black pixel is output at all other pixel positions. Three examples of the use of a halftone screen are shown in Figure 8-14.

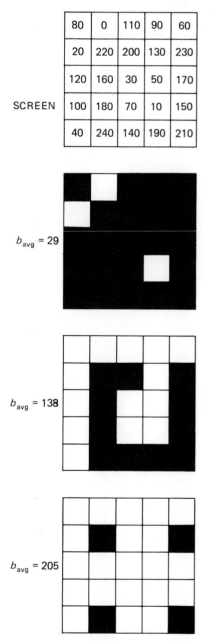

Figure 8-14. Three examples of the binary pixel patterns produced with the halftone screen shown at the top, for three different intensity values in the input image.

Figure 8-15. Halftone representation of the image shown in Figure 4-34a.

		196	182		
	142	57	43	128	
255	114	28	14	99	241
	170	85	71	156	
		227	213		

Figure 8-16. Halftone screen used to produce the halftone image shown in Figure 8-15.

Advanced digital halftoning techniques will utilize adjacent image segments, and apply a larger thresholding screen to the input image (e.g., in a two by two pattern of threshholding screens, each four by four group of pixels might be employed). This introduces a random effect in the output halftone image, and prevents a "blocky" appearance near edges or image discontinuities. A full discussion of digital halftoning techniques can be found in Reference 3.

Figure 8-15 shows a halftone rendition of the same image as shown in Figure 4-34a. The halftone screen used to produce this image[4] is shown in Figure 8-16.

REFERENCES

1. Hunter, R. and A. H. Robinson, "International Digital Facsimile Coding Standards," *Proc. IEEE 68,* 7, July 1980 (p. 854).
2. International Telegraph and Telephone Committee (CCITT), *Terminal Equipment and Protocols for Telemation Services,* Red Book Volume VII-Fascicle VII.3, VIII Plenary Session, 1985.
3. Hou, H. S., *Digital Document Processing,* New York, John Wiley and Sons, 1983.
4. Young, J. and E. Wels, Personal communication.

9
Image Processing on Personal Computers

INTRODUCTION

Increasingly powerful personal computers are now making it possible to implement fairly comprehensive image processing systems for less than the cost of a new automobile. Personal computer (PC) -based image processing systems can incorporate many features of minicomputer or mainframe based systems, scaled down for the personal computer environment.

The main limitations imposed by processing on a personal computer as opposed to the minicomputer or mainframe-based systems described in the previous chapters of this text include:

Display resolution. In a PC environment, image display is performed using the display screen associated with the PC. PC-based image processing generally does not involve the use of expensive special purpose dedicated image display peripheral devices that are found on minicomputer or mainframe-based systems. Special-purpose boards are available that improve the available display resolution for PCs, but generally PC-based image processing is limited to display resolutions on the order of 512 × 512 or 640 × 480 pixels. The color resolution available for display is generally 8 bits (256 colors). Without the use of special-purpose boards, many PCs support even less display resolution, but the trend is toward increasing display resolution and increasing color resolution.

Processing Speed. Most PCs are generally slower than minicomputer or mainframe systems. The processing speed of PCs is adequate for many image processing operations that are not CPU-intensive. Operations such as digital filtering, Fourier transforms, and geometric transformation will be extremely time consuming if performed on PCs. For this reason, there are special-purpose hardware boards available that provide high-speed computation for many desirable image processing operations. These boards are described later in this chapter.

Solid State Memory. PCs are limited in both solid state and peripheral memory when compared with minicomputers or mainframes. Image processing operations that are computationally intensive proceed more slowly on PCs because the PC memory cannot hold the entire image, or even large segments of the image, and processing a full image requires a significant amount of disk to memory data transfer. Even though the microprocessor used within a particular PC might have an inherent processing speed equivalent to a minicomputer or mainframe processor, the memory limitations of the PC cause the PC-based system to operate more slowly than the larger processor.

Peripheral Memory. As of this writing, PCs are available with 40 megabyte Winchester disk drives, and 100 megabyte drives are being forecast. Although this memory capacity is more than adequate for many conventional PC functions (word processing, spreadsheet, graphics packages, etc.), the large memory demands of digital image processing can exceed these storage capacities very quickly. A 512 × 512 8-bit image requires 262 kilobytes, and a 40 megabyte disk would hold approximately 150 images if it could be fully dedicated to image storage. Generally, the full disk can not be devoted completely to image storage, since the operating system and applications programs will be stored on the Winchester disk, so a 40 megabyte disk will fill up rapidly with images in operational use. Even a 100 megabyte disk will not accomodate a large number of images.

Peripheral disks on PCs generally operate at transfer speeds lower than disk storage units on minicomputer or mainframe processors. The PC environment does not require high-performance high-speed disk drives, since PCs are not generally used in a multiuser shared environment, and the cost of high-performance drives inhibits their introduction into the PC market. Consequently, disk drives on PCs tend to perform at lower data transfer rates than drives on larger systems. The net effect of the lower data transfer rate to and from disk, and the memory restrictions of PCs, combine to limit the speed at which image processing can be performed in a PC environment.

This chapter describes PC-based image processing systems, and the peripherals most commonly utilized in that environment. A description of special-purpose hardware boards now available to support PC-based image processing operations is also included. The number of products and the functionality of available products is increasing rapidly in this area, and the information in this chapter has been developed as a basic introduction to the commercial product base. Interested readers should consult current trade literature to insure that they are obtaining the most advanced available products when developing a PC-based system, since the field is dynamic and the rate at which new products are being introduced into the market is increasing rapidly as of this writing.

PC-BASED IMAGE PROCESSING SYSTEM ARCHITECTURE

Figure 9-1 shows a typical PC-based image processing system. The system includes the same general elements as systems utilizing minicomputers or mainframes as host processors—equipment for image acquisition, image processing, and output operations. The implementation in a PC environment is quite different, however.

System Bus. The system bus is a data transfer mechanism within computer systems. The bus handles high-speed data transfer within the processing system. The system bus is the path on which digital data travels between the central processing unit, memory, and peripheral devices. It is generally a high-speed transfer path incorporating data transfer protocols and formats designed for high performance. In the PC environment, many manufacturers make it possible to attach additional devices to the system bus for special-purpose applications. A variety of special-purpose products for supporting image processing applications has become available, and the majority of these products attach directly to the PC system bus.

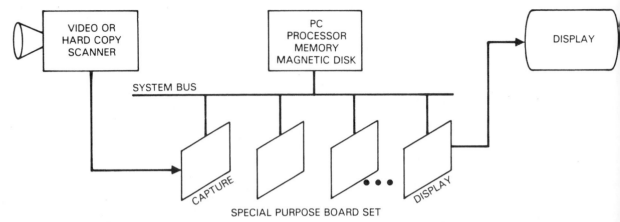

Figure 9-1. PC-based system architecture.

Video or Hard Copy Scanners. PC-based image processing systems are generally used to process image data originally captured in hard copy or video format. Commercially produced paper scanners are available that scan hard copy images (paper, photographic prints, etc.) in black and white or color formats. Video digitizers are also available, similar to those described in Chapter 2. These digitizers digitize a single frame of video data, where the video data is in a conventional commercial television format. The scanner used for image capture is attached to the system bus using an interface card provided by the manufacturer of the device. Image data can be transferred to magnetic disk via the PC memory for slow-speed paper scanners, or to a memory buffer provided within the bus interface for the higher speed capture of video frames.

Special-Purpose Boards. Various types of commercially available boards provide large image storage memory buffers and programmable hardware for performing image processing operations at high speeds. These boards provide performance far in excess of the limited performance that would be achieved using the PC with its limitations on data transfer rates and solid-state memory capacity for specific functions. These boards are described later in this chapter.

Display. Display controller boards are generally used to improve on the resolution that might be directly available with the PC. These boards control monitors with resolution generally up to 640 × 480 pixels, and boards supporting black and white or color display are available. Hard copy output of images processed on PC-based systems is generally produced by photographing the screen of a display. There are currently no low-cost digital film recorders available for PC-based systems.

SPECIAL PURPOSE IMAGE PROCESSING BOARDS

Figure 9-2 shows the data transfer and control paths generally associated with the use of special purpose boards for image processing applications on PCs. The details of the interconnectivity, and the exact data transfer paths, vary with the manufacturer of the board sets. Figure 9-2 is meant to represent the type of equipment currently available commercially, but does not represent equipment from any specific manufacturer.

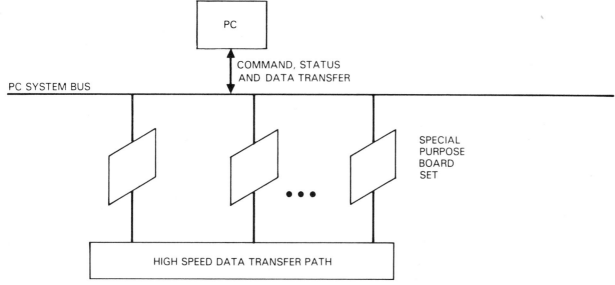

Figure 9-2.   Data transfer and control paths using special-purpose board sets.

Most commercially available board sets do not utilize the system bus of the PC for the transfer of large volumes of digital imagery. Generally, a board set will incorporate a high-speed data transfer path that links all boards used in an image processing system. This data transfer path allows high-speed transfer of image data between boards as required by the application. The data transfer occurs at higher speeds than would be possible on the PC bus. This approach makes high-speed transfer of image data between boards possible, and avoids interference or contention on the PC bus. As one example, data transfer is generally required between the board performing image acquisition and the processing board. Figure 9-3 shows a commercially available example. The image acquisition board, shown on the left, is linked to a processing board via a ribbon cable connection. The protocols for transferring image data between boards are generally specific to the manufacturer of the board set selected, and may not conform to any network or bus transfer standards (such as Ethernet* or Multibus**).

The PC provides control of image processing operations performed on the special purpose board set. Software in the PC controls all board operations, including image acquisition, processing, and display. The interface between the board set and the PC operates across the PC bus. Data transfer across the PC bus to and from the board set includes the transfer of commands from the PC directing operations on the board set, and status information passed from the board set back to the PC. Status information generally indicates that operations have been completed (e.g., the scan and digitization of a video frame has been completed, or a digital operation on a line of digital image data has been completed).

PC control of image processing operations on the special purpose boards is generally achieved using a set of subroutines provided by the board manufacturer. These subroutines provide control of basic image processing operations (e.g., initiate image digitization on the image acquisition board). Control commands are transferred

---

*Trademark of Xerox Corporation
**Trademark of Intel Corporation

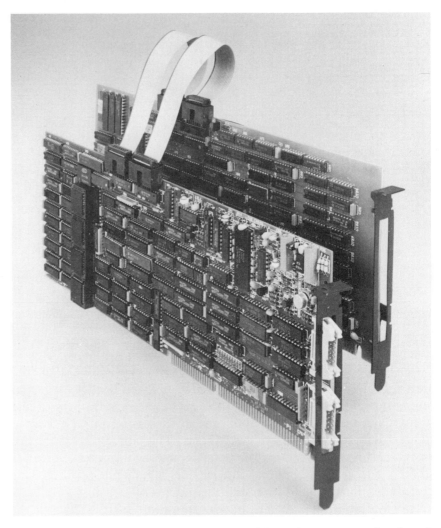

Figure 9-3. An image acquisition board linked with an image processing board using a high-speed data transfer path. The board on the left accepts video signal input and digitizes a video frame. The board on the right provides high-speed computational support. The two ribbon cables handle high-speed image data transfer between the boards under control of the PC (Data Translation Inc.).

to the appropriate board across the PC bus through the use of these low-level subroutines.

The PC bus interface with the board set also provides for the transfer of image data when required. Image segments or entire images can be transferred across the PC bus into the PC memory for further use. The PC processor can perform image processing operations on image data not available using the special-purpose board set. The PC is also used to store and maintain an image data base on PC peripherals. Some boards provide Direct Memory Access (DMA) to the PC memory.

The remainder of this section describes the types of special-purpose boards that are commercially available.

Image Acquisition Boards

Figure 9-4 shows a functional block diagram of a typical video image digitizing board used with PC-based systems for image acquisition. This diagram is illustrative

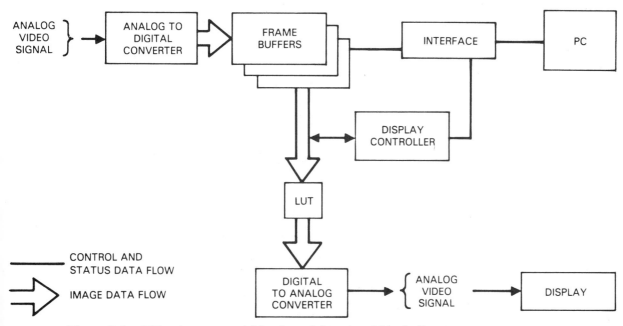

Figure 9-4. Video image acquisition board functional block diagram.

of the types of commercially available boards, and does not represent any specific commercial product. The majority of PC-based systems utilize commercially available video cameras as the input source of the imagery to be processed. If an image in hard copy format is to be processed, it is generally placed in front of a video camera for digital capture.

The PC controls the acquisition of video imagery. A command to initiate video frame capture is passed from the PC across the PC bus to the special-purpose board used for image capture. A single video frame is processed by the analog to digital converter and a raster image is produced. Some boards provide three separate color component (red, green, and blue) images from color video input.

The raster image is stored into a frame buffer generally available directly on the image acquisition board (some manufacturers utilize a high-speed data transfer path to transfer image data to another board containing the frame buffers as the video signal is digitized). For color imagery, three frame buffers are filled. After the frame is digitized and the image data is available in the frame buffers, a status signal is sent to the PC signifying completion of video digitizing.

Some commercially available image acquisition boards also support video display. These boards provide the ability to display the digitized image directly on a monitor as it is captured. These boards can also serve as the display controller for any image data that is to be displayed. Image data can be transferred from the PC, or from other special-purpose boards via the manufacturers data transfer path, into the frame buffers. The display controller on the board controls continual read from memory and display refresh operations. Look-up tables (LUTs) that provide contrast enhancement of the image to be displayed are generally provided on the board. The LUTs can be addressed directly by the PC via the PC interface, and the PC is used to compute and load the LUTs for the specific application.

Commercially available boards generally produce 512 square or 256 square digital imagery, with 8 bits per pixel. Color images are represented as three 8 bit images at either 256 or 512 square pixel resolution. Manufacturers provide boards for interfacing with various standard video signal data, and the user must select a board in combination with the selection of the video camera to be used for image acquisition.

Image processing operations are often available on these boards as built-in hardware features. Features commonly found on these boards include:

- image arithmetic, including frame averaging, frame addition, multiplication, subtraction, and division
- multiplication or division by a constant
- logical operations between multiple images (e.g., AND and OR operations)
- image windowing for display, including roam and zoom control (for boards that combine display with capture support)
- bit-mapped graphics overlay of image data

Figure 9-5 shows an example of a commercially available image acquisition board. Figure 9-6 shows a block diagram of the board shown in Figure 9-5.

Image Processing Boards

Image processing peripheral boards generally provide high-speed image processing functionality through the use of specially designed processing hardware components. The basic concept is to provide image processing performance that is an order of magnitude or more improvement over use of the PC system itself, with a goal of

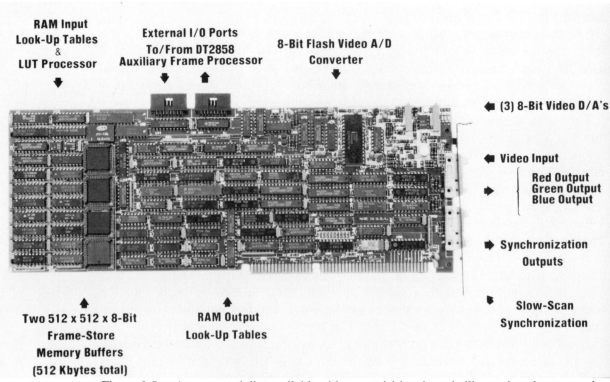

Figure 9-5. A commercially available video acquisition board, illustrating the processing components and board interfaces. The external I/O ports support data transfer to and from a high-speed image processing board (Data Translation Inc.).

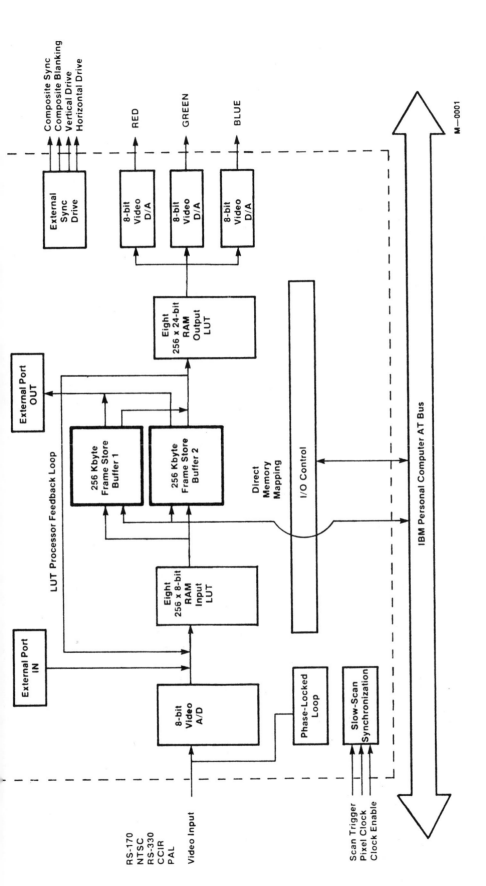

DT2851 HIGH RESOLUTION FRAME GRABBER

Figure 9-6. Block diagram of the video acquisition board shown in Figure 9-5 (Data Translation Inc.).

providing image processing operations that can be performed in less than a second on 512 pixel square 8 bit imagery.

Use of special-purpose boards can provide responsive interactive image processing on small images in a PC-based environment. Figure 9-7 shows a functional diagram of a special-purpose processing board. The PC controls the processing of imagery through transfer of commands and control data across the PC bus to the special-purpose boards. The PC bus can also be used to transfer image data to and from digital frame buffers on the special-purpose boards, when required. Generally, however, image data transfer will occur via a data transfer path internal to the special-purpose board set, as discussed earlier in this chapter.

In the case of special-purpose processing boards, the digital image data to be processed resides in image frame buffers. The frame buffers can be located either directly on the board performing the processing, or can be located on other boards within the system (e.g., the video image acquisition board). Image data is transferred sequentially to a selected high-speed processor that executes the specific algorithm requested. As processing proceeds, the processed (output) image data is transferred back to an image frame buffer that is also located on the special-purpose board set. The data transfer path shown in Figure 9-7 can either be a direct memory transfer between on-board memory and processors, or can be via the manufacturers internal data transfer connection between boards.

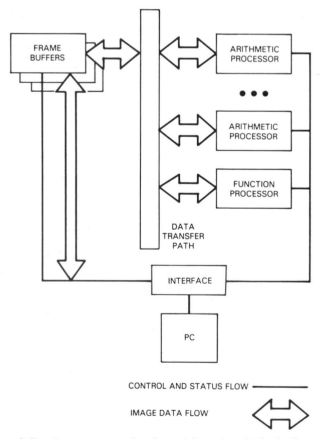

Figure 9-7.   Image processing board functional block diagram.

The arithmetic and function processors shown in Figure 9-7 are hardware components that are specifically optimized to perform a small number of arithmetic processes at high speed. They are limited in functionality, and optimized for performance. Functions that are available generally include:

- Histogram computation
- Convolutional filtering
- Image arithmetic (both on a frame to frame basis and on a local pixel neighborhood basis)

The processors are designed to accept a stream of pixels from the input image, perform the required arithmetic operations at high speed, and transfer the processed pixel stream back out to memory.

Processing speeds of approximately 10 million pixels per second are common for these processors. At that speed, it is possible to perform point operations (an arithmetic computation involving only a single pixel per operation) at a computation speed that provides processing of a full frame at 512×512 pixel resolution in less than the refresh time of the output display (1/30 sec). Even more complex operations, such as a 3×3 or 5×5 convolutional filter of a 512×512 pixel image can be performed in less than two seconds using these special purpose components. This processing speed provides "real-time" image processing on a PC-based system. Figure 9-8 shows an example of a commercially available processing board. Figure 9-9 shows a block diagram of a commercially available floating point processing board designed to support a PC for image processing applications and other signal processing applications.

Special-purpose processing boards remove many of the restrictions, discussed at the start of this chapter, imposed by working in a PC-based environment. Despite the evolution of these processing aids, even the best available commercial equipment

Figure 9-8. A commercially available image processing board (Imaging Technology Incorporated).

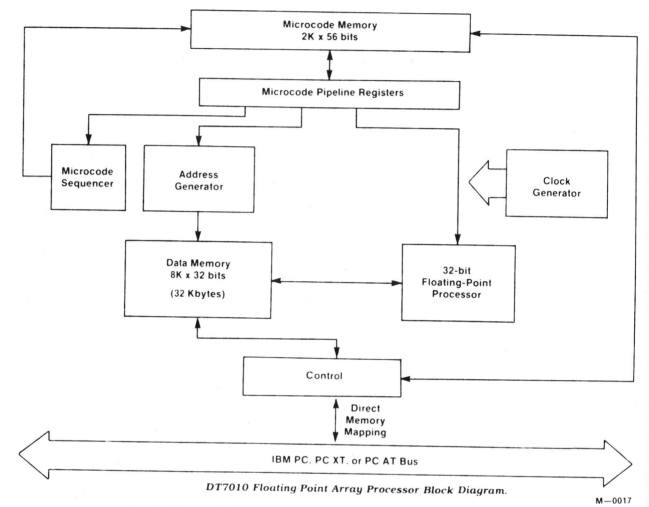

DT7010 Floating Point Array Processor Block Diagram.

M—0017

Figure 9-9.   Block diagram of a commercially available board for high-speed floating point processing supporting a PC (Data Translation Inc.).

does not remove all of the restrictions associated with operating in a PC-based environment. The major restrictions that still remain include:

- The majority of PC-based image processing is oriented toward images that are 512 by 512 pixels or less. This is primarily due to the fact that video signal data (approximately 512×512 resolution) is the primary low-cost source of imagery processed on PC-based systems. With currently available technology, processing of 1024 by 1024 pixel imagery will probably be available within a few years for the PC environment.
- The emphasis on the currently available image processing boards has been on supporting the subjective enhancement operations (Chapter 3), and on high-speed image filtering. Other quantitative operations, such as geometric transformation, multispectral classification, and others discussed in Chapter 4 can benefit from the use of the high-speed arithmetic processors provided with the special-purpose boards, but the boards are not specifically designed to optimize those computations.

The use of special-purpose boards thus provides a low-cost system solution for a system that can be effectively applied to selected problems. Complex processing of large imagery generally still requires the resources of a minicomputer or mainframe-based system. Despite the restrictions, PC-based systems can be effectively applied in a large number of applications. Figure 9-10 shows a PC-based image processing system configured with commercially available components.

SOFTWARE CONSIDERATIONS

The software design concepts discussed in Chapter 7 generally apply to the PC-based system environment. PC-based systems should be designed with the same modularity as systems developed in more complex environments (minicomputer and mainframe environments). The image formatting and header record considerations also apply to the PC-based environment, but the level of image annotation and the amount of information stored within each header record will generally be much less in a PC environment. A PC-based system will generally be used for highly interactive and adaptive image processing, and the requirements for large volumes of indexed imagery are generally not present in that environment. PC-based image processing generally involves real-time acquisition of an image from a video source, image processing and enhancement, and capture of the enhanced image by photographing a display monitor. Occasionally, an image may be retained on the peripheral storage devices on the PC, but the limitations of those devices, discussed previ-

Figure 9-10.   A commercially available PC-based image processing system. The PC and standard PC monitor are on the left; the display on the right supports a higher resolution gray scale image display, and the video camera used for image acquisition is shown on top of the image display (Imaging Technology Incorporated).

ously in this chapter, generally preclude accumulation of large volumes of archival image storage.

A PC-based system will involve all the software components described in Chapter 7 (individual processing modules, general purpose subroutines, the image processing executive, the image DBMS, and the computer operating system). In addition, the user may get involved in selection of a lower level set of software subroutines, board interface software. Reference 1 contains an overview of a PC-based image processing software structure, including examples of each category and C-language software for selected image processing operations. This section contains a description of board interface software, and a discussion of the other categories of software and how they are affected by implementation in a PC-based environment.

Board Interface Software

Board manufacturers generally provide a library of software routines that can be called from higher level programs in the PC. These routines provide direct interface between the PC and the board components. Commands can be forwarded to the board components to perform low-level image operations.

Board interface software provides the detailed low-level control of all elements of the image processing performed on the board set. These routines control the detailed execution of the components of all operations. They control the timing of operations occurring on the boards, the transfer of data between elements of the boards, downloading of information to board elements (e.g., loading of look-up tables, loading of microcode for performing arithmetic operations within an arithmetic processor, etc.), and other functions. They also provide PC control of total operational flow by fielding and handling interrupts and status messages transferred to the PC from the board components.

The developer of a PC-based image processing system generally does not have to develop this set of subroutines. The board manufacturers provide support software for their products. The developer must review the software provided with board sets that are under consideration during system design. The designer should insure that a large amount of low-level software development is not required in order to achieve optimal performance from the board set that is selected for a particular application.

Other Software Considerations

The general-purpose subroutines operate at the next level above the board interface software. They provide the same functionality as described in Chapter 7. The main difference in the PC-based environment is that the system developer may get involved in a lower level of interface than in the mainframe or minicomputer environment (the board interface software).

The operating systems and data base management systems available for PC systems are generally more restricted in functionality than minicomputer or mainframe-based systems. The functionality is still adequate for image processing system development and operation.

Commercially available software for the PC image processing environment is becoming available. This software is generally provided as part of an integrated system (an integrated PC, video acquisition system, display, board set, and display and support software), but software can be acquired separately for different operating

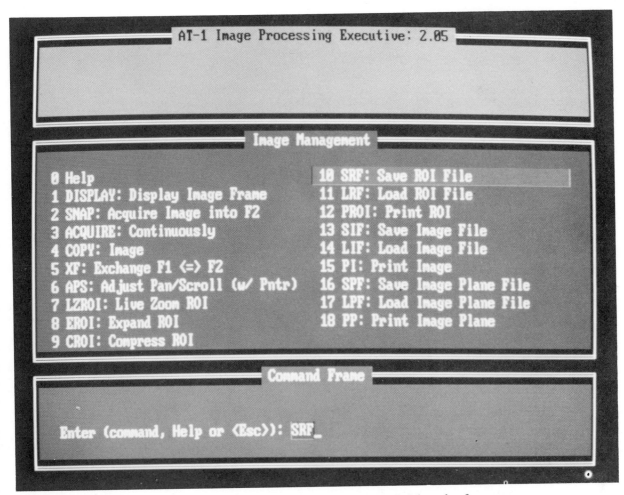

Figure 9-11.   Second-level menu screen for a commercially available PC-based software system (Datacube).

systems and special purpose board sets. The available software generally exploits the interactive command and menu structures supported by most PC operating systems and commercially available software products. Figure 9-11 shows one example of a command menu from a commercially available software system linked to PC-compatible image processing hardware. This menu is at the second level down in a tree-structured menu system.

Figure 9-12 shows a series of displays produced by a commercially available set of PC software. The various screens demonstrate histogram computation, enhancement processing, and selection of regions of interest within the image for customized processing.

REFERENCE

1. Dawson, B. M., "Introduction to Image Processing Algorithms," *BYTE,* March 1987, p. 169.

Appendix A1—
Data Sources

EARTH IMAGING DATA

Earth imaging data are available from several sources in a variety of formats. Data are available in photographic form, and in digital format in some cases. Table A1-1 summarizes the various sources for earth imaging data within the United States, and lists the types of data available from the various satellite and aircraft remote sensing programs. Sources of LANDSAT data outside the United States are listed in Appendix A2.

The following distribution agencies should be contacted for additional information regarding data availability and cost:

EOSAT: Earth Observation Satellite Company
            4300 Forbes Blvd.
            Lanham, MD 20706
            Telephone: 800-344-9933 or 301-552-0500

EDC: EROS Data Center
            Sioux Falls, SD 57198
            Telephone: 605-594-6511

SPOT: SPOT Image Corporation
            1897 Preston White Drive
            Reston, VA 22091-4326
            Telephone: 703-620-2200

NSSDC: National Space Science Data Center
            Code 601
            Goddard Space Flight Center
            Greenbelt, MD 20771
            Telephone: 301-286-6695

NOAA/SDSD: Satellite Data Services Division
            National Oceanic and Atmospheric Administration
            Room 100, World Weather Building
            Washington, D.C. 20233

NESDIS: National Environmental Satellite Data and Information
            Service
            Director of Operations, FOB-4 Room 2069
            Suitland, MD 20233

Offices of the National Cartographic Information Center (NCIC) can provide information regarding the availability of cartographic data (maps, geodetic control, aerial photography, and space imagery):

TABLE A1-1   DISTRIBUTION AGENCIES FOR EARTH IMAGING DATA

DATA SOURCE	SENSOR DESCRIPTION	DISTRIBUTION AGENCY
Apollo 6, 9	Multispectral terrain photography	EDC
Apollo 16	Far ultraviolet camera	NSSDC
ATS 1, 3	Spin scan cloud camera	NOAA/SDSD
Defense Meteorological Satellite Program	Scanning radiometer auroral imagery	NSSDC
ESSA Series	TV camera	NOAA/SDSD
Gemini Missions	Synoptic terrain photography	EDC
ISIS 2	Auroral photometers	NSSDC
LANDSAT	Multispectral scanner and return beam vidicon	EOSAT
SPOT	Multispectral scanner	SPOT
Nimbus Series	Vidicon camera	NOAA/SDSD
Nimbus Series	Scanning radiometer	NSSDC
NOAA Series	Visible and IR scanning radiometers	NOAA/SDSD
SMS and GOES Series	Visible spin scan radiometer-Archival products	NOAA/SDSD
	Real-time products	NESDIS
TIROS Series	TV camera and IR radiometers	NSSDC
U2 and Other	Aerial photography	EDC
Skylab	Multispectral photography	EDC
SEASAT	Synthetic-aperture radar imagery	NOAA/SDSD

NCIC
   U.S. Geological Survey
   507 National Center
   Reston, VA 22092
   Telephone: 703-860-6045

Mid-Continent Mapping Center
   U.S. Geological Survey
   1400 Independence Road
   Rolla, MO 65401
   Telephone: 314-341-0851

Rocky Mountain Mapping Center
   U.S. Geological Survey
   Stop 504, Box 25046
   Federal Center, Building 25
   Denver, CO 80225
   Telephone: 303-236-5829

NCIC
   U.S. Geological Survey
   National Space Technology Laboratories
   NSTL Station, MS 39529
   Telephone: 601-688-3541

Western Mapping Center
   U.S. Geological Survey
   345 Middlefield Road
   Menlo Park, CA 94025
   Telephone: 415-323-8111, ext. 2427

TABLE A1-2 ASTRONOMICAL AND PLANETARY DATA
AVAILABLE FROM NSSDC

DATA SOURCE	SENSOR DESCRIPTION
SOLAR OBSERVATIONS	
OSO-4	Soft X-ray telescope
OSO-6	EUV spectroheliometer
Skylab	White light chronograph
Skylab	X-ray spectrographic telescope
Skylab	Harvard College Observatory experiments
Skylab	X-ray and EUV experiments
LUNAR OBSERVATIONS	
Lunar Orbiter	Film scanner
Ranger	Vidicon camera
Surveyor	Facsimile video camera
Luna and Zond	Miscellaneous
Apollo	70-mm still, 16-mm motion picture, 35-mm stereo, topographic camera
MARS	
Mariner 4, 6, 7, 9	Vidicon camera systems
Viking Orbiter	Vidicon camera systems
Viking Lander	Facsimile camera system
VENUS	
Mariner 10	Vidicon camera
MERCURY	
Mariner 10	Vidicon camera
JUPITER, SATURN	
Pioneer 10, 11	Spin scan imaging photopolarimeter
Voyager 1, 2	Vidicon camera
URANUS	
Voyager 2	Vidicon camera

NCIC-Alaska Operations
U.S. Geological Survey
4230 University Drive
Anchorage, AK 99508-4664
Telephone: 907-271-4159

Newsletters are available from some of these agencies. *LANDSAT Application Notes* is available from EOSAT; *Satellite Data User's Bulletin* is available from NOAA/SDSD; *SPOTLIGHT* is available from SPOT Image Corporation.

ASTRONOMICAL AND PLANETARY IMAGING DATA

A summary of astronomical and planetary imaging data available through NSSDC is listed in Table A1-2. NSSDC should be contacted for details concerning the format and type of data available from each source. Generally, some data are available on magnetic tape for some of the nonimaging sensors, whereas NSSDC generally retains only photographic products for the planetary missions. The archival magnetic tapes for the Mariner, Viking, and Voyager imaging experiments are located at the Jet Propulsion Laboratory (JPL), 4800 Oak Grove Drive, Pasadena, CA 91103.

Appendix A2—
Worldwide Landsat Receiving Stations and Data Distribution Centers

Landsat data is acquired by ground stations around the world. The following table lists the status of ground receiving stations as of mid-1987. Data distribution centers are also listed. This table is reprinted from LANDSAT Data User Notes, courtesy of EOSAT.

TABLE A2-1 LANDSAT RECEIVING STATION CAPABILITIES

Station	Date Established	Reception And MSS	Processing TM	Status	Data Distribution Center
Argentina	Dec. 1980	X		Off-line	Comision Nacional de Investigaciones Especiales (CNIE) Centro de Procesamiento, Avenue Dorrego 4010 1425 Buenos Aires, Argentina Tel.: 722-5108; Telex: 17511 LANBA AR
Australia	Nov. 1980	X		TM upgrade scheduled	Australian Center for Remote Sensing (ACRES) P.O. Box 28 Belconnen, Act 2616, Australia Tel.: 062-52 4411; Telex: 61510 ACRES AA
Brazil	May 1974	X	X	Operational	INPE-DGI Caixa Postal 01, Cachoeira Paulista, SP CEP 12630, Sao Paulo, Brazil Tel.: (125) 611507; PBX: (125) 611377; Telex: 1233562 INPE BR
Canada	Aug. 1972	X	X	Operational	Canada Centre for Remote Sensing (CCRS) 2464 Sheffield Road Ottawa, Ontario, Canada K1A 0Y7 Tel.: 613-952-2717; Telex: 0533777 CA
People's Republic of China	Dec. 1986	X	X	Operational	Academy of Sciences, Landsat Ground Station P.O. Box 2434, Beijing, China Tel.: 284861; Telex: 210222 RSGS CN
ESA (3) Fucino Kiruna Maspalomas	Nov. 1982 Apr. 1975 Mar. 1983 Spring 1984	X X X X	X X X X	Operational Operational Seasonal operation	ESA-ESRIN, Earthnet User Services C.P. 64, 00044 Frascati, Italy Tel.: 39-6-9401360 or 39-6-9401216 Telex: 610637 ESRIN I
India	Jan. 1980	X	X	Operational	National Remote Sensing Agency (NRSA) Department of Space, Balanagar Hyderabad - 500 037, Andhra Pradesh, India Tel.: 262572 X 62, 63; Telex: 01556522 NRSA IN
Indonesia	July 1982	X	X	Off-line TM upgrade announced	Indonesian National Institute of Aeronautics and Space (LAPAN) JL Pemuda Persil No. 1, P.O. Box 3048 Jakarta, Indonesia Telex: 49175 LAPAN IA
Japan	Jan. 1979	X	X	Operational	Remote Sensing Technology Center of Japan (RESTEC) Uni-Roppongi Bldg., 7-15-17 Roppongi Minato-Ku, Tokyo 106, Japan Tel.: TOKYO 3-403-1761; Telex: 2426780 RESTEC J
Pakistan	TBD	X	X	Scheduled mid-1987	Pakistan Space and Upper Atmosphere Research Commission (SUPARCO) 43-1/P-6 Pecks, P.O. Box 3125, Karachi-Az, Pakistan Telex: 25720 SPACE PK
Saudi Arabia	Jan. 1987	X	X	Operational	King Abdulaziz City for Science & Technology P.O. Box 6086, Riyadh 11442, Saudi Arabia Tel.: 01-478-8000; Telex: 201590 SJ
South Africa	Dec. 1980	X			National Institute for Telecommunications Research Attn: Satellite Remote Sensing Center, P.O. Box 3718 Johannesburg 2000, Republic of South Africa Tel.: 27-12-26-5271 Telex: 3-21005 SA
Thailand	Nov. 1981	X		TM upgrade scheduled	Remote Sensing Division National Research Council of Thailand (NRCT) 196 Phahonyothin Road, Bangkhen Bangkok 10900, Thailand Telex: 82213 NARECOU TH; Tel.: 5791370-9 Cable: NRC BANGKOK
United States	July 1972	X	X	Operational	Earth Observation Satellite Company (EOSAT) 4300 Forbes Blvd., Lanham, MD 20706 Tel.: (301) 552-0500 or 800-344-9933 Telex: 277685 LSAT UR

Appendix A3—
Bibliography and Sources of
Information

TEXTS

General Texts and Reprint Collections

Andrews, H., *Computer Techniques in Image Processing,* New York, Academic Press, 1970.

Andrews, H., and B. R. Hunt, *Digital Image Restoration,* Englewood Cliffs, NJ, Prentice-Hall, 1977.

Castleman, K. R., *Digital Image Processing,* Englewood Cliffs, NJ, Prentice-Hall, 1979.

Chellappa, R., and A. A. Sawchuk, *Digital Image Processing and Analysis* (2 Volumes), IEEE Computer Society, 1985.

Gonzalez, R., and P. Wintz, *Digital Image Processing,* Addison-Wesley Publishing Company, 1977.

Hou, H. S., *Digital Document Processing,* New York, John Wiley & Sons, 1983.

Okoshi, T., *Three Dimensional Imaging Techniques,* New York, Academic Press, 1976.

Pratt, W. K., *Digital Image Processing,* New York, John Wiley & Sons, 1978.

Rosenfeld, A., *Picture Processing by Computer,* New York, Academic Press, 1969.

Rosenfeld, A., and A. A. Kak, *Digital Image Processing* (2 Volumes), New York, Academic Press, 1982.

Pattern Recognition and Classification

Ahuja, N., and B. Schachter, *Pattern Models,* New York, John Wiley & Sons, 1983.

Andrews, H. *Introduction to Mathematical Techniques in Pattern Recognition,* Wiley-Interscience, 1972.

Duda, R. O., and P. E. Hart, *Pattern Classification and Scene Analysis,* John Wiley-Interscience, 1973.

Fu, K. S., *Syntactic Pattern Recognition and Applications,* Englewood Cliffs, NJ, Prentice-Hall, 1982.

Hall, E. L., *Computer Image Processing and Recognition,* New York, Academic Press, 1979.

Nevatia, R., *Machine Perception,* Englewood Cliffs, NJ, Prentice-Hall, 1982.

Tanimoto, S., and A. Klinger, Eds., *Structured Computer Vision,* New York, Academic Press, 1980.

Tou, J., and R. Gonzalez, *Pattern Recognition Principles,* Addison Wesley, 1975.

Young, T. Y. and K. S. Fu, *Handbook of Pattern Recognition and Image Procesing,* New York, Academic Press, 1986.

Remote Sensing

Manual of Remote Sensing, 2nd Edition, American Society of Photogrammetry, 1983.

Bernstein, R., *Digital Image Processing for Remote Sensing,* IEEE Press, 1978.

Siegal, B. S., and A. R. Gillespie, *Remote Sensing in Geology,* John Wiley & Sons, 1980.

Digital Filtering and Signal Processing

Huang, T. S., Ed., *Picture Processing and Digital Filtering,* Springer, 1975.

Oppenheim, A., and R. Schafer, *Digital Signal Processing,* Englewood Cliffs, NJ, Prentice-Hall.

OTHER SOURCES

Special Journal Issues

Special issues on digital image processing: *Proc. IEEE 60*, 7 (July 1972), *69*, 5 (May 1981).
Special issue on encoding of graphics: *Proc. IEEE 68*, 7 (July 1980).
Special issue on computerized medical imaging: *IEEE Trans. on Biomed. Engr. BME-28*, 2 (Feb. 1981).
Special issue on computer analysis of time-varying images, *IEEE Computer*, August 1981.
Special issue on computer architecture for pattern analysis and image database management, *IEEE Trans. Comput., C-31* (Oct. 1982).
Special issue on computerized tomography, *Proc. IEEE, 71* (March 1983).
Special issue on image processing: *IEEE Computer*, August 1977.
Special issues on optical and digital image processing: *Optical Engineering 19*, 2 and *19*, 3 (1980).
Special issue on knowledge-based image analysis, *Pattern Recog. 17*, 1 (1984).

Journals That Contain Papers on Digital Image Processing on a Regular Basis

IEEE Transactions on Pattern Analysis and Machine Intelligence
IEEE Transactions on Medical Imaging
IEEE Computer Graphics and Applications
Computer Vision, Graphics and Image Processing
Pattern Recognition
Photogrammetric Engineering and Remote Sensing
International Journal of Remote Sensing
International Journal of Geographic Information Systems
Optical Engineering
IEEE Transactions on Acoustics, Speech and Signal Processing
Journal of the Optical Society of America
Applied Optics

Conferences That Feature Image Processing Technology or that Generally Include Sessions on Image Processing

SPIE Annual Meeting and special topical meetings
IEEE Computer Society Pattern Recognition and Image Processing Conference
Association for Computing Machinery Special Interest Group on Computer Graphics (SIGGRAPH)
IEEE Acoustics, Speech and Signal Processing annual conference
Society for Information Display annual conference
American Society of Photogrammetry
Association for Information and Image Management (AIIM)

Index

Index